The New Planning for Results

A Streamlined Approach

Sandra Nelson
FOR THE
Public Library Association

American Library Association
Chicago and London
2001

Project manager: Joan A. Grygel

Cover and text design: Dianne M. Rooney

Composition by the dotted i in Stempel Schneidler and Univers using QuarkXPress 4.04 for Macintosh

Printed on 50-pound white offset, a pH-neutral stock, and bound in 10-point coated cover stock by Data Reproductions

The paper used in this publication meets the minimum requirements of American National Standard for Information Sciences—Permanence of Paper for Printed Library Materials, ANSI Z39.48-1992. ∞

Library of Congress Cataloging-in-Publication Data
Nelson, Sandra S.
    The new planning for results : a streamlined approach / Sandra Nelson for
the Public Library Association.
        p.   cm.
    Includes bibliographical references and index.
    ISBN 0-8389-3504-4 (alk. paper)
    1. Public libraries—Planning.   2. Public libraries—United States—Planning.
3. Public libraries—Administration.   4. Public libraries—United States—
Administration.   5. Resource allocation.   I. Public Library Association.
II. Title.
Z678.N454   2001
025.1'974—dc21   00-045388

Printed in the United States of America.

05   04   03   02   5   4   3   2

Contents

Part Two
Public Library Service Responses

145

Part Three
Tool Kit

221

Part Four
Workforms

279

Index

309

Figures

Foreword

Planning for Results: A Library Transformation Process was published in March 1998, and *The New Planning for Results: A Streamlined Approach* was published in January 2001, slightly less than three years later. That is in sharp contrast to earlier versions of the Public Library Association (PLA) planning model, which were published seven to ten years apart. There are a number of reasons for this shift. The first is implicit in the subtitle of this book: *A Streamlined Approach*. This new book is intended to simplify and streamline the processes recommended in *Planning for Results* in response to feedback from many of the librarians who used that process.

The most notable change is in the format of the publication. *Planning for Results* was published in two volumes—a 125-page *Guidebook* that introduced people to the various planning steps and tasks and the service responses and a 100-page *How-To Manual* that provided very detailed information on how to complete each task. Many of the librarians who used the process thought it was confusing to have the information in the *Guidebook* and the *How-To Manual* separated. A number of librarians also found the level of detail in the *How-To Manual* daunting. This is a perfect example of the law of unintended results, in which any large-scale activity, no matter how well intentioned, is often accompanied by unforeseen repercussions that can overshadow the original purpose of the activity. The *How-To Manual* originally was developed in response to many requests for more explicit and practical help on how to complete the planning tasks. However, to provide a comprehensive tool that would meet everyone's needs, the manual ended up very long and very detailed. Instead of reassuring planners that there was a place for them to get the answers they needed, the manual seemed to suggest that planning was even more complicated than they had thought it was—not at all the intended outcome.

In the *New Planning for Results,* the format has changed, but the core elements of *Planning for Results* have not. In Part Two the service responses are reprinted exactly as they were in *Planning for Results*. The definitions of goals, objectives, and activities are the same, and so are the three recommended ways to measure library progress. The six steps will look familiar to those of you who have used *Planning for Results,* too, although you will notice that the order has been changed slightly. Most of the changes that have been made deal with the planning process and not the planning priorities. For example, the recommended time line in *Planning for Results* was eight to ten months; the planning time line here is four to five months to complete the plan. The twenty-three planning tasks in *Planning for Results* have been combined into twelve planning tasks here. (See figure 1: Comparison of Planning Steps and Tasks.)

The only instances in which significant changes in the content of *Planning for Results* have been made are in the areas of resource allocation and monitoring the implementation of the plan. The librarians and consultants who wrote *Planning for Results* realized even before the publication of that document that library planners would need additional tools to help them make the resource allocation decisions required to implement their plans. By the time *Planning for Results* was published, a PLA committee was working with three consultants to develop a companion volume on resource allocation. *Managing for Results: Effective Resource Allocation for Public Libraries* was published in January 2000. It is intended to be used as a companion to *The New Planning for Results* and references to it have been integrated when appropriate throughout this book.

FIGURE 1
Comparison of Planning Steps and Tasks

PLANNING FOR RESULTS	*THE NEW PLANNING FOR RESULTS*
Prepare: Planning to Plan	**Prepare: Planning to Plan**
Task 1: Read the *Guidebook* and the *How-To Manual*	Task 1: Design the Planning Process
Task 2: Estimate the Level of Effort for Each Task, Set the Planning Timetable, and Develop the Planning Process Budget	Task 2: Prepare Board, Staff, and Committee
Task 3: Prepare for Keeping People Informed	**Imagine: Identifying Possibilities**
Task 4: Select the Planning Committee	Task 3: Determine Community Vision
Task 5: Orient the Planning Committee	Task 4: Identify Community Needs
Envision: Imagining the Future	**Design: Inventing the Future**
Task 6: Articulate a Community Vision	Task 5: Select Service Responses
Task 7: Scan the Community	Task 6: Write Goals and Objectives
Task 8: Identify Community Needs	
Task 9: Scan the Library	**Build: Assembling the Future**
Task 10: Determine Which Community Needs the Library Should Address	Task 7: Identify Activities
Task 11: Write the Library Vision Statement	Task 8: Determine Resource Requirements
	Communicate: Informing the Stakeholders
Design: Inventing the Future	Task 9: Write the Plan and Obtain Approval
Task 12: Select Service Responses	Task 10: Communicate the Plan to Staff and Community
Task 13: Write the Library Mission Statement	
	Implement: Moving into the Future
Build: Assembling the Future	Task 11: Reallocate Resources
Task 14: Set Goals	Task 12: Monitor Implementation
Task 15: Review Library Measurement and Evaluation Techniques	
Task 16: Develop an Array of Objectives	
Task 17: Select Objectives	
Implement: Moving into the Future	
Task 18: Determine Available Resources	
Task 19: Identify Activities Necessary to Meet Objectives	
Task 20: Revisit the Impact of Your Choices	
Communicate: Informing the Stakeholders	
Task 21: Compile the Draft Plan	
Task 22: Obtain Final Approval	
Task 23: Publish and Distribute the Final Plan	

Acknowledgments

The New Planning for Results is the latest in a long line of planning models published by PLA, and it builds on all of the work that went into those earlier models. The real strength of these publications is the collaboration between practitioners and consultants, which ensures that the final products work in the *real* world and not just in the never-never land of theory. The librarians and consultants who have helped to develop these models are acknowledged below.

The Present

Having worked with the staff and the board of the Daviess County to field test a number of the new processes in this book, I am particularly grateful to the Daviess County Library Director, Deborah Mesplay, for her thoughtful recommendations on ways to involve staff more effectively in the planning process.

The draft of this book was reviewed by four of the most experienced library planners in the country—Jane Eickhoff, June Garcia, Ruth O'Donnell, and Rhea Rubin. Not surprisingly, their suggestions were on-target and insightful, and the final document is better because of their efforts.

The other person who deserves thanks for this book is the editor, Joan Grygel. She also edited two earlier books I cowrote, *Wired for the Future* and *Managing for Results,* and in doing so taught me how to write a book. I will always be grateful to her.

And the Past

PLA's interest in library planning began in 1971 when the PLA Standards Committee, chaired by Rose Vainstein, decided the *Minimum Standards for Public Library Systems* did not meet the needs of modern libraries and appointed three task forces to consider the needs of different age groups. Mary Jo Lynch and Ralph Blasingame responded to the work of the task forces with a commentary that said "most people think of a standard as a rule for sameness" and suggested that "what public librarians need now are not rules for sameness but tools which will help them analyze a situation, set objectives, make decisions and evaluate achievements."[1] That suggestion was endorsed by the committee and set the stage for all four of the planning models that have been published by PLA, not only in terms of intent but also in terms of process. Each of the planning models was developed though a collaborative effort between practicing librarians and library consultants. This ensured that each new model incorporated the actual experiences of the librarians who used the preceding model and resulted in an evolving process that produced ever-more-effective planning models.

Two library leaders deserve special recognition for their contributions to public library planning. The first is Dr. Lowell Martin whose work and writings provided the philosophical foundation upon which all of the public library planning models have been based. The second is Charles Robinson who served as an adviser to the consultants who wrote the first three planning models. Mr. Robinson was also one of the first library directors in the country to integrate the PLA planning approach into the ongoing operation of the library he directed, and his successes at the Baltimore County Public Library showcased the value of planning.

Following is a list of the librarians and consultants who were responsible for the first three planning models. They all dedicated countless hours to designing and refining the PLA planning models, and the results of their labors have improved public library services for everyone in the country.

A Planning Process for Public Libraries, 1980

> Consultants and authors: Vernon E. Palmour, Marcia C. Bellassai, and Nancy V. DeWath
>
> Steering committee: Genevieve M. Casey, Agnes M. Griffen, Mary Ann Heneghan, Peter Hiatt, Henry Shearouse, Joseph Schubert, and Ella Gaines Yates
>
> Adviser to the consultants: Charles W. Robinson

Planning and Role-Setting for Public Libraries: A Manual of Operations and Procedures, 1987

> Consultants and authors: Charles R. McClure, Amy Owen, Douglas L. Zweizig, Mary Jo Lynch, and Nancy A. Van House
>
> New Standards Task Force: Karen Krueger (chair), Carolyn A. Anthony, Kathleen M. Balcom, Nancy M. Bolt, Mary Jo Detweiler,

Ronald A. Dubberly, James H. Fish, June M. Garcia, Claudya B. Muller, Charles W. Robinson, Eleanor Jo Rodger, Elliot Shelkrot

Planning for Results: A Public Library Transformation Process, 1998

Consultants and authors: Ethel Himmel and William James Wilson

Special consultant for evaluation methodology: Dr. George D'Elia

ReVision Committee: Sandra Nelson (chair), Ron Dubberly, Susan Baerg Epstein, June Garcia, Toni Garvey, Luis Herrera, Sam Morrison, Kathleen Reif, Charles Robinson, Greta Southard, and Barbara Weaver

NOTE

1. Mary Jo Lynch, "Foreword" in *A Planning Process for Public Libraries* (Chicago: American Library Assn., 1980), xii.

Introduction

The New Planning for Results was built on three basic assumptions:

1. Excellence must be defined locally—it results when library services match community needs, interests, and priorities.
2. Excellence is possible for both small and large libraries—it rests more on commitment than on unlimited resources.
3. Excellence is a moving target—even when achieved, excellence must be continually maintained.[1]

These assumptions provided the framework for the earlier public library documents *Planning and Role-Setting for Public Libraries* and *Planning for Results,* and they are as powerful today as they were when they were first published in 1987. The first statement, "excellence must be defined locally—it results when library services match community needs, interests, and priorities," is critical to the development of your library plan. Prior to 1987 most public libraries thought of excellence as meeting or exceeding state or national standards. That approach assumed a "one-size-fits-all" approach to library planning that doesn't make much sense when you consider the extraordinary diversity in our communities. Programs that exemplify excellent services in one community may be all but irrelevant in another community.

It just takes one simple example to underscore this diversity. Consider the Mesa Public Library and the Sun City Public Library. Both are located in Maricopa County, Arizona, but the demographic profiles of the communities the two libraries serve are polar opposites. In Sun City, a popular retirement community, less than 1 percent of the population is under the age of 18 and 85 percent of the population is 65 or older. In Mesa, on the other hand, 30 percent of the population is under 18 while only 12 percent is 65 or older.[2] The Mesa Public Library allocates a significant proportion of its resources to providing services for children and young adults; the Sun City Public Library allocates virtually nothing for that age group. Both are making the right decisions for the communities they serve.

The second statement, "excellence is possible for both small and large libraries—it rests more on commitment than on unlimited resources," is even more true now than it was in 1987. The explosion of information resources available electronically has made it possible for small and rural libraries to offer a level of access to information that was unimaginable in 1987. However, managers in small and rural libraries cannot take full advantage of the opportunities they have if they don't plan carefully. The commitment that is required for excellence has to be based on clearly defined goals that address community needs.

Of the three statements, the third, "excellence is a moving target—even when achieved, excellence must be continually maintained," is perhaps the most difficult for library managers to address. Imbedded in that statement is the assumption that excellent public libraries continually monitor their results and that change is an integral part of their organizational culture. Many public libraries have a long way to go before that is true, but library managers all over the country have begun putting into place the processes that will lead to this environment. Foremost among those processes is structured, ongoing planning using a tool like *The New Planning for Results.*

A Preview of the Process

As you and your staff work through the planning process you will complete six planning steps, each of which is divided into two tasks. Figure 2 presents an overview of those steps and tasks. A more complete overview of the process follows. It includes not only the steps and tasks but also a list of the milestones or things you will accomplish during each of the six steps. This will give you and your colleagues some idea of

---

FIGURE 2
The New Planning for Results Planning Steps and Tasks

Prepare: Planning to Plan
Task 1: Design the Planning Process
Task 2: Prepare Board, Staff, and Committee

Imagine: Identifying Possibilities
Task 3: Determine Community Vision
Task 4: Identify Community Needs

Design: Inventing the Future
Task 5: Select Service Responses
Task 6: Write Goals and Objectives

Build: Assembling the Future
Task 7: Identify Preliminary Activities
Task 8: Determine Resource Requirements

Communicate: Informing the Stakeholders
Task 9: Write the Plan and Obtain Approval
Task 10: Communicate the Results of the Planning Process

Implement: Moving into the Future
Task 11: Allocate or Reallocate Resources
Task 12: Monitor Implementation

---

the scope of the planning effort. It can also serve as an easy reference tool to check where you are in the process as you move from step to step and to help you keep track of the big picture.

Step 1   Prepare: Planning to Plan

Task 1: Design the Planning Process

Task 2: Prepare Board, Staff, and Committee

Milestones

- develop a planning time line and budget
- explain the responsibilities of planning committee members, library staff, library board members, and local government officials
- identify the stakeholders and community representatives you want to serve on the planning committee
- provide a planning orientation for the library staff and the board
- provide an orientation for the planning committee
- develop a plan to inform your community about the planning process and its results

Step 2   Imagine: Identifying Possibilities

Task 3: Determine Community Vision

Task 4: Identify Community Needs

Milestones

- gather data about your community
- look to the future to develop a vision for your community
- identify current conditions in your community and compare them with the vision for the future
- determine what needs to be done to move the community closer to the vision for the future
- present data about current library programs and services
- identify which community needs the library can help the community meet

Step 3   Design: Inventing the Future

Task 5: Select Service Responses

Task 6: Write Goals and Objectives

Milestones

- make the connection between community needs and library service priorities
- assess the effect the proposed library service priorities will have on existing services and programs
- select the library priorities for the current planning cycle and write the library mission statement
- write goals that reflect the library priorities
- select measures that will help you track the progress the library is making toward meeting the goals
- write objectives that incorporate the selected measures

Step 4   Build: Assembling the Future

Task 7: Identify Preliminary Activities

Task 8: Determine Resource Requirements

Milestones

- involve library staff members in the identification of activities that will result in the library's making progress toward reaching its goals and objectives
- help the staff understand the difference between efficiency and effectiveness
- identify the most important resources that will be required for each possible activity
- select the activities for the current year
- explain the gap analysis process to the board and staff
- use the gap analysis process to determine the staff, collections, facilities, and technology requirements for the selected activities

Step 5   Communicate: Informing the Stakeholders

Task 9: Write the Basic Plan and Obtain Approval

Task 10: Communicate the Results of the Planning Process

Milestones

- write the basic library plan
- present the draft of the basic plan to the staff and the members of the planning committee for review and comment
- submit the final draft of the basic plan to the library board or your local government for review and approval

- review your public relations plan to ensure that all appropriate audiences have been identified
- select the portions of the basic plan that need to be included in communications to each target audience
- determine the formats and languages in which the plan should be published

Step 6   Implement: Moving into the Future

Task 11: Allocate or Reallocate Resources

Task 12: Monitor Implementation

Milestones

- allocate or reallocate the resources required to implement the activities in the plan
- integrate the activities in the plan into the ongoing operations of the library
- monitor the progress the library is making toward achieving the goals and objectives in the plan
- adjust the plan as needed when circumstances change or planning assumptions prove to be invalid
- develop activities for the second and third years of the current planning cycle
- use what you have learned in this planning cycle in your next planning process

How to Use This Book

The first planning assumption presented at the beginning of this chapter was "excellence must be defined locally—it results when library services match community needs, interests, and priorities." The same holds true for the planning process itself. Every library is unique, and the staff and boards of every library will start the planning process from a different place. Some libraries have had a history of developing new plans regularly and using those plans as the basis for making management decisions. Other libraries have never had a formal, written strategic plan. Yet other libraries have plans that were developed to meet a state mandate and were never intended to be used as management tools.

This book can be used by library managers no matter what their previous experiences have been. The staff and board of each library are strongly encouraged to adapt the processes described here to meet local needs and conditions. This flexibility is one of the most important aspects of all of the PLA planning models. There is no *one* right library plan. The right plan for your library may not look anything like the right plan for the library in a neighboring county or state. The key is to begin the planning process and develop a plan that works for you and your colleagues right now and then to continually update that plan as conditions change.

Levels of Effort

Most libraries will want to complete the planning process as quickly and efficiently as possible, and the best way to do that is to streamline the level of effort put into completing each of the twelve tasks. "Level of effort" was a concept introduced in *Planning and Role-Setting for Public Libraries:*

> Choosing a level of effort is one of the most significant ways in which you can adapt the planning process to your library's needs, purposes, and resources. This manual presents three levels of effort for each phase—basic, moderate, and extensive.[3]

In *Planning for Results* the concept of level of effort had evolved, and two levels were suggested, basic and enhanced:

> The different methods for carrying out each task are designated as levels of effort. The basic level represents the minimum effort that will get the particular task done. The enhanced level is typically more staff intensive but is designed to yield greater insight, broader participation, or a sharper focus on specific areas of interest or concern.[4]

This book, as implied by the word "streamlined" in the subtitle, suggests that library managers expedite their planning activities. The underlying assumption is that all tasks will be completed with the minimum level of effort required to accomplish them effectively. Certain tasks will include suggestions for different approaches that might be appropriate depending on the complexity of the planning environment, but there has been no attempt to include suggested levels of effort for every task.

Do's and Don'ts

On the first page of each chapter in Part One you will find a box containing tips from experienced planners to help ensure that you have a successful planning experience. The tips are presented in a "do/don't" format. The "do" items are suggestions for ways to enhance your planning experience. The "don't" items are warnings about common pitfalls in the planning process. You may find it helpful to review the tips several times as you go through the tasks in each step. They provide a convenient way to be sure that you are still on track in the process.

The Anytown Public Library Planning Experience

The Anytown Public Library was introduced in the original *Planning for Results* and appeared again in *Wired for the Future* and *Managing for Results*. Anytown is a mythical community somewhere in the United States. The Anytown Public Library serves a countywide population of 100,000 people and has an authority board. It operates from a single facility with no branches, although it does provide bookmobile services throughout the county.

In the earlier books, the Anytown Public Library was used as the basis for a variety of case studies, each of which illustrated a specific issue. In this book you will find a series of descriptions of Anytown planning efforts with a focus on the processes that were used rather than the issues being considered. This is a significant difference. For example, in *Managing for Results* readers reviewed a case study that described the problems the Anytown staff had in scheduling their single meeting room. A second case study looked at how the Anytown staff could find the computer time needed to develop a series of marketing tools. In contrast, in this book you will have the opportunity to attend several of the planning meetings of the Anytown planning committee, staff, and board. There are five parts to the Anytown planning experience; you will have a front-row seat when the

1. facilitator leads the planning committee members through the community visioning process
2. planning committee members complete the community SWOT analysis
3. committee members identify community needs
4. committee members make the preliminary selection of service responses
5. Anytown Library director leads a series of meetings to brainstorm the activities that the library might undertake to accomplish the goals and objectives in the plan

These experiences are certainly not intended to be prescriptive. Every planning process is different. However, most of us are more comfortable in situations that are familiar than we are doing something we have never done before. The Anytown planning experience descriptions are written in the present tense to help you feel like you are there participating in the process. That may make it easier for you to visualize how you intend to accomplish the various tasks in your own library.

It might help you to become a part of the Anytown planning process if you know something about the planning committee. The committee has twelve members and a trained facilitator. The members of the committee include the president of the chamber of commerce, a city councilwoman, an architect, the current president of the PTO, a representative from the day-care providers in town, the superintendent of schools, the woman who heads a coalition of social service agencies to provide services to the migrant population, the vice president of a local industry, a retiree who is active in the local genealogical society and uses the library regularly, the president of the student body at the local community college, the president of the library staff association, and a member of the library board. The members of the committee reflect the ethnic, age, and gender demographics of Anytown.

The committee members attended an orientation meeting before the meeting described in Part One of the Anytown planning experience. During that meeting they received some basic demographic information about the community. It included data on trends in the age, ethnic background, education, and income levels of the people in Anytown over the past twenty years and projections in the same areas for the next ten years. They also received a brief summary of library services, programs, and resources, again with trend data to put the information into a context that would be useful for planning.

Part Two, Service Responses

The second part of the book includes the library service responses that were originally introduced in *Planning for Results: A Public Library Transformation Process:*

> What is a service response? . . . In simple terms, a service response is what a library does for, or offers to, the public in an effort to meet a set of well-defined community needs. . . . Service responses . . . are very distinctive ways that libraries can serve the public. They represent the gathering and deployment of resources to produce a specific public benefit or results.[5]

More information on the service responses and how to use them is given in Task 5 of the planning process.

Part Three, Tool Kit

As you work through the planning process you will find that certain issues come up again and again. Four of the most important of these issues are helping groups identify options, helping groups reach agreement, keeping staff informed about the planning process, and presenting data effectively. Rather than spreading information about these important topics throughout the book, each has been addressed in the Tool Kit, Part Three of this book.

The first section of the Tool Kit is "Groups: Identifying Options." This planning process, like most, is based on working with a variety of groups of people. You will be dealing with group process issues when you select the planning committee, during your planning committee meetings, when you work with staff committees, and when you present the draft of your plan to the members of the library board for consideration and discussion. This Tool Kit section describes some of the reasons groups have difficulty identifying options and provides you with complete guidelines for four different mechanisms to help groups work through these problems. The next section of the Tool Kit, "Groups: Reaching Agreement," continues this discussion of group process issues. This section includes information on how to work with individuals who are disrupting a group and how to help groups reach agreement.

The third section of the Tool Kit focuses on internal communication practices. This is a theme that runs throughout the planning process. Any successful planning process must keep the staff informed and involved from the beginning through the implementation. This section includes some common library communication problems and recommendations to help everyone in the library to communicate more effectively.

The final section of the Tool Kit focuses on presenting data. You will have to develop a package of information about the community and the library for the planning committee. You will look at data collection and presentation issues again when you develop the objectives for your plan and when you make the resource allocation decisions required to implement your plan. Finally, you will be looking for ways to present data effectively to help the members of the community understand the value of the services and programs the library staff provide. The information in this section of the Tool Kit will give you practical guidelines to ensure that the data in your presentations are clear and easily understood by the people receiving them.

Part Four, Workforms

Thirteen workforms have been included in Part Four. These workforms can serve a variety of purposes; the most obvious purpose is to provide a place to record information. A second, and more important function, is to provide you with suggestions for the types of data you need to collect, particularly in the case of Workform B: Community Data and Workform E: Library Data. The workforms can also serve as process guides for both the community-based planning committee and staff committees.

It is rare for the planners in any library to use all of the workforms in any planning book. Each library planning process is different, and one way that planners can tailor this process to meet their needs is to select from among the workforms those that are appropriate to specific circumstances. If a given workform will help you simplify your work, organize your thoughts, or explain a process to others, then use it. If a workform does not appear to be useful, skip it, modify it, or develop a tool that works better for you.

Putting It All Together

All of the tools you will need to develop an effective strategic plan for your library have been included in this book. All that is left is to "just do it."

NOTES

1. Charles R. McClure and others, *Planning and Role-Setting for Public Libraries: A Manual of Options and Procedures* (Chicago: American Library Assn., 1987), 1.
2. 1990 U.S. Census Data.
3. McClure, *Planning and Role-Setting for Public Libraries,* 4.
4. Ethel Himmel and William James Wilson, *Planning for Results: A Public Library Transformation Process* (Chicago: American Library Assn., 1998), 8.
5. Himmel and Wilson, 54.

Part One

The Planning Process

Chapter 1

PREPARE
Planning to Plan

MILESTONES

By the time you finish this chapter you will know how to

- develop a planning time line and budget

- explain the responsibilities of planning committee members, library staff, library board members, and local government officials

- identify the stakeholders and community representatives you want to serve on the planning committee

- provide a planning orientation for the library staff and the board

- provide an orientation for the planning committee

- develop a plan to inform your community about the planning process and its results

The planning process is almost always easier to manage and more effective when the people responsible spend the time required planning to plan. The reverse is true as well. One of the primary reasons that library planning efforts fail is lack of preplanning. Unfortunately, a lot of us think "planning to plan" is an oxymoron. As a result too many managers jump right into planning without taking the time to consider

> what they want to accomplish with the process
>
> who should be involved
>
> how long the process should last
>
> what resources will be required to complete the process
>
> at what points in the process preliminary recommendations should be reviewed and by whom they should be reviewed

Even worse, these same managers often neglect to think about how they are going to keep the staff and board involved throughout the process.

This step, *prepare,* helps library planners set the stage for a successful planning effort. Several key decisions have to be made. The first is quite basic: what is the purpose of your plan? In other words, what do you hope to gain by going through a planning process? Once you know the answer, you are ready to begin to consider the general composition of your planning committee. This is your second decision because the reason you are developing a plan will affect the type of committee you appoint. The choices you make here are critical; they will have a profound effect on the structure of your planning process and the content of your final plan. As you are considering the kind of planning committee you want to appoint, you will also be developing the planning time line and deciding who should lead the planning effort. When those decisions have been made, you will be ready to select the actual planning committee members and invite them to participate in the process.

However, you still won't be ready to actually begin the planning process. Another set of decisions remains to be made, and these decisions

DO	read through all six chapters of this planning manual before you begin
DO	involve the staff and board in planning decisions from the beginning
DO	consider using an outside facilitator to lead the planning committee meetings
DON'T	limit your vision by not including community members on the planning committee
DON'T	get so involved in planning that you forget that it is just the beginning; implementing the plan is what is important
DON'T	make things harder than they have to be; follow the rule of KISS (keep it simple, sweetie)

are at least as important as the purpose for planning and the composition of the planning committee. First, you will have to think about how you are going to ensure that every staff member in the library and every board member is aware of and involved in the planning process from the beginning through the final implementation. Unfortunately, this consideration is too often left until the end of the planning process, at which point you are presenting the staff and the board with a completed plan. Then it is too late to encourage the ongoing active participation in the process that is necessary if the plan is going be successfully implemented. You will also want to consider how you are going to inform the members of your community that library managers are working to reshape library services to meet changing community needs. This will be the first part of an ongoing marketing program that you will be developing to publicize the planning process and the priorities that result from that process.

As you can see, you and your colleagues will have a lot to think about and many decisions to make as you work through the *prepare* step. Fortunately, while this step has lots of elements, they are for the most part fairly straightforward and easy to manage. The decisions are interconnected, and once your first choices are made, your next options become quite clear. As you and your colleagues consider your options and make your decisions, you will be setting the stage not only for the planning process itself but for the implementation that will follow.

The two tasks you will accomplish in the *prepare* step are

> **TASK 1**
> Design the planning process
>
> **TASK 2**
> Prepare board, staff, and committee

TASK 1: Design the Planning Process

You probably learned about the 5 *W*s—why, what, when, where, and who—in high school. The 5 *W*s are often taught in English class as a way to help students structure factual writing assignments. The 5 *W*s provide you with an equally effective methodology to design your planning process. When you have answered the 5 *W*s, you will have made all of the decisions required for a successful planning effort.

Decide Why You Need a Plan

Before you can begin to design your planning process, you need to be very clear in your own mind about what you want to accomplish. There are dozens of reasons for planning. They range from a desire to create a blueprint that will help the library provide quality services to the community for the next three to five years, to a need to develop services and programs for a new client group, to a response to a significant budget increase or decrease, to a requirement by your state library agency that a plan be developed. The decisions you make concerning what, when, where, and who will probably be different in each of these scenarios.

One way to clarify your thinking about the reasons you are embarking on a planning process is to put those reasons in writing. The following questions might be helpful as you do that:

Who decided we should develop a plan?

What was the stated reason for beginning a planning process?

What were the unstated reasons (if any) for beginning a planning process?

Are there are other reasons that we should develop a plan?

What is the most important outcome of this planning process?

What other positive outcomes are likely?

Are there any negative outcomes that might result from planning?

If there are potential negatives, how can they be reduced or eliminated?

What are the consequences or negatives if we fail to plan?

If we don't begin a planning process now, when will we begin such a process?

When you have finished responding to these questions, consider asking others on the management team to go through the same exercise. In some libraries, it might be a good idea to include key board and staff members as well. Then compare all of the answers and discuss the similarities and differences in your perceptions. Taking the time to be sure everyone is operating with the same assumptions before you begin to plan can save untold trouble and confusion later in the process.

Determine the Composition of the Planning Committee

Once you know why you are planning, you have the information you need to decide what kind of planning committee you want. This is basically a question of the desirable balance between community involvement and staff participation. If you are developing a plan solely to meet the requirements of your state library agency, you may decide to restrict the planning committee to staff or a combination of staff and board members. If the purpose of your plan is to develop a blueprint for library services for your community, it is critical that you involve community members in the planning process.

Including community members is hardly a new concept. Every planning process the Public Library Association has published since 1980 has strongly recommended that community members be included on the planning team. Even so, not all libraries have involved community members in their planning efforts, and when they have, the results have been mixed. In some cases having community members on the planning committee has been an unqualified success. In others cases community participation in the process has led to problems. Problems, when they do occur, tend to fall into two main categories: dealing with the individuals selected to serve on the committee and dealing with the scope of the responsibility the committee is given.

As anyone who has ever served on a committee knows, each member is a unique personality, which can make it difficult for members to work together effectively. (For dealing with disruptive committee members, see "Groups: Reaching Agreement" in the Tool Kit.) Occasionally, individuals selected to represent a particular constituency feel so strongly about that constituency that they block any attempts to address other issues. The best solution to this problem is to be very careful when making committee appointments, which will be discussed in detail later. A more common and potentially more serious problem occurs when committee members are not given a clear understanding of the scope of their responsibilities. On occasion, community-based planning committees have focused their attentions not on how the library could better meet community needs but on how the library is allocating resources. Some committees have tried to interfere with the selection of materials, the placement of bookmobile stops, the development of programs, the performance of a specific staff member, and other issues that are clearly the responsibility of the library staff and board.

Planning Responsibilities

The ideal relationship between community members and library staff in the planning process is illustrated in figure 3. In this model, the planning committee, composed primarily of community members, is an advisory committee to the library staff and board and is responsible for helping the library identify community needs. After all, who is better qualified to talk about what will be required to move the community forward than the people who live in the community? The planning committee is also responsible for helping the library select the service priorities that will most effectively meet the identified community needs.

Once the preliminary service priorities have been selected, the staff and board members become more involved in the process. Their first responsibility is to review the committee's preliminary recommendations concerning service priorities and to tell the committee what would happen to existing services and programs if the new priorities were selected.

FIGURE 3
Planning Responsibilities

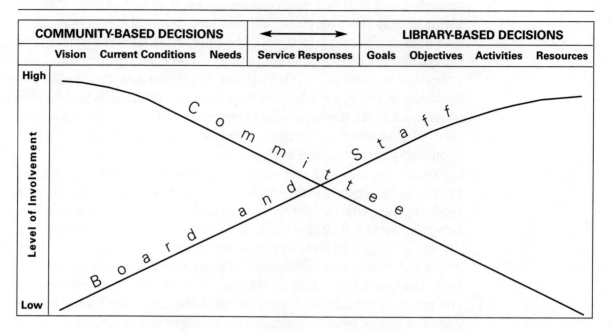

COMMUNITY-BASED DECISIONS			Service Responses	LIBRARY-BASED DECISIONS			
Vision	Current Conditions	Needs		Goals	Objectives	Activities	Resources

The committee will use this information when they make their final service priority recommendations.

As you can see in figure 3, most of the planning committee's responsibilities end with the selection of service priorities. They will meet only one more time, and that will be at the end of the process to review the completed draft of the plan. The planning committee's recommended service priorities will be passed on to staff committees. These staff groups will be responsible for developing goals, objectives, and activities and for making the resource allocation decisions required to implement the plan. This planning model allows all of the participants to use their strengths. A diverse and well-selected group of community members is in a far better position to talk about the desired future for the community than are library staff members. Community members also bring fewer preconceived ideas about library service priorities to the table than staff members do, which allows the community members to think more creatively about how the library might help meet community needs. Similarly, library staff use their training and skills to translate the recommendations of the committee into programs and services that will lead to the outcomes all have agreed are important.

Committee Size

There is no hard-and-fast rule about the number of people who should be appointed to a planning committee. Planning committees have ranged in size from five to fifty. However, there are two factors to consider when deciding how large your committee should be. On the one hand, you want a committee that is large enough to include people with diverse points of view and representatives of all segments of your community. On the other hand, you want to keep the committee small enough to work effectively. In view of those two guidelines, it seems safe to say that a committee with five people is probably too small to be inclusive and that a committee with fifty people is probably too large to work effectively. Most library managers find that committees of nine to fifteen people work well. As you will see later, the decision you make about the size of the committee will affect the options you have about the leadership of the committee.

Establish the Planning Schedule

The most important thing to remember when determining your planning time line is that planning is the means to an end and not the end itself. Over the years, staff in many libraries have spent an enormous amount of time and energy on their planning processes, and they have felt a real sense of accomplishment when the plan was finally written and approved. However, that sense of accomplishment can get in the way of actually implementing the plan. Staff sometimes finish the process with a form of planning fatigue, and they just don't want to think about the plan anymore. As a result, the plan ends up on a shelf, and it is only looked at occasionally thereafter.

It is not uncommon to hear a library director say "I looked at our plan the other day, and I was surprised by how many of our objectives we have accomplished." The director is right to be surprised; any progress made toward reaching the objectives was coincidental. It is much like asking an architect to design a building, putting the resulting building plan in a safe place, and then working with different contractors to construct the building without ever referring to the plan again. The building you end up with will not look much like the one in the plan, and it is very likely to have required significantly more time and money than you anticipated.

Planning Time Line

Figure 4, Sample Time Line, provides an outline for a planning process that takes approximately five months. It includes both descriptions of the meetings to be held during that time and the activities to be completed between one meeting and the next. This time line is based on several assumptions:

> The library is going to use existing data about the library and the community rather than collecting an extensive amount of new or additional data.

The library is going to plan "from the top down" using a single community-based planning committee rather than multiple planning committees or subcommittees from each area served by a branch or outlet.

The process will include two or three four- to five-hour planning meetings rather than ten or twelve one- to two-hour meetings.

Figure 4 also includes three suggested approval points. An approval point is a time in the planning process when some significant decision that will affect subsequent decisions is made. It may appear to slow the process slightly to get these interim approvals, but that appearance is deceiving. In fact, it makes sense, both in terms of time and of buy-in, to have the recommended decision reviewed by staff, board, and any other governing body before moving on. If there are problems with the recommendation, they can be resolved in a timely manner, and that resolution will not affect later parts of the plan. If you wait until the end of the process to share the work of the committee and then find out that people have concerns, you will face serious problems with the committee and with the staff, board, or governing body. The committee is likely to be unhappy because their work is being attacked, and the people with concerns are likely to feel that they were excluded from the process and that the entire plan is flawed and unworkable. Obviously, this is the exact opposite of what you are trying to accomplish. As you develop your own planning time line, you will want to identify the approval points that are appropriate for your library.

Schedules for Meetings

We are all way too busy. Every day is already full, and adding any new activity is difficult. This, while too bad, is the reality of our lives—and of the lives of all of the people we will be asking to participate in our planning process. One way to simplify the scheduling problems associated with the planning process is to select the times for all of the meetings before you make any committee appointments. That will allow people to check their schedules before committing to participate in the process. The alternative is to ask people to serve on the committee and then to try to find a time that is acceptable to all of them, a thankless task at best.

Select Meeting Locations

Before you can confirm your planning schedule you will have to decide where the various meetings will be held. This is the least complex of the 5 *W*s to resolve. There are really only two choices: in the library or not in the library. Most planning committees meet in a library meeting room because it is the most inexpensive option and it sends a continual subliminal message to the committee members about why they are meeting.

FIGURE 4

Sample Time Line

Task	Approval Point	Action	Date
Task 1 ↓	**Approval Point**	***Design Your Planning Process*** • Decide why, what, when, where, and who. • Develop a marketing strategy for the plan.	**Month One**
Task 2 ↓ **Tasks 3, 4, and 5** ↓	 **Approval Point**	**ORIENTATION MEETING FOR STAFF AND BOARD** Two-hour meeting, repeated as often as necessary. ***Before the Committee Orientation Meeting*** • Develop fact sheets about the community and the library. **COMMITTEE ORIENTATION MEETING** 2 hours Note: This is optional; it may be combined with the first meeting. **FIRST PLANNING COMMITTEE MEETING** 10:00–3:00 with box lunch *or* 4:00–9:00 with box dinner Note: This may be divided into two meetings. • Identify a community vision and needs and select preliminary library service priorities. ***Before Second Planning Committee Meeting*** • Send committee members, staff, and board notes from the first meeting and photocopies of the full descriptions of the preliminary service responses. • Ask library board to review the committee work and approve or recommend changes. • Meet with staff to identify current library strengths and weaknesses in relation to the draft priorities and to identify threats and opportunities if drafts become the library priorities.	**Month Two**
Tasks 6 and 7 ↓		**SECOND PLANNING COMMITTEE MEETING** 10:00–3:00 with box lunch *or* 4:00–9:00 with a box dinner • Review the library board's response to the vision, needs, and draft service priorities, and take any action necessary. • Give a presentation of the staff review of the preliminary service responses. • Select final service responses and identify target audiences for each. ***Before Meetings with Staff Teams*** • Develop goals and objectives based on the service responses and target audiences identified by the planning committee. • Appoint staff committees to develop a preliminary list of activities for each goal.	**Month Three**

(continued)

FIGURE 4
Sample Time Line (continued)

Task	Approval Point	Action	Date
Tasks 7 and 8		**MEETINGS WITH STAFF TEAMS** As many 1–1½ hour meetings as needed • Develop a composite list of activities to include in the plan. • Based on this list, determine what resources will be required. • Develop preliminary plans to obtain those resources.	**Month Three (cont.)**
Task 9	Approval Point	***Before the Third Planning Committee Meeting*** • Prepare a final draft of the library plan. • Distribute it to the planning committee at least one week prior to its meeting. **THIRD PLANNING COMMITTEE MEETING** 2 hours or less • Review final draft. • Recommend any needed changes. ***Before Presenting the Plan to the Board*** • Revise the plan as needed. • Send it to the board members two weeks prior to their meeting. **BOARD MEETING** • Present the plan to the library board for approval. Note: If you are a city or county department, do what is necessary to get the plan officially reviewed and approved.	**Month Four**
Task 10		***Communicate Your Plan*** • Distribute the final plan to the committee, staff, and board. • Continue to implement the marketing strategy for the plan.	**Month Five**
Tasks 11 and 12		***Implement Your Plan*** • Reallocate resources. • Monitor implementation.	**Ongoing**

Occasionally, planning committee meetings are held in nonlibrary space. There are a variety of reasons for this. Some libraries simply don't have any meeting room space. If the committee includes a number of staff members, the director may feel they will concentrate on the planning issues more if they are away from the distractions of their phones, e-mail, and desks. Wherever you decide to hold the meeting, be sure that all of the committee members receive directions to the meeting location and specific information about the name or number of the room in which they will be meeting.

Identify Whom to Include in the Process

As noted in the "Determine the Composition of the Planning Committee" section earlier in this chapter, before you can decide whom to appoint to the committee you have to decide whether to use a community-based planning committee. If you decide to appoint a committee composed only of staff members or of staff members and board members, the process is fairly straightforward. The most difficult task will be identifying those staff members who have something significant to contribute to the process. Some libraries, usually those with relatively few staff members, actively involve all their staff members by assigning each one to serve on a subcommittee. In larger libraries it is helpful to include staff members from various classifications and departments on a staff-based planning committee. Look for people with special skills or knowledge who are involved in their jobs and care about the future of the library. Select people who enjoy the challenge of working in a continually changing environment rather than people who always seem to be looking to the past with longing. Identify the informal leaders in the various units of the library, and involve them in the process. The credibility they have with their colleagues will be a valuable asset when the time comes to involve the entire staff in developing implementation strategies.

The appointment process is a little more complex if you plan to use a community-based committee. The responsibility for appointing committee members from the community varies depending on the governance structure of the library. If your library has an administrative library board, it probably has the final responsibility for such appointments. If your library is a city or county department, the city or county manager or council may have the final say. Regardless of who has the final responsibility, library staff should be involved in identifying potential committee members. This can be done as a collaborative process in a meeting or by developing a list of potential members and sending it to the appointing authority. If the library board is making the appointments, a collaborative approach is usually the most desirable option.

Role of Staff and Board Members on the Community-Based Planning Committee

Most community-based planning committees include one or two staff people and one board member as formal participants. In general, it is better to have a staff person other than the library director or one of the senior managers serve as the official member of the committee. When the library director or a senior manager serves as a formal member of the committee, there is a tendency among the community members of the committee to look to the director and manager for answers rather than working through issues on their own. Furthermore, at several points in the process the director will be making presentations to the committee, and this can be awkward if he or she is a member of the committee. The library director and senior managers are more effective as ex-officio members of the committee who attend all meetings but do not take an active part in discussions or decision making.

The role of the one or two staff members who serve as formal committee members is twofold. First, and most important, they will provide a communications link with the rest of the staff about the process and what actually happened during the committee meetings. This is a critical function. The community committee members will be identifying the needs the library should address. It is important that all staff understand the process used to identify the needs and believe that it was unbiased and driven by the community members and not by some hidden agenda of library management. Obviously, this is easier to do if the director and senior managers are ex-officio to the committee. The staff members selected to serve as actual committee members should have credibility with their colleagues. The president or past president of the staff association or the union may be a good choice. You might also consider appointing a long-time staff member or another informal leader who is respected by staff throughout the organization.

Staff committee members will also answer questions about current library services and priorities and participate fully in the discussions leading up to the selection of community needs. Therefore, you will want to select staff members who can participate in discussions as equals without becoming defensive if the library or particular policies are criticized or without feeling that their role on the committee is solely to be the expert on all library topics.

The board member who serves on the committee has roles similar to those of the staff members. His or her most important responsibility is to serve as a link between the board and the committee. In most cases, the community-based planning committee is advisory to the library board. However, it serves no purpose to appoint a committee of respected community members and then ignore their recommendations. The board representative on the committee can help ensure that there are no misunderstandings during the process and that board concerns about the committee's deliberations are heard before final recommendations are made. The board member will also serve as a resource on current programs and services of the library. It is just as important that the board member on the committee is able to respond nondefensively to criticism or suggestions for change as it is for the staff on the committee to be able to do so.

Chair or Facilitator

Before you can begin to identify which community members to invite to participate on the planning committee, you need to decide who will chair the committee. There are two choices: One is to appoint a respected community leader as the chair; the other is to appoint or hire a facilitator to direct the process work of the committee but not be involved in the actual content decisions being made. The pros and cons of each choice are described in figure 5.

One factor to consider when deciding who should lead the committee is the number of people you intend to appoint. In general, larger committees are more difficult to manage than smaller groups. If the planning committee will have nine or fewer members, you may not need a trained facilitator. If the committee will have more than nine members, it might be helpful to have a trained facilitator; if it will have more than fifteen members, it is highly likely that you will need a facilitator.

FIGURE 5

Who Should Lead?

COMMUNITY LEADER		TRAINED FACILITATOR	
Pro	**Con**	**Pro**	**Con**
Respected in the community and brings credibility to the process	May not have the skills needed to ensure that all members fully participate in the decision making	Trained to ensure that groups work together effectively	Can be difficult to identify good facilitators
May be able to help identify other community leaders	May become too involved in managing the committee to participate effectively in decision making	Has the skills to manage difficult committee members without confrontation	May need an extensive orientation to the library planning process if a nonlibrary facilitator
Participation may encourage others to participate	May be too busy with other commitments to manage chair responsibilities effectively	Can focus solely on the group interactions without being distracted by content issues	May charge a fee
		Perceived by the group and by staff as being neutral	

Selection of Community Members to Serve on the Committee

The three categories of people to consider when making committee appointments are stakeholders, people with certain skills, and community representatives. Stakeholders can be defined as people or groups who can affect or will be affected by an action. Clearly, staff and board members are library stakeholders and as such they have been included on the committee. Other library stakeholders to consider include specific user groups (children, literacy students, etc.) and organizations that rely on the library (schools, businesses, etc.).

There are also community stakeholders to consider. Identifying community stakeholders may be more challenging than identifying library stakeholders. We, after all, are quite familiar with our clients and the organizations with whom we already collaborate. Reaching out into the community to identify those individuals and groups that can affect us or that could be affected by our actions is more difficult, yet these are the very people and groups that need to be included if the community needs assessment process is going to be valid. Start by identifying community decision makers. Who in your community can influence elected officials? Who are the leaders of the various groups and organizations that combine to make up the fabric of your community? It might help to review the groups listed in figure 6 and to check those that apply to your community.

Once you have identified the groups that are stakeholders in your community, the next step is to decide who can speak for and to that group effectively. In the past, many libraries have selected committee members who happened to belong to a group or organization and assumed that those members could speak for the group. That isn't necessarily true. Furthermore, it is equally important that the people who serve on your committee have credibility with the groups they represent so that they can tell the members of the group how the library is designing services to meet their needs. This means that you are looking for people in leadership positions in the groups that you have identified as stakeholders.

Library directors and board members have on occasion been hesitant to ask business and professional leaders to serve on library committees. In fact, it hasn't been uncommon for a wife of the leader to be asked to serve instead, presumably on the theory that she would influence the leader while they are eating breakfast. That won't do for this process. The library is a critical community resource, and the library planning effort is vital to the effective appropriation and use of public monies. It is important that the right people come together to identify the community needs that will serve as the basis for the library's priorities.

FIGURE 6
Community Stakeholders

Businesses/Chambers of Commerce/Economic Development Organizations

Major employers, minority business owners, small business owners, visitors' centers, chambers of commerce (city, county, and ethnic, if any), economic development councils, industry councils

Community Services Organizations/Associations/Clubs

Rotary, Lions, Kiwanis, United Way, AARP, AAUW, American Red Cross, literacy organizations, Soroptimists, National Organization for Women, YWCA, YMCA

Cultural Groups

Theater groups, art leagues, dance supporters, arts commission

Educational Organizations

Public schools, private schools, colleges/universities, PTA or PTO, school boards, home school organizations

Ethnic Organizations

Ethnic chambers of commerce, NAACP, tribal councils, Latino/Hispanic groups, Asian groups, Urban League, refugee rights associations

Family Services Organizations

County department of social services, family service agency

Financial Representatives

Bankers, credit unions, financial planners, stockbrokers

Government/Political Representatives

Mayor, city/county manager, city council, county supervisors, city/county fiscal office, city/county planning office, law enforcement officers, job training programs

Health Organizations

American Cancer Society, American Heart Association, hospitals, public health nurses, public health clinics

Legal Organizations

Legal aid, ACLU

Library Representatives

School media center staff, college or university librarians, special librarians

Media Representatives

Newspaper, radio, TV, ethnic media, local magazines and newsletters

Organizations Serving the Disabled

Center on Deafness, Council of the Blind, state/county/city health and human services, Easter Seal, Goodwill, independent living centers, United Cerebral Palsy

Professional Groups

Medical associations, board of Realtors, bar association, business and professional women's groups

Religious Groups

Ministerial alliance, youth groups, Jewish community center

Senior Centers/Service Organizations

Area agency on aging, senior centers, nursing homes

Youth Services Organizations

Big Brother/Sister, Boy Scouts, Girl Scouts, FFA, FHA, child abuse agencies, city/county recreation programs, Junior Achievement, Head Start, Even Start, child care associations, local Association for the Education of Young Children, school-age care and enrichment programs

Adapted from a training handout prepared by Gail McGovern and Rhea Rubin.

A second category of people to consider are those with special skills. The skills that you want to have available on your committee will vary depending on local circumstances. Many libraries have found that people with technology skills (telecommunications, computer literacy, local networks, etc.) are useful committee members. Another person with unique skills who has much to contribute to the committee is the city or county planner. Other skills and knowledge that might be useful include law, fund-raising, architecture, marketing, local government, literacy, early childhood education, etc.

The third category of people to consider are representatives of the various demographic and socioeconomic groups in your community. Essentially, this means that you want the committee to look like your community. It should include young people and seniors, people with college educations and people with high school educations, parents, representatives from major businesses or industries, people from the various ethnic groups in the community, etc.

An issue that has been of some concern in the past when making committee appointments is the relative importance of library users and nonusers on the committee. If you follow the planning model recommended in figure 3, this is not a serious concern. You are likely to select some library users for their special skills and as representatives of demographic or socioeconomic groups. If you identify the leaders of stakeholder groups to include on the committee, you are almost sure to have some infrequent or nonusers, as well. Remember, the primary role of the community-based planning committee members is to identify community needs. It is far more important that the members understand the dynamics of the community than it is that they be library users. You will have lots of library experts on staff, and they will be responsible for making decisions that require library expertise. Many libraries have found that one side benefit of this planning process is that the community leaders who were nonusers and served on the committee learned about the library and became strong library supporters and advocates.

You might find it helpful to use Workform A: Selecting Planning Committee Members as a tool to record possible committee members in each of these categories. (See Part Four of this book.) It would be even more useful to ask a number of library staff and board members to complete Workform A and then compare the results. Names that appear on multiple lists would be serious candidates for the committee. You may also find that the same name appears in more than one category. For instance, John Smith might be listed as a stakeholder because he is president of the Rotary Club, appear on the skills list because he is a professional fund-raiser, and show up on the community representative list because he is active in the local African-American Chamber of Commerce. Clearly, Mr. Smith would be a great committee member.

There is no question that the process of identifying possible committee members and then balancing the stakeholders, the desired skills, and the community representation is going to be challenging. It is easier to complete the list in a group rather than doing it alone, and it is something that will take time. The time you spend will be worth it if you get a committee that can effectively identify the community needs the library should be addressing. One final point: because you are balancing so many different elements, when you select potential committee members it is helpful to have two or three possible candidates to fill each slot. Then if Mr. Smith can't serve, you will have already identified someone who has a similar profile and can ask that person instead. If you don't have this backup, you may find that the final committee doesn't look at all like what you thought it would when you began the appointment process.

Committees for Library Systems and Regional Libraries

As noted earlier, effective planning is based on identifying local needs. If you work in a large library system with multiple branches serving unique neighborhoods, or in a county system with library outlets in several communities, you will want to consider how you will identify local needs in each of those neighborhoods or communities. There are several choices. The simplest option is to have a single planning committee with representatives from each area served by the library, assuming that the representatives speak for their neighbors. Another possibility is to sponsor a series of focus groups in each area served by the library and then provide the data from those focus groups to the planning committee. A third choice would be to appoint a planning committee in each area served by the library to identify needs and select preliminary service priorities and then to bring those committees, or representatives from each, together to develop a composite list of priorities. Yet another alternative would be to develop a systemwide plan and then appoint a committee in each area the library serves to adapt that plan to meet local needs. You and your colleagues will have to decide which of these choices is right for your library. Needless to say, each of these options, except the first, will extend the planning time line.

Effective Invitations to Potential Committee Members

One of the biggest concerns for many library directors is how to convince the people they select as potential committee members to agree to serve on the planning committee. Too often librarians have had great difficulty in getting people to accept committee or board appointments. In fact, these negative experiences have made some librarians very reluctant to consider community-based planning committees at all.

The good news is that this process is different from earlier planning models (and certainly from board appointments) in one critical way—it has been streamlined. You will not be asking people to commit to an endless string of evening or weekend meetings lasting over a period of eight months to a year. Instead you will be asking them to attend two or three meetings within a month and a short final meeting at the end of the planning process. You will even be able to give them the dates of those meetings.

Another important thing you can do to encourage people to accept your invitation to serve on the committee is to tell the person *why* he or she is being asked to serve. After all, you have gone through a very thorough review and selection process to identify the people you are inviting. Tell them about it, and emphasize the skills and knowledge that each of them brings to the planning process. Tell them also about the services that you hope the library can provide to the constituencies they represent. That brings up another point. Beginning with your first conversation with potential committee members, you will want to define their responsibilities as twofold: They are being asked to represent certain stakeholders and constituents to the library, and they are also being asked to represent the library to those stakeholders and constituents. This two-way communication is vital to the successful completion and marketing of the library plan.

There are several practical details to decide before you can issue invitations to potential committee members. They include who will issue the invitations, when the initial calls will be made, how long you can wait for someone to decide if he or she will accept the appointment, and how you will coordinate the process if more than one person is issuing invitations. The following is a list of points to be covered during the preliminary phone call to a potential committee member:

> the name of the person calling and his or her relation to the library
>
> the purpose of the planning process
>
> why the person being called was selected to be included on the committee
>
> who else will be serving on the committee (if you already have some people who have agreed to serve)
>
> the timetable for the planning process
>
> the date, time, and place of the first planning committee meeting
>
> the date and time of the subsequent meetings
>
> the planning committee's role and responsibilities, including the limits of the planning committee's authority and its relationship to the library board and local government
>
> the process for reimbursement of any expenses incurred (mileage, parking, etc.), if applicable

You will want to write a confirming letter to each person who agrees to serve on the committee. Include in the letter all of the information covered in the phone call, and ask for a formal written acceptance of the appointment. Another option would be to include a stamped postcard for the committee members to use to formally accept their appointments to the committee.

Staff Planning Responsibilities

There are two final aspects of whom to consider before you are finished with Task 1. You will need to decide who is going to be responsible for managing the various tasks in the planning process and who will provide the needed clerical support for the planning process. This isn't always easy. Staff members are already fully occupied with their current responsibilities, and they don't necessarily respond enthusiastically to new assignments. It might be helpful to review the current responsibilities of the staff you want to involve in the planning process to see if some of those responsibilities can be deferred or handled by a temporary employee or another staff member.

Task 2: Prepare Board, Staff, and Committee

Planning by its very nature is about organizational change. Library managers across the country are working to create flexible organizations that can respond rapidly and effectively to the continually changing environment in which we all operate. The key to their efforts is effective communication.

Communication starts with the members of the library board or governing authority. It is critical that they understand and endorse the planning process. In a very real sense, most planning committees are working in an advisory capacity to the governing authority. You will want to be sure to keep the people on the board or in your government chain of command informed at every step of the process. To avoid confusion and potential discord, it is important that all understand their roles and responsibilities.

Organizational change does not happen from the top down; it only happens when staff at all levels understand why change is necessary and how the change process will operate. Furthermore, they need to have these things explained *before* the process begins, not after it is over. Staff also need to know that they will have a role in the planning process that will allow them to use their unique skills and expertise to help shape the organization's services and programs.

The members of the planning committee, too, must understand their roles and responsibilities. Not only must they be clear about the part the committee will play in helping define the library's priorities but they must also have some awareness of the library itself. Although the committee members' primary responsibility will be to identify community needs, they will also be making recommendations about the services the library should offer to meet those needs, and they will need a context for those recommendations.

One final group that needs to be kept informed about the planning process and the evolving library service priorities is the public. It is, after all, their library, and it is their money that pays for the services under discussion. It has been general practice for libraries to issue a press release at the end of the planning process. In many cases, it would be more effective to use the planning process itself as a way to increase awareness of the library and to underscore the library's commitment to providing services that respond to changing community needs.

Managers in each library will handle the public relations part of the planning process a little differently depending on their ongoing public relations programs. What is important is that this process be integrated into that ongoing public relations program from the beginning. That might start by announcing the planning process and publicizing the names of the committee members. The adoption of the library mission statement might provide another opportunity to publicize library priorities. Remember that library staff are not the only ones who will be publicizing the process. The community members who serve on your committee also have a responsibility to share the library story with their constituents.

Provide Orientation for the Board or Governing Authority

The orientation for the board or governing authority will probably be twofold. You will have to provide a preliminary introduction to the process to get approval to initiate a planning effort, but that should not be the only orientation the board or governing authority receives. After the planning process has begun, you will want to provide a more in-depth orientation to the process to ensure that everyone has the same expectations.

The key to providing a successful preliminary introduction to the process is to keep it simple. There is a tendency in these situations to overwhelm people with information. Remember that the goal is to get approval to initiate the process, not to make your board or supervisor within your governing authority an instant expert on library planning. You might want to organize your presentation around four of the *W*s discussed in Task 1 (the *where* doesn't seem too relevant in this context). Taken together why, what, when, and who cover the essential points that the members of the board or your governing authority will need to know to authorize the planning process. At this point the *why* and the *what* are the most important elements, and you will want to focus your verbal presentation on these areas. The *why* will differ for each library. The critical question to be addressed in the *what,* however, will be the same for most libraries: What kind of planning committee should be used? If you plan to recommend the use of the community-based committee, then you will need to be ready to explain the reasons for your recommendation. It might be helpful to review the *what* and *who* segments of Task 1 as you prepare your presentation.

People respond best when they receive information in several formats. It would be a good idea to develop a one-page handout covering the basic points of the planning process to distribute during your presentation. Figure 7 suggests one format you could use for such a handout. If you think there is a possibility you may encounter resistance to the idea of a community-based committee, consider including a copy of figure 3, Planning Responsibilities, as a handout as well.

FIGURE 7
Sample Orientation Handout

PUBLIC LIBRARY PLANNING OUTLINE

Why

The city is growing and changing, and library services and programs need to continue to grow and change with it. Library staff and board went through the long-range planning process four years ago, and we have worked hard to accomplish most of the goals and objectives in our plan. It is time for us to look again to be sure that we are using our resources effectively to meet the changing needs of the taxpayers.

What

We intend to use the standard public library planning process, *The New Planning for Results,* as the framework for developing the library plan. This process is a collaborative effort between community residents and staff. First, a planning committee, made up of community members representing various stakeholders and constituencies, will help the library identify the community needs. Then library staff will use their skills to develop new programs and services to address the needs identified by the committee.

When

The whole process will take less than six months. The emphasis will be on preparing for implementation and not on planning as an end in itself. We would like to start the process in early February and expect to have a completed plan in time to incorporate the new service priorities into next year's budget in August.

Who

Marie Garza, the director of the library, will work with members of the library board and staff to identify community members to be asked to serve on a library planning committee. She will also work with senior library managers to identify the staff members to be involved at each step of the process. The library board recommends that a professional facilitator be hired to help Ms. Garza manage committee meetings and work with staff to reach consensus on the programs and services that would best meet the needs identified by the committee. If we hire a facilitator, the total cost will not exceed $_____.

A second level of orientation is required for boards or governing authorities after the planning process has been approved. In general, library boards are more interested in the details of the planning process than other governing authorities will be, so if you are a part of a city or county government, you need to use your judgment with this part of the process. This phase of the board orientation will probably take one to two hours, which means the first decision to make is whether to try to do it during a regular meeting or to call a special meeting of the board. If your board is not overwhelmed with business, it is probably preferable to do the orientation at a regular meeting. Sometimes board members are not overly enthusiastic about additional meetings, and you want them to be in a positive frame of mind for your presentation.

Your presentation will be built on the information you presented when requesting approval to begin the planning process and will be organized in the same way. In this presentation you want to put most of your emphasis on what, when, and who. The main points to introduce in the *what* segment are the roles and responsibilities of the committee, the board, and the staff; the visioning process that will be used to identify community needs; and the library service responses. The *when* portion will include the specific time line for the project, with special emphasis on the decision points. It is at those points that the board will review and respond to committee or staff recommendations, which need to be clearly identified. The *who* part of the orientation has three purposes. First, it is intended to reiterate the relative roles and responsibilities of all of the participants. It may seem a bit repetitive, but it is critical that everyone understands and accepts these roles and responsibilities, particularly if you are using a community-based planning committee. It will also help the members of the planning committee to understand the three categories of people to consider including on the committee. Finally, you can end this portion of your presentation by actually beginning the process of selecting potential committee members, which provides a nice transition from orientation to implementation.

Once again, it is helpful to have a packet of printed materials to support your presentation. It won't hurt to include the planning outline you used in your first presentation in this packet. It provides a concise overview of the process. Other useful handouts include

planning steps and tasks (see figure 2)

planning responsibilities (see figure 3)

community vision statements (see Workform C)

library service reponses (see figure 10)

the library's planning time line

list of possible community stakeholders (see figure 6)

process to select planning committee members (see Workform A)

Most of these figures and workforms are for illustrative purposes only, but you and the board will use Workform A during your deliberations concerning the membership of the committee.

Obviously, the orientation for your board or governing authority is just the first step in what will be an ongoing series of communications about the progress of your planning efforts. You need to be sure that meetings have been scheduled at appropriate times in the process to review the recommendations that have been identified as decision points. You also probably want to make plans to send board members or the people in your chain of command copies of all communications sent to the members of the planning committee and the staff about the planning process.

Inform and Involve the Staff

The implementation of the final library plan rests solely in the hands of the library staff. It's very simple: Management cannot make meaningful changes without staff buy-in. We all know this, and yet some managers still resist involving all levels of staff in planning activities. There are lots of reasons for this resistance, and many of them are quite valid. We are all overworked, and it is both difficult and expensive to pull staff from their regular duties to attend one or more meetings about planning. Furthermore, some staff members don't have any real desire to be involved in the planning process on the front-end, although they often feel quite free to criticize the results during the process or after the fact. For some managers, information is power, and it is hard to share power. Other managers believe that written communications—these days usually in the form of e-mail—are sufficient to ensure that everyone is informed. Still other managers trust the traditional library communication hierarchy to spread the word about the planning process, often in the face of significant evidence that this is not a particularly accurate or effective mechanism.

Communicating with staff about the planning process begins even before the board or governing authority has approved the process. Library managers and supervisors should be included in discussions about the need to initiate a planning process. They can provide valuable insights into the *why* portion of your planning effort. Once the planning process has been approved, it is time to involve the rest of your staff. The most effective way to do this is to hold a series of orientation meetings for all staff. If possible, it is best to have the same person or people present the information about the planning process at each meeting. This ensures that everyone in the organization hears exactly the same message about the plan and can reduce complications later.

The staff orientation is similar to the board orientation, although there will be more emphasis on the library-specific parts of the process. It should be organized around *why, what, when,* and *who.* Staff members are going to be most interested in what and who, although clearly you need to explain why to provide them a context for the process.

Several important points should be conveyed during the staff orientation. First, staff need to clearly understand the distinction between identifying community needs and developing library programs and services to meet those needs. Figure 2: *The New Planning for Results* Planning Steps and Tasks, figure 3: Planning Responsibilities, and Workform C: Community Vision Statement may be helpful here. Second, you want to be very sure that staff understand that they will have ample opportunity to be heard during the process. It is particularly important for staff to know that they will be given an opportunity to review and respond to the committee's recommended service priorities before those recommendations are acted on (this is part of Task 5: Select Service Responses). You also want to emphasize that the planning committee will not be involved in the development of library programs or services or in any resource allocation decisions. These are tasks that require the special skills and knowledge that staff have worked for many years to develop.

It is just as important to keep the staff informed about progress on the plan as it is to keep the board informed. Some libraries have established a planning Web site for staff on the library intranet and posted all planning-related documents on that site. Others rely on memos and e-mail. Generally, it takes a combination of delivery methods to ensure that most staff receive information in a timely manner. Remember, communication does not occur until the message has been received and understood. Too many of us still think that communication occurs when the message has been sent. See "Library Communication" in the Tool Kit for more information on keeping staff informed about the planning process.

Introduce the Committee to the Process

The easiest way to design the committee orientation process is to use the now familiar 5 Ws—why, what, when, where, and who. The *why* seems fairly self-evident: You want to introduce the committee members to one another; you want them to understand their responsibilities; and you want to give them an overview of the planning process that will be used. Basically, you want to be sure that all of the committee members have a common understanding of the task before them and of the process that will be used to accomplish that task.

The *what* and *when* are a little more complex, and they are intertwined. If you decide to present the committee orientation as part of the first formal meeting of the committee and plan to go on in that meeting to discuss vision and current conditions, you automatically restrict the amount of orientation information that can be presented. If, on the other hand, you decide to have a separate committee orientation meeting, then you have opened up the options for what you can include in that orientation.

There are pros and cons to either choice. If you have a separate orientation meeting, the committee members will have a chance to think about their task for a week or so before they begin planning, which may be helpful. They may work together more effectively in their first planning meeting because they had a chance to get to know each other during an orientation, and that might lead to more open discussions and more effective recommendations. However, a separate orientation meeting will add to the time commitment you are asking committee members to make and will lengthen the overall planning process by one or two weeks. If you live in a small or medium-sized city and your committee members are likely to be acquainted with one another and with the library, you can probably do the orientation as a part of the first working meeting with no problems. If you live in a large city or serve a region or county and have put together a committee made up of people who have never met each other and have little in common, it might be worth the investment of time and energy to have an orientation meeting.

In either case, you need to design an orientation program that fits the time available and leads to the outcomes you have identified as important for the orientation. Special emphasis should be placed on helping committee members to understand the planning process to be used. Figure 2: *The New Planning for Results* Planning Steps and Tasks and figure 3: Planning Responsibilities provide the basic information the committee members will need. It might also be helpful to include the planning outline developed for use with the board. (See figure 7: Sample Orientation Handout.) That would provide some background and help the members of the committee understand why the library initiated the planning process in the first place. In fact, a lot can be said for using the same orientation handouts with different groups whenever possible: It is a good way to ensure that everyone is getting the same message.

You will also want to give the committee members some basic information about the library. There are several ways to do this. You can put together a one-page overview of library services and another page that includes a summary of the library budget, the number of staff, the number of items in the collection, etc. (See "Presenting Data" in the Tool Kit for more information.) If you have a separate orientation meeting, it makes sense to have it at the library regardless of where the following committee meetings will be held. This allows you to offer tours of the library to committee members following the meeting. One library with multiple units made arrangements to take committee members on a tour of branch libraries. That gave the committee members an excellent feel for the scope of the system and for the diversity of the neighborhoods served by the library. It is also nice to be sure that each committee member has a library card. If any do not, you might want to include an application form in their orientation materials and take them to the desk to get their cards after the meeting.

Timing is not an issue if you combine the orientation with the first working meeting of the committee. However, if you decide to have a separate meeting, *when* becomes important. Ideally, the orientation meeting should be scheduled no more than a week to ten days before the first working meeting. If the meetings are farther apart than that, you lose most of the benefits of having a separate orientation meeting. Committee members aren't going to remember much about the orientation if too much time goes by before the first working meeting.

The final decisions to be made are who will develop the orientation materials and who will lead the orientation meeting. The responsibility for developing materials can be assigned to anyone who has access to the information required and the skills needed to present it effectively. The question of who should lead the meeting is a little less clear-cut. The who section of Task 1 recommended that the library director and senior staff serve as ex-officio members of the committee rather than serving as leaders or full members. The one instance in which this may not hold true is the orientation meeting. The library director and senior managers could present this meeting quite effectively because it is an information meeting and not a working meeting. Staff expertise would be a positive thing when laying the groundwork for the planning process and introducing the committee to the library, whereas that same expertise might get in the way of eliciting opinions from the committee members later in the process.

Prepare to Communicate with the Public

The last decade has been an interesting time for libraries on many levels. One of the most challenging issues concerns the relationships among libraries and governments and the citizens they serve. For many years, although both users and nonusers had generally positive attitudes about libraries, they also perceived libraries as peripheral to government, on the very fringes of power with little or no influence. The changes in information technology in the past decade have radically altered that perception by both government officials and the public, and libraries are more closely tied to government than ever before. Unfortunately, this is occurring at the same time that public trust in government is dropping, and as a result that distrust is beginning to have an effect on libraries. Therefore, it is more critical than ever that we make sure that the taxpayers who support the library understand that we are committed to spending their tax dollars wisely to provide services that meet changing community needs. This planning process is tailor-made for that message.

However, as Himmel and Wilson noted in *Planning for Results:*

> All too frequently, libraries fail to think about the communications aspects of the planning process until the plan is being prepared for publication. The right time to think about this topic is before you begin to plan.[1]

The way to do that is to develop a public relations plan. According to the Public Relations Society of America (PRSA) "public relations helps an organization and its publics adapt mutually to each other."[2] The PRSA emphasis on multiple publics is particularly appropriate for libraries, which serve diverse groups throughout the community.

The public relations plan you develop should be specific to the planning process. You do that by listening to your publics. You can use figure 6: Community Stakeholders as a starting point for zeroing in on your diverse publics. Next, review the library's planning time line and identify points at which it would useful to disseminate information. These public communications might include the reasons for initiating the planning process, the results of the community needs assessment, the identification of the library goals, and a list of some of the more innovative activities that result from the plan. The key here is to identify the most important messages you want to deliver to your community. It is better to focus your public relations activities on a few critical points than to deliver a hodgepodge of miscellaneous information with no central theme.

There are lots of different ways to deliver your message to the various publics you have identified. They include newspapers, radio, television, announcements in local newsletters, flyers, inserts in local utility bills, Web pages, booths at school fairs, and presentations. You can even encourage others to reprint library stories in their school, association, or work newsletters. It is important to match the delivery mechanism and the audience. If you want to reach teens, it won't do you much good to put articles in senior newsletters. On the other hand, if you want to reach seniors, it won't be particularly effective to concentrate all of your efforts on Web-based delivery tools. Don't underestimate the power of personal communication when you develop your public relations plan. It may well be that a presentation by the library director to the chamber of commerce will be the most effective way to reach that particular group. Furthermore, library staff members shouldn't be the only people delivering the message. The members of the committee can serve as effective advocates for the library planning efforts.

Public relations programs don't have to be expensive, but there will be some costs associated with even the most bare-bones efforts. Obviously the delivery mechanism has a lot to do with the cost of the process. When you develop your public relations budget, don't forget to include printing and mailing costs. If your public relations plan will require extensive staff time, you may want to budget for that as well. Some libraries make arrangements for professional public relations firms to develop their marketing plans. These firms often work for the libraries at reduced rates or pro bono. Different people can be assigned to carry out the various parts of your public relations plan, but someone needs to be responsible for monitoring the implementation of the overall plan and for making the inevitable adjustments. See Task 10: Communicate the Results of the Plan to the Public for more information about marketing the plan after it has been approved.

Review Your Plan to Plan

Before you move on to the *imagine* step, take a little time to review the decisions you made during the *prepare* step. It takes a lot of work to plan to plan, and it involves a lot of people. However, there is no question that any time and energy put into the process at this point will be repaid many times over as the planning process moves forward. If the staff and the board understand and endorse the process before you begin, you reduce the chances of covert or overt resistance later on. Similarly, if the committee members understand their roles, you are far less likely to have to deal with inappropriate questions about library policy or personnel during their meetings. Finally, if you have developed a time line and allocated the resources required to complete the process, you will finish your plan in a timely manner and be able to begin implementation with a committed team of library and board members who understand how library priorities relate to the larger vision for the community.

NOTES

1. Ethel Himmel and William James Wilson, *Planning for Results: A Public Library Transformation Process* (Chicago: American Library Assn., 1998), 15.

2. PRSA Tampa Bay, *Public Relations: An Overview from the PRSA Foundation Monograph Series.* Available: http://tampa.prsa.org/pr101.html on 2/2/00.

Chapter 2

IMAGINE
Identifying
Possibilities

MILESTONES

By the time you finish this chapter you will know how to

- gather data about your community

- look to the future to develop a vision for your community

- identify current conditions in your community and compare them with the vision for the future

- determine what needs to be done to move the community closer to the vision for the future

- present data about current library programs and services

- identify which community needs the library can help the community meet

This may be the most exciting time to be a public librarian since Melvil Dewey first developed the Dewey decimal system. Of course, that is both the good and the bad news. Many of us could learn to live with a little less excitement and a little more stability. However, excitement is what we have, and it does create a wonderful planning environment. When we look to the future we see an infinite number of possibilities. The services we might offer are limited only by our own imaginations and the imaginations of our staff and of the people involved in our planning process.

This step, *imagine,* provides a framework to help planners consider how the library can take advantage of the possibilities to provide improved services to the community. In essence, in this step you identify the priorities that will become the foundation for the rest of the plan and therefore for the services and programs your library will be offering over the next several years. You can't build a strong plan on a weak foundation any more than you can build a strong house on sand.

Planning, at the most basic, is about defining priorities, and the first thing any planning process must do is provide the criteria that will be used to identify those priorities. All three of the previous public library planning models have recommended that "community needs" be used as the basis for determining priorities, although the term has been defined a little differently in each version of the planning process. In *A Planning Process for Public Libraries,* the authors stated:

> The first planning process step begins with a description of the community and its people. This usually entails creating a community profile, that is, a summary of the information available from secondary sources such as the census, and collecting some new information directly from the community's residents and knowledgeable individuals: primary sources.[1]

The underlying assumption in that book—that effective library services must be developed to meet unique community needs—was a new con-

DO use the resources available from local and state planning offices to gather data about your community

DO be open to new ideas when determining which community needs the library can help meet

DO keep the staff informed about the committee's activities and recommendations

DON'T assume that you already know everything there is to know about your community

DON'T limit your vision for the future to those areas that seem to relate directly to the library

DON'T forget that you are part of local government and should be working with other agencies to help the community reach its vision

cept to many library managers. So was the idea that they didn't already know everything there was to know about the communities they served. The processes and forms used to collect the information needed to create the community profile took up nearly two-thirds of that book, and the data collection and statistical manipulation required for the kind of community profiling recommended in it was both staff- and time-intensive. Many managers in small and medium-sized libraries discounted that entire planning process because they couldn't imagine how they would find the resources to complete the community analysis. In some larger libraries, managers became so bogged down in collecting and analyzing data that they never moved along into the planning process.

The committee members and consultants responsible for the second planning model, *Planning and Role-Setting for Public Libraries,* responded to concerns about the extensive community analysis component of *A Public Library Planning Process* by sharply reducing the emphasis on community data collection. In fact, the whole process was renamed "looking around" in an effort to make it more user friendly. A minimum level of data collection was recommended: "At the basic and moderate levels of effort, the planning committee selects only a small set of data and confines its information gathering to existing sources of information."[2] The actual community data collection instrument was two pages long—a far cry from the 150 pages of recommended data collection instruments and instructions in *A Public Library Planning Process.* This abbreviated process worked well for some library managers, but it seemed somewhat cursory to others. After all, if library excellence is defined locally, then library managers had better know a good bit about all of the people in the community before they begin selecting library service priorities.

The committee members and consultants responsible for *Planning for Results: A Public Library Transformation Process* reviewed the issues surrounding the collection of community data and discovered something interesting: It didn't appear to matter how much or how little data library managers collected about their communities; library priorities (roles) were almost always selected based on the personal beliefs of the people making the selections. It seemed that the major problem wasn't the amount of data collected but rather the way the data was used. Neither of the two planning processes published in the 1980s provided planners with a way to put the data gathered about their communities into a context that could be used for decision making.

Planning for Results provided the context needed for planners to use data about the community to identify community needs and then to connect those needs to library service priorities. That context came from a three-pronged process. First, the planning committee created a vision for the future of the community, a picture of what the community would look like in ten years if everything were perfect. Then the committee identified current conditions in the community in relation to their vision for the future. Finally, they looked at the difference between where the community was today and where they hoped it would be in ten years. Those differences were the needs to be addressed if the vision were to be achieved. The process can be clearly diagrammed:

$$\text{Vision} - \text{Current Condition} = \text{Needs}$$

This book takes the same approach, and the two tasks you need to accomplish the *imagine* step are

> TASK 3
> Determine community vision
>
> TASK 4
> Identify community needs

Task 3: Determine Community Vision

When undertaking Task 3, it becomes clear just how critical the composition of the planning committee really is. The members of the committee will be the people who identify a vision for the future of your community and decide what, in their opinions, needs to be done to reach that vision. This in turn will provide the criteria used to determine library services priorities. It is obviously vital that all community stakeholders be represented on the planning committee. It is also critical that the planning committee membership reflect the demographic composition of your community. The community vision upon which everything else will be based is valid only if it is fair and inclusive.

While it is important that the members of the committee have a first-hand knowledge of the community and its strengths and weaknesses, it is unreasonable to expect them to know everything about everything. A part of this task will be to decide what data about the community the members of the committee need for informed decisions, to collect that data, and then to format the data in such a way that the committee members can use it. As noted earlier, this is not easy to do, and more than one library manager has become so entangled in data collection that the planning process itself became secondary or was abandoned entirely—not a desirable outcome.

Collect Data about the Community

Several questions need to be answered before you begin to collect data about the community. The first, and most important, question is what kinds of information the committee will need to make informed recommendations. The answer will depend on two factors: the composition of the planning committee and the complexity of your planning environment. If you have selected a planning committee that includes community leaders and is broadly representative, you will probably find that they already know a lot about the community and won't want or need extensive background materials. Workform B: Community Data provides a basic list of suggested community data elements to consider. Most of the information called for on Workform B should be available from your city or county planning office.

If you are working with a staff or board committee, you may very well need more community data to ensure that all community elements are considered. Even with a community-based committee, you may decide that one or more of the community stakeholder groups are underrepresented. You may have similar concerns if you are planning for a large county system that serves a variety of communities. In this complex environment it will probably be necessary to provide the members of the committee with additional data about each of those communities. As you review your committee and your planning environment, it may help to make a list of the kinds of information that the committee will need during their deliberations that is unlikely to be provided by the members themselves.

Next you need to decide what specific data will be needed to support the information you intend to provide the committee. For example, if you decide that a stakeholder group is not represented on the committee, you may be concerned that specific issues of great interest to that group will not be discussed. Therefore, you will want to collect data that presents those interests. You will not be interested in collecting general demographic data about the stakeholder group in question. If you are planning in a large county, you may be concerned that the committee members will not understand the diversity of the county. Therefore, you will collect data that underscores that diversity and not data that provides a generic look at services and programs throughout the county. The key here is to focus on collecting data that meets a preidentified information need.

The third, and potentially most vexatious, question is how to collect the data you need as quickly and easily as possible. Many data collection methods are available, including questionnaires, individual interviews, focus groups, observations, expert opinions, number gathering, and compilations of existing data. The question is how to select from among them. Debra Wilcox Johnson recommends that you use two criteria for selecting a data collection method: meaningfulness and practicality. *Meaningfulness* relates to usefulness of the data collected. *Practicality* refers to the affordability of the data collection process in terms of intrusiveness, ease, and cost.[3] If we apply these criteria to the case of the stakeholder group not represented on the planning committee, it seems likely that a focus group composed of representatives from that stakeholder group will provide the most meaningful information in the most affordable way. By holding a focus group, we can actually ask people what they think and quickly and easily write up the results for the planning committee to review. A questionnaire might ultimately give us similar information, but it would be much more expensive to administer and tabulate. Compilations of existing data, on the other hand, would be unlikely to provide any meaningful data to support the information needed (the issues and concerns of the stakeholder group) and therefore would be pointless, no matter how easy they might be to put together.

The final question to consider is how you will present the data to the committee so that it can be easily understood and used. See "Presenting Data" in the Tool Kit for more information.

Understand Why Planning Starts with Community Vision

Some librarians and board members have asked why a library planning process should begin by defining a community vision. Shouldn't we be more concerned with the library's vision than that of the whole community? Doesn't this focus on community create a risk that the unique characteristics of the library will be lost in the big picture? These questions reflect the long-standing attitude among some library managers and supporters that the library can and should exist separately from the rest of the city or county. Nothing could be farther from the truth in today's environment. Public libraries are tax-funded institutions, and taxpayers increasingly expect all tax-funded bodies to work together to provide services and programs. Collaboration is the name of the game, and library managers who have learned to play that game well are reaping big rewards.

On the other hand, library managers who continue to insist that the library is unique and can't be expected to plan in conjunction with other city or county departments place themselves—and the libraries they lead—in considerable jeopardy. One such library manager was the director of the library in a middle-sized community when the city council hired a new city manager. The city manager's first act was to initiate a planning process based on developing a community vision and defining how various city departments could help reach that vision. When the draft goals and objectives were sent to the city department heads for review and comment, the library director responded by saying: "Only one of these ten goals applies to the library. We are going to develop our own plan based on library users and the services and programs they need." The city manager replied: "You can develop whatever kind of plan you want to. The city will be providing funding for programs that support the goals and objectives in the citywide plan."

This story ended with the departure of the library director, to no one's surprise. However, to quote Paul Harvey, it is the "rest of the story" that is truly interesting. The city hired a new library director who looked at the city goals and objectives and said: "Of course, our programs and services can support these outcomes." The goals addressed such issues as providing services for children at risk, establishing job training programs, improving education opportunities for children and adults, strengthening multicultural relationships, and retaining a strong sense of the community's heritage. These are all issues to which libraries can make significant contributions.

You might wonder how the first director could have been so blind as to not see the connections between the city's goals and objectives and possible library services. However, before you get too judgmental, remember how insular the library vocabulary is and how many of our staff focus on doing things the way they have always done them. Remember, too, that no one is excited about being told by an "outsider" how to do business, and it is easy to say, "He doesn't understand libraries; therefore nothing he says could possibly have any merit." The increasing emphasis on communitywide collaboration to provide tax-funded services is relatively new, and like all new ideas, it takes some time to get used to it. However, one message comes across loud and clear: Library managers who consider themselves separate from other city or county departments and not responsible for looking at the needs of the whole community do so at their own peril.

Another question that is occasionally raised is whether it is appropriate for a library planning committee to develop a vision for the community as a whole. This question implies that it is somehow presumptuous for the library to consider the broader community in its planning efforts. If the library planning committee members were being asked to develop a community vision that would then be used as the basis for communitywide planning, there might be some legitimate concerns about the need to validate the vision with other groups and organizations. However, the visioning component of this process is intended to provide a framework for library planners to identify community needs and nothing else. This piece of the process is certainly not intended to take the place of a full-scale community visioning process. In fact, in some communities it has generated interest in initiating such a process.

The final question that has been raised about community vision concerns how to handle this part of the process if your community has already developed a community vision statement. If you are in this fortunate position, you should be glad that you live in a progressive community interested in planning, and you should use the existing vision as the starting point for the committee's deliberations. In many instances existing community visions have been refined and combined to the point that some of the details have been blurred or lost. One way to handle this is to ask the committee members to deconstruct the vision statement, moving from the general to the specific. This allows the members of the committee to look at the assumptions upon which the vision was based and to create a list of vision statements that grow naturally from the more concise existing community vision.

Sometimes library planners discover that although their city or county does not have a vision statement, various organizations in the community have gone through visioning processes. It may be helpful to gather copies of these visions for the committee members to review before the meeting in which they will develop their community vision statements. It never hurts to consider a variety of points of view—and it often results in a stronger final product.

Create the Community Vision Statements

Derek Okuba, the director of the National Civic League Community Assistance Team, defines community vision as a shared sense of the future. He goes on to say:

> A community's vision should reflect the common values of the community; at the same time, however, it needs to be inclusive of the diverse populations which make up that community. Moreover, a community vision is not a "cookie cutter" type of document. A vision should reflect those qualities that make a community unique.[4]

In essence, the purpose of the visioning component of this process is to describe a destination; the rest of the plan then provides the road map for reaching that destination. It is important to remind the committee members that they are not creating a single vision statement. No single vision of the future could possibly encompass the entire community. Rather, they will be looking into the future to describe a range of ideal conditions they hope will exist in their community in ten years. It is not only possible, but probable, that some of the vision statements developed by the committee will be contradictory. That is fine. There is room for more than one picture of the future, and discussion of the differences and similarities in the vision statements will help committee members better understand themselves and each other.

It is also important to keep the focus of the vision statements on the community and not on the library. Sometimes committee members, knowing that they are working on a library plan, limit their vision statements to things that they think will affect the library. This can be a particular problem with a planning committee composed solely of library staff and board members. When the committee members have completed their work, at least some of the vision statements should be as applicable to the police department, the department of parks and recreation, the development office, and schools as they are to the library. If this is not the case, the committee members have restricted the library possibilities before the planning process really begins. The visioning process is supposed to help us look at how library services can be redefined to meet new and changing community needs. If we keep firmly focused on things the library is doing now, we make that difficult to do.

As committee members begin to describe their ideal future, they should be encouraged to consider specific constituent groups. The strongest vision statements will identify a target population, then describe the desired condition or circumstance of that population in the ideal future, and finally state the result of that condition or circumstance:

Target population: All children

Desired condition or circumstance: . . . will have the education they need to find jobs

Result: . . . that provide wages that allow them to live a comfortable lifestyle.

However, some vision statements may address the community as a whole:

Target population: Anytown

Desired condition or circumstance: . . . will be a desirable tourist destination

Result: . . . and that will generate increased tax revenues to support needed services.

The members of the planning committee can use Workform C: Community Vision Statement to help structure their discussions. You might get other ideas about helping the committee members develop vision statements by "participating" in the Anytown Planning Experience: Part 1—Creating a Community Vision that follows. (A description of the Anytown Public Library and the Anytown planning committee was presented in the introduction to this book.)

THE ANYTOWN PLANNING EXPERIENCE

PART 1 Creating a Community Vision

At the first meeting of the planning committee the facilitator (or chairperson) reviews Workform C: Community Vision Statement with the committee, answers any questions they may have, and makes sure that everyone understands the purpose of the workform and the process to be used to complete it. The facilitator then divides the twelve members into four groups of three. (These can be self-selected or assigned groups, depending on the facilitator's preference.) The four groups are given approximately one hour to complete Workform C. Because some groups finish in 45 minutes and others need an hour and a quarter, the facilitator monitors the progress of each group and adjusts the time as needed.

At the end of the small-group work sessions, each group reports a vision statement, taking turns in a round-robin process: The spokesperson for the first small group reads one of their vision statements, then the second group reads one of theirs, and so forth. Then the process starts again. The facilitator records the vision statements on newsprint and posts them on the walls in the meeting room. This reporting generates a reasonable amount of conversation. The first small group reports that one of their vision statements is "Preschool children in Anytown will enter school ready to learn." Groups two and three chime in "We said that too." The facilitator does not record similar vision statements more than once and doesn't indicate the relative priority or weight of the various statements at this point. As the groups discuss their visions during the reporting process, they identify additional vision statements. The facilitator encourages the committee members to expand on each other's work.

However, the facilitator discourages arguments about the relative merits of the various vision statements at this point, stating that the purpose of this exercise is to record all of the statements of the committee that describe the desirable future of the community, no matter how many—or how contradictory. One group says "Anytown will retain its rural character and restrict growth to ensure that it continues to provide a healthy and attractive environment." A second group says "Workers in Anytown will have access to a wide variety of jobs in both retail and industrial settings so that they have employment opportunities that match their skills." The facilitator records both vision statements without debate.

When all groups have reported and all of the possible visions for the community have been recorded, the facilitator suggests that the group review the visions and combine those that are similar, clarify those that seem ambiguous, and debate any that seem contradictory or incompatible. While not trying to help the group reach consensus, the facilitator makes sure that everyone understands all of the vision statements listed and that the visions are not unduly repetitious. When this part of the process is over, there are still vision statements that are contradictory to one another on the list, thus reflecting an appropriate diversity of the community and of the committee. The facilitator gives the group a short break.

Task 4: Identify Community Needs

In Task 4, the members of the planning committee will compare the idealized future described in their vision statements with the current conditions that exist in the community. When they have reached agreement on where they are now in relation to where they want to be, they will identify a list of the needs to be addressed if the community is to achieve their vision for its future.

This list of needs will be used as the basis for the second part of this task, in which members of the committee will discuss which needs might be addressed by the library. However, before they do that, committee members will be given more information about current library services and programs, including data on usage patterns over the past five or ten years. As they review the current library services, committee members may identify a critical community need that the library is currently meeting that did not emerge during the visioning process and decide to add that need to their list.

At the end of this task, the members of the committee will make a preliminary selection of the community needs that the library could address through targeted services and programs. They will base their selections on the suitability of the library to address the need in question and on the number of other agencies working to meet the need.

Define Current Conditions in the Community

The planning committee will identify the strengths in the community that support the efforts of residents to reach the future described in the vision and the weaknesses that exist in the community that may impede progress toward the desired future. They will also look at the opportunities that might be available to help move the community forward and the threats that might affect the community's ability to grow and change.

This may seem like a monumental undertaking, but it is a more manageable process than it appears to be on the surface. In the first place, committee members will not be trying to describe every detail of every part of the community. Instead they will be looking at the present in relation to the future they described in the vision statements. That automatically focuses their discussions and provides a context for their conclusions.

Furthermore, the process of defining current conditions doesn't happen in an unstructured environment. The committee will use a powerful strategic planning tool called a SWOT analysis as the framework for their discussion. SWOT is a mnemonic device:

S = Strengths
W = Weaknesses
O = Opportunities
T = Threats

The strengths and weaknesses in a SWOT analysis normally refer to existing conditions. Potential strengths and weaknesses include the educational environment, the economic base, recreational opportunities, the transportation infrastructure, housing, medical care, etc. The opportunities and threats refer to potential scenarios that may occur as the community moves toward the future. Opportunities might include a proposed bond referendum, the inclusion of the community in a regional transportation plan, the possible construction of a new hospital, or the expansion of the local community college system. Threats might range from national conditions, such as a recession, to state issues, such as unfunded mandates from the legislature, to local circumstances, such as the fact that the community has a narrow economic base or that a major employer might go out of business.

Workform D: SWOT Analysis of the Community will help the committee members structure their discussions and provide a place for them to record the responses. The Anytown Planning Experience: Part 2 presents additional suggestions for helping the members of the planning committee complete a community SWOT analysis.

THE ANYTOWN PLANNING EXPERIENCE

PART 2 Completing the SWOT Analysis of the Community

After their break, the facilitator (or chair) asks the committee members to return to the same three-member groups that worked together to identify vision statements, thus letting the members of each work group continue their discussions from the point at which they quit their deliberations to report their vision statements. The facilitator distributes Workform D: SWOT Analysis of the Community to the committee members and explains the SWOT analysis process, with special emphasis on the fact that committee members should be considering current conditions in the context of the future described in the vision statements.

The facilitator gives the work groups approximately an hour to complete the SWOT analysis. One group is able to complete the process more quickly, but the other groups need a little additional time. The facilitator notes the time every 15 minutes to encourage the groups to move ahead to the next section of the SWOT analysis. When one of the work groups seems to be bogged down, the facilitator joins that group to see if she can help the members move forward. During this exercise, lunch is served.

At the end of the time allotted for the SWOT analysis, the facilitator records the decisions of the groups on newsprint, starting with the strengths each group identified. Once again, to ensure that each group has an equal voice, the reports from the groups are taken in a round-robin process. As in the earlier exercise, this reporting generates conversation as groups note the similarities or differences in their responses.

When all of the strengths have been recorded, the facilitator posts them on the walls in the meeting room and moves on to the list of weaknesses. These are reported in the same way as the strengths and again posted on the walls. The same item is reported as both a strength and a weakness, according to the points of view of the members of the group discussing the item. A group interested in economic development defines the fact that a commuter railroad is being built as a strength, while another group, more interested in preserving the character of the community, defines the same thing as a weakness. Because this is perfectly appropriate, the facilitator makes no effort to resolve any differences of opinion or to reach consensus. The facilitator comments, "We are trying to create a picture of the community, and the more complex the picture is, the more likely it is to be accurate."

The facilitator next records the lists of opportunities and then the lists of threats, posting them on the walls as each is complete. Again, some of these repeat items listed as strengths and weaknesses, and again the facilitator notes that classification of opportunity or threat depends on the perception of the group making the classification. Then the group takes another short break.

List Community Needs

When the facilitator has listed all of the strengths, weaknesses, opportunities, and threats on newsprint and posted them on the walls of the meeting room, it is time for the members of the committee to identify the community needs reflected in all that information. In this instance, *community need* can be defined as a description of what will be required to move from a specific current condition to one of the vision statements defined by the members of the committee.

The members of the committee might want to consider several questions as they compare the vision statements and the current conditions:

Which community strengths provide the strongest foundation for making progress toward the visions?

Are there current community strengths that are not likely to contribute to helping make progress toward the visions? If so, can they be reshaped to be more useful in the areas that we believe are going to be important in the future?

Which of the weaknesses in the community have the potential for being the most detrimental to efforts to make progress toward the visions? How can they be addressed?

What can be done to ensure that the community takes full advantage of the opportunities that are likely to occur?

How can the members of the community prepare to deal with the threats that might impede progress toward the visions?

There is a real danger that during the process of defining needs, the specificity implicit in the vision statements and the results of the SWOT analysis will be lost. Remember, the intent is to *summarize,* not to homogenize. It is important to define community needs as explicitly as possible. These needs will be used as the criteria against which various library service priorities will be measured later in the planning process. The more clearly and concisely the needs are defined, the easier they will be to use. Many of the vision statements developed by the committee refer to specific target audiences. Encourage the committee members to continue to refer to those audiences as they identify needs. This will help everyone involved in the planning process stay focused on the specific outcomes defined in the vision statements.

The Anytown Planning Experience: Part 3 that follows presents a suggested process for helping members of the committee identify community needs.

<table>
<tr><td>

**THE
ANYTOWN
PLANNING
EXPERIENCE**

**PART 3
Listing
Community
Needs**

</td><td>

The facilitator defines community needs and goes over the discussion questions listed before the break. The facilitator encourages questions about the process to be used and then asks the committee members to return to their original work groups for one final session. The groups are given 10 to 15 minutes to list the community needs they see resulting from the visioning process and the SWOT analysis. (The time allotted for this part of the process is limited on purpose, as it forces the members of the group to focus their thoughts quickly.)

</td></tr>
</table>

The groups report in the now-familiar round-robin format, and the facilitator records their comments on newsprint. When all of the groups have reported, the facilitator reads the needs out loud and asks if anyone has any additions to the list. The facilitator then goes through the list one at a time and encourages the members of the committee to make any needed clarifications, to specify target populations, or to do whatever else is necessary to make the needs as explicit as possible. (Note: This is not the end of the meeting; discussion of it continues in chapter 3.)

Review Current Library Services

The vision, SWOT, and needs identification process is an effective way to encourage planning committee members to think about the community and the services that tax-supported organizations could and should provide to make it a better place to live. The outward focus inherent in this process to this point is a critical component of any successful library planning effort. However, this focus on the community does not give planning committee members the whole picture.

As mentioned previously, to complete the identification of needs prior to making recommendations about library service priorities, the members of the committee will also have to understand how people currently use the library. They will also have to consider what the current use patterns suggest in the way of community perceptions and expectations for library services and programs. This does not mean that we have come this far in the process only to now decide that we will continue business as usual so as not to upset our regular users—or our staff. That would be as inappropriate as developing an entire plan without ever factoring into the needs assessment process information on how the library is currently being used.

Presenting information about current library services and programs to the members of the committee can be tricky. On one hand, you want them to understand the library's current strengths and the trends you and the staff have observed. On the other hand, you don't want to seem to be preaching to retain the status quo or in any way appear to be defensive about the possibility of change. Obviously, you expected that the committee would recommend some changes when you began the planning process; otherwise, there would have been little point in investing all of this time and effort in planning. That does not mean that it is easy to sit in a room and hear people who don't know much about the library talk about its future. In Task 1 it was recommended that the library director and senior staff members serve as ex-officio members of the committee rather than as full participating members. It is at this point in the proceedings that the wisdom of that recommendation may become most apparent.

Normally, the most appropriate person to present information about current services and programs to the committee is the library director. The presentation should be no longer than twenty minutes and should be supported with suitable written documentation. This presentation will provide a more in-depth look at the library than the introductory presentation that may have been made during the committee orientation, but it should not be so data-dense that it overwhelms the listeners.

Library Data Issues

As you develop the presentation, you might want to review recommendations given for gathering data about the community in Task 3. As in that process, first you decide what information about the library the members of the committee will need to make informed recommendations. That will probably include information about the major services of the library and some sense of how those services have been and are being used. It will also probably include information about the library's resources: number of outlets, budget, number of staff, number of items in the collection, level of automation, etc.

Next, you will decide what data will provide the committee with the information they need. This will no doubt include usage statistics, budget information, etc. Consider providing trend data in these categories to give committee members some idea of how services have been used over a period of five or ten years and what kinds of changes have occurred in the library's resource base during the same period. It can also be helpful to provide some information about use and resources in comparable libraries to give the committee members a context for the data they are reviewing.

Collecting the library data you decide you need will be less onerous than collecting data about the community, because you probably have almost all of the library data you need in some format already. The problem will be to find it and then to format it in such a way that the committee will be able to easily understand it. Be careful to select data that will be meaningful to the committee. There is a tendency to include data that isn't particularly relevant just because we have it readily available; this is not a situation in which more is better. Workform E: Library Data and the "Presenting Data" section in the Tool Kit may both be useful when preparing the data for the committee.

It is critical that you present the data as fairly and honestly as you can. As British politician and author Benjamin Disraeli noted: "There are lies, damned lies, and statistics." We all know that statistics can be manipulated to reflect a particular point of view or belief. Most of us would have little reason to manipulate the data about our community; however, sometimes the temptation to use data to support a strongly held library belief or to present the library in a particular way can be almost overwhelming.

Skewing of data can happen in a variety of ways. For example, a library director creating a chart comparing the library's resources with similar libraries might choose only those libraries that have significantly more resources to include in the chart, thereby presenting an inaccurate picture of the relative resources available to the library. Another director might decide not to include data on circulation trends because he is unhappy about the continued decline in the circulation of print nonfiction materials and doesn't want the committee to focus on that. Yet another director might lump together children's and adult circulation figures rather than have to explain to the committee why the children's collection, which gets so much use, receives such a relatively small percentage of the collection budget.

The directors who skew data in these ways are running real risks. All of the statistics about your public library and the other public libraries in your state and across the country are public documents. They are available to anyone who asks or who knows where to look. All it takes is one person who decides to get more information to create a potentially unpleasant situation. At the very least, the director who presented the data will have to explain why certain data elements were excluded. In the worst-case scenario, the director's credibility will be seriously damaged. It is both easier and safer to present all of the pertinent data and deal with questions that result openly and honestly.

Additions to the Needs List

When the library director has completed his or her presentation about the library, the members of the planning committee should be given a chance to ask questions and to discuss current library services in the context of the preliminary list of needs they developed after completing the community SWOT analysis process. It is not uncommon for them to decide to add one or more needs to the list based on what they have heard. For example, a number of planning committees have reached this point in the process and determined that there was a need for citizens to have a place to go to get answers to their questions if the community was going to be able to achieve its vision. Other committees have decided that the recreational need being filled by the library was not clearly represented on the preliminary needs list. Any additional needs the committee members identify should be added to the list of needs to be considered by committee members as they continue their deliberations.

Select the Needs the Library Can Address

The final activity in this task is for the members of the committee to review the list of needs they have identified in their first meeting and select from among those needs the ones that might be effectively met using current or potential library resources and staff skills. The committee members will have to consider two basic questions as they make their selections. The first question concerns how well suited the library is to meet a given need, and the second concerns how many other organizations are working on the need under review. These questions are presented in the form of a decision tree as shown in figure 8.

FIGURE 8
Needs Decision Tree

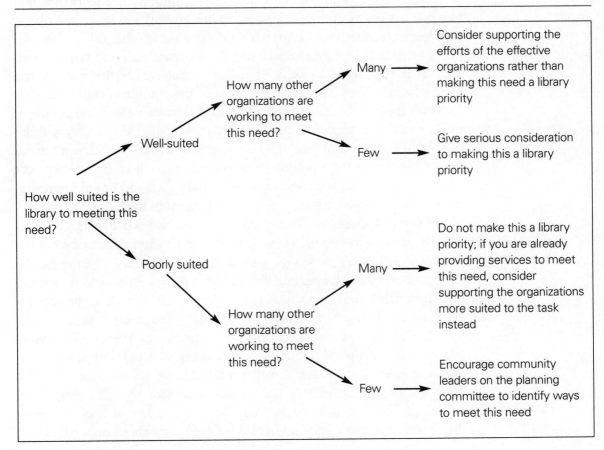

Needs the Library Is Suited to Address

The issue of suitability is the more important of the two questions to answer. It also can be the more difficult to assess, although in some instances the answers seem fairly obvious. For example, many communities need to improve the transportation infrastructure. While this is no doubt an important need, there clearly isn't much the library can do to build roads. Library managers and staff don't have the equipment, the training, or the responsibility for road work. Therefore the library is not the suitable agency to take the lead in meeting this need. Depending on community conditions, however, this need might be identified as an area in which library staff could support the work of other community groups to provide people in various neighborhoods with a forum to discuss transportation issues.

Unfortunately, the question of suitability is not always this clear-cut. Remember the story about the library director who didn't think the library was well-suited to address such issues as services for children at risk, job training, improved education opportunities for children and adults, strengthened multicultural relationships, and retaining a strong sense of the community's heritage.

This is yet another point in the planning process when it is often easier to work with a committee made up of community residents than it is to work with a committee composed of library staff and board members. Residents are much less likely to have their sense of what is possible limited by the blinkers of tradition and habit than are staff and board members. It is that sense of what is possible that makes this part of the process work. After all, the whole point of the planning effort is to look for ways the library can be more relevant and responsive to the people in the community, which, in turn, clearly implies that the library will be serving new client groups and addressing new needs. That doesn't make the process of identifying those new client groups or seeing the connections to those new needs any easier for library staff and board members, many of whom have a long-term vested interest in the status quo.

The truth is that many library staff members and board members enter any planning process with a clear picture in their own minds of what the results should be. Anyone who was involved in selecting roles using the 1987 process from *Planning and Role-Setting for Public Libraries* can remember long arguments about the various roles. Almost all of those arguments revolved around the words "I believe" and "in my experience." As noted earlier, only rarely was a connection made between the roles under review and the data gathered about the community, the theoretical basis for choosing roles. In contrast, consider the processes recommended in this book. All of the activities in Tasks 3 and 4 provide the members of the committee with the information they need to decide which of the needs they have identified can be addressed by the library based on what is best for the community and not what is currently standard operating procedure in the library or the belief structure of any individual.

The members of the committee may want to ask several questions to assess the suitability of the library to address a given need. These include the following:

> What special skills, if any, are required to address this need?
>
> Are these skills that library staff members have or could acquire?
>
> What special materials or pieces of equipment, if any, are required to address this need?
>
> Are these materials or pieces of equipment the library has or might obtain?
>
> Can you easily think of several specific services or programs the library might provide to address this need? If so, list them.
>
> Would the members of the target population consider the library an appropriate organization to address this need?
>
> Are there any other organizations that are clearly more suitable than the library to address this need? If so, list them.
>
> Can the library play a supporting role in addressing this need?

Needs Being Addressed by Other Organizations

Once the members of the committee have decided that the library is well-suited to meet a specific need, they will want to think about whether other organizations are working to meet the need in question. There are more than enough community needs to go around; the library certainly doesn't want to allocate resources to take a leadership role in meeting a need that is being adequately addressed by one or more other organizations.

The public library world is full of examples of turf wars between school and public libraries, between libraries and historical societies, and between libraries and recreation departments, to name but a few. In one community, a new public library director with an interest in genealogy was hired. She decided to expand the very small local history and genealogy collection in the library even though the local historical society had spent a lot of time and money creating the premier collection of these types of materials. The members of the historical society took exception to what they saw as an attack by the public library director on their most important service, and the battle was on. In another community, the children's staff at the library and the staff of the recreation department waged a war every summer, fighting for the fleeting interest of the community's children. That situation became even more confused and disruptive when the librarian in a local alternative school received grant funding to keep the school library open during the summer. In a third community the public library director and the director of the community college are fighting over which agency should take the lead in providing Internet training for the public.

From the outside looking in it seems obvious that the resolution to all of these conflicts is cooperation, but that is easier said than done. In almost every cooperative activity there is a lead agency and one or more supporting agencies. The real question is what agency takes the lead and what agencies are expected to provide support. The lead agency normally gets to set the priorities, evaluate the services, and reap the bulk of the rewards. The supporting agencies sometimes feel like their resources are valued but their opinions and concerns are ignored.

In the past these questions have made it difficult to establish and sustain cooperative relationships between two or more agencies, and this, in turn, has discouraged many agencies from even considering such relationships. However, as taxpayers continue to expect more services for the same or fewer tax dollars, public managers must rethink their approaches to collaboration. The library, in particular, must carefully define the areas in which it intends to take a leadership position and those areas in which it can provide useful support to other agencies. As the members of the planning committee review the needs the library is well suited to meet, they will be helping the library make these decisions.

NOTES

1. Vernon Palmour and others, *A Planning Process for Public Libraries* (Chicago: American Library Assn., 1980), 8.

2. Charles R. McClure and others, *Planning and Role-Setting for Public Libraries: A Manual of Options and Procedures* (Chicago: American Library Assn., 1987), 17.

3. Debra Wilcox Johnson, "Choosing an Evaluation Method," in *The Tell It Manual: The Complete Program for Evaluating Library Performance* (Chicago: American Library Assn., 1996), 127.

4. Derek Okubo, "Building Your Community's Problem Solving Capabilities: Insights from the Community Assistance Team." Available: http://www.ncl.org/ncl/cat1.htm on 2/8/00.

Chapter 3

DESIGN
Inventing the Future

MILESTONES

By the time you finish this chapter you will know how to

- make the connection between community needs and library service priorities

- assess the effect the proposed library service priorities will have on existing services and programs

- select the library priorities for the current planning cycle and write the library mission statement

- write goals that reflect the library priorities

- select measures that will help you track the progress the library is making toward meeting the goals

- write objectives that incorporate the selected measures

During the *imagine* step of the planning process, most of the focus was on the community and not the library. With the *design* step, attention shifts to the internal operations of the library as we begin to define the library services and programs that will best meet the community needs identified by the planning committee. It is at this point that library staff members are likely to become more interested in the process as it moves from what some may see as a fairly theoretical discussion of vision and needs to the nuts and bolts of library priorities, goals, and objectives. It is also at this point in the process that the responsibility for making planning recommendations shifts from the members of the planning committee to staff committees and teams.

The selection of library service priorities has been the core element of all of the public library planning processes. The conceptual framework that is still being used by public libraries to define their priorities was developed by Dr. Lowell Martin in the 1960s and 1970s. As Charles McClure and others stated, Dr. Martin

> observed that public libraries try to do too much and as a result find it difficult to provide the quality of services desired. He suggested that the complex set of services public libraries provide their communities could be grouped under a set of service profiles, or roles, from which each library could choose a few on which to focus.[1]

The librarians and consultants who developed *Planning and Role-Setting for Public Libraries* built on Dr. Martin's work and proposed eight roles that they defined as profiles of library service emphasis:

Community Activity Center
Community Information Center
Formal Education Support Center
Independent Learning Center

DO be sure that the planning committee members clearly understand the implications of the priorities they are recommending

DO assure the library staff that changes will be implemented over a period of time and that appropriate training and resources will be available

DO select measures that are time- and cost-effective

DON'T forget that you asked the planning committee to make recommendations and that you need to take those recommendations seriously

DON'T write more goals and objectives than you can manage in this planning cycle

DON'T confuse objectives and activities

Popular Materials Library

Preschoolers' Door to Learning

Reference Library

Research Library

Library planners were encouraged to select three of the roles as priorities during each planning cycle.

We have already seen that some libraries had problems using the eight roles as an effective means of identifying priorities because many staff, board, and planning committee members based their selections on personal beliefs and not on community needs. Planners had two additional problems with the roles as well. People tended to put their own interpretations on each of the roles, which made defining actual priorities difficult. For instance, one member of a planning committee might think that *research library* referred to the library's local history and genealogy section—people do research there, after all. Another member might define the role as providing the resources to create new knowledge. There is a big difference between the local history collection in a small town library and the New York Public Library, but that distinction was not always clear to the people making the role selections.

A third problem was almost as prevalent. People found it very difficult to limit their choices to three roles. It seemed both artificial and unrealistic to try to narrow the focus of what a library does to that extent. While this validated Dr. Martin's thesis that many public libraries try to do too much, it didn't help library planners who were trying to make difficult resource allocation decisions during the recession of the early 1990s and to deal with the rapidly changing information environments of the mid and late 1990s. It is virtually impossible to make good resource allocation decisions without a clear understanding of what is important to the organization.

The librarians and consultants who wrote *Planning for Results* built upon and refined the concept of the library roles when they developed the thirteen library service responses that were introduced in that book. A library service response was defined as "what a library does for, or offers to, the public in an effort to meet specific community needs."[2] The authors made no hard-and-fast recommendation as to the number of service responses a library might select. Instead, libraries were encouraged to link their service priorities to community needs and then to rank the service responses they selected in order of their importance in meeting those community needs. Based on that ranking, library managers would allocate their resources, first funding the most important services and then moving through the list. Clearly, when library managers ran out of resources, they couldn't address any more priorities.

The thirteen service responses were enthusiastically received by the library community and have been included, unchanged, in Part Two of this book. (See figure 9.) From a planning perspective, one of the most valuable things that the service responses do is provide a common vocabulary and frame of reference for planning committee members and staff. That common understanding will be critical as the planning committee members and staff work together to select the appropriate library service priorities for the current planning cycle.

Once the priorities have been determined, the members of the planning committee will have completed their primary responsibilities. Library staff will then take the lead in writing the mission statement, creating goals that reflect the library's new priorities, and deciding how to measure the progress being made toward reaching those goals.

The two tasks to be completed in the *design* step are

TASK 5
Select service responses and write mission statement

TASK 6
Write goals and objectives

TASK 5: Select Service Responses

The thirteen service responses provide library planners with a mechanism for linking identified community needs with specific library services and programs. However, there is no hard-and-fast rule about the organizational framework in which those links will be made. During the discussion of levels of effort in Task 1 it was noted that libraries have very different planning environments. Libraries with a single outlet obviously have the least complex environment and will have the easiest time when it comes to selecting service responses. They will be identifying service responses for the entire organization.

The situation is less clear in organizations with multiple outlets. Will the service responses selected apply to the whole system? Will one set of service responses be selected for the central library and a different set for the branch libraries? Will service responses be selected for each separate outlet and then clustered under a systemwide mission? While not exhaustive, these questions provide some idea of the questions planners may have at this point in the process.

Some general guidelines can help planners answer these questions. The first has been mentioned before: Try to make choices that keep things as simple as possible. This does not mean that you should avoid making a choice that is clearly more labor-intensive and complex if there are good reasons for doing so. Instead, it is a reminder that you don't want to automatically select a complex option without good reasons for doing so. The second reminder is that service responses must link to

FIGURE 9
Library Service Responses

Basic Literacy

A library that offers Basic Literacy service addresses the need to read and to perform other essential daily tasks.

Business and Career Information

A library that offers Business and Career Information service addresses a need for information related to business, careers, work, entrepreneurship, personal finances, and obtaining employment.

Commons

A library that provides a Commons environment helps address the need of people to meet and interact with others in their community and to participate in public discourse about community issues.

Community Referral

A library that offers Community Referral addresses the need for information related to services provided by community agencies and organizations.

Consumer Information

A library that provides Consumer Information service helps to satisfy the need for information to make informed consumer decisions and to help residents become more self-sufficient.

Cultural Awareness

A library that offers Cultural Awareness service helps satisfy the desire of community residents to gain an understanding of their own cultural heritage and the cultural heritage of others.

Current Topics and Titles

A library that provides Current Topics and Titles helps to fulfill community residents' appetite for information about popular cultural and social trends and their desire for satisfying recreational experiences.

Formal Learning Support

A library that offers Formal Learning Support helps students who are enrolled in a formal program of education or who are pursuing their education through a program of homeschooling to attain their educational goals.

General Information

A library that offers General Information helps meet the need for information and answers to questions on a broad array of topics related to work, school, and personal life.

Government Information

The library that offers Government Information service helps satisfy the need for information about elected officials and government agencies that enables people to participate in the democratic process.

Information Literacy

A library that provides Information Literacy service helps address the need for skills related to finding, evaluating, and using information effectively.

Lifelong Learning

A library that provides Lifelong Learning service helps address the desire for self-directed personal growth and development opportunities.

Local History and Genealogy

A library that offers Local History and Genealogy service addresses the desire of community residents to know and better understand personal or community heritage.

community needs. It will be almost impossible to select different service responses for each outlet if you haven't already identified the unique needs of the clients served by those outlets. If, as in an earlier example, you are planning for a county system serving a number of different communities and you have decided to collect data about each community for the committee to use in its needs identification process, then you will probably want to select unique service responses for each community as well. If you are planning for an urban library system serving a single community, no matter how complex, you will probably select system-wide service responses and tailor them to meet the unique conditions in each neighborhood served by a branch.

Remember, the key to successfully completing this task is to keep the focus on deciding what library services and programs will be most effective in meeting the needs identified by the planning committee. If that focus is blurred or lost, people will automatically fall back on their personal value structures as the criteria they use to select library priorities, and all of the work of the committee to this point will have been for nothing. More importantly, library managers and staff may well find themselves in the position of providing services that don't really meet the needs of the people they are intended to serve.

Review the Thirteen Service Responses

A list of the thirteen library service responses with short definitions of each can be found in figure 9: Library Service Responses. While figure 9 serves as a convenient tool for planning committee members and staff, it is only a very abbreviated introduction to the service responses. Considerably more information about each service response is provided in Part Two of this book, including

examples of needs addressed by this service response

what the library does and provides

some possible components of the service response

target audiences and service aspects

resource allocation issues to consider

possible measures to consider when developing objectives

stories that describe the services and programs provided by real libraries in the area under discussion

All of this adds up to five or six pages of information about each service response for a total of nearly seventy pages of text, and that can be more than a little overwhelming for the members of the planning committee. Instead of expecting the members of the committee to read the full descriptions of all thirteen service responses, it is often more effective to give them a verbal overview of the service responses and allow time for questions and discussion. The easiest way to do this is to give each member of the committee a copy of the information in figure 9 and to go over that information with the group, spending a few minutes talking about each service response.

The person who makes this presentation does not have to be the facilitator or chair of the committee. In fact, the presenter doesn't have to be a member of the committee at all. He or she does have to have a complete understanding of the library service responses and the ability to make the distinctions among the service responses clear. It is very possible that the best person to do this is the library director or a senior staff member.

Before introducing the thirteen service responses, the presenter will want to point out to the members of the committee that none of the thirteen service responses refers to a specific target audience. Each might be focused on a variety of groups, whether defined by age, educational level, ethnic background, or some other characteristic important in your community. This is intentional and allows library planners the maximum degree of flexibility as they work to match the identified community needs—many of which are defined by target audience—and library services and programs.

As an example of how this works, let's consider the question of what service response might be selected to meet the community need identified by the Anytown planning committee in Part 1 of the Anytown planning experience: "preschool children in Anytown will enter school ready to learn." If Anytown is a suburban community with a relatively affluent and educated population, planners might select Lifelong Learning as the appropriate service response to meet this need. In that case, the library would work in partnership with parents to encourage children to develop a love of reading and learning. However, if Anytown is a poor community with a relatively undereducated population or a community with a large number of non-English speaking immigrants, then planners might select Basic Literacy as the appropriate service response, recognizing the need to focus library services for preschoolers on reading-readiness programs. This is not just a matter of semantics. As any children's librarian will tell you, there is a big difference between the kinds of materials needed to support reading-readiness programs and those that support the more standard story programs, just as there is a difference in the staff skills required to design reading-readiness programs and those required to develop programs that encourage children to love books and reading. There is even a third possible scenario: Perhaps Anytown is a community in which most parents work and most preschool children are in licensed day-care centers. In that instance, planners might decide that Formal Learning Support is the best choice, with the intent that the library focus its preschool program on helping day-care providers prepare children to succeed in school.

Make Preliminary Selections

When the committee members have reviewed the thirteen service responses, asked any questions they might have, and seem to understand the general intent of each, they will make their preliminary selections. The scenario presented in the Anytown Planning Experience: Part 4 is one way in which committee members might approach the selection process.

THE ANYTOWN PLANNING EXPERIENCE

PART 4 Selecting Preliminary Service Responses

When the presenter of the service responses is finished, the facilitator (or chair) makes sure that each committee member is comfortable with his or her understanding of the service responses, and all questions are referred to the presenter. Then the facilitator posts the final list of needs so that all members can see them easily. The facilitator reads the needs aloud one last time and reminds the members of the committee that they will be selecting the service responses they believe will best meet these needs. The facilitator also reminds the committee members that the service responses are supposed to reflect the most important services the library can offer, and that means that some service responses will not be selected. The facilitator suggests, but does not require, that the committee members select no more than six service responses.

The facilitator tells the committee members that they will individually select the service responses. The facilitator gives the group five or ten minutes to make their choices, monitoring the members' progress carefully to ensure that they have the time they need. While the group is working, the facilitator writes the thirteen service responses on a page of newsprint. When all of the members have completed their selections, the facilitator reads the list of service responses, asking the committee members to raise their hands each time a service response they selected is read. The facilitator counts the votes for each service response and records the tally next to the service response on the newsprint.

When all of the votes have been cast, the facilitator rewrites the list, this time in priority order with number of votes each service response received clearly noted. Only those service responses receiving at least two votes are included on this list. The facilitator reviews the list with the group, and they decide together which service responses received a sufficient number of votes to be included on the preliminary list of recommendations. The five or six top service responses receive significantly more votes than the others and the break between the top and bottom groups of service responses is clear. One of the committee members asks what would happen if there had been seven service responses in the top group.

The facilitator says, "That is fine, but that is the upper limit. If there had been more than seven service responses in the group that received the most votes, we would repeat the voting process, restricting the choices to those service responses in the top group and asking people to choose no more than four."

The facilitator ends the session by describing the next tasks in the process. Committee members are reminded that their primary responsibilities relate to community needs and that the library staff will be responsible for developing programs and services to meet those needs. The facilitator continues, "The responsibilities of the two groups converge with the selection of the service responses. The selections that were made during this meeting are preliminary, and both the members of the committee and the members of the staff and board will be given a chance to review and discuss the decision in the next couple of weeks."

The facilitator continues, "Everyone involved—you, staff members, and board members—will receive the notes from today's meeting along with more complete descriptions of each of the preliminary service responses that have been selected. Before the next committee meeting staff and board members will be given an opportunity to formally react to your preliminary selections. Staff and board reactions will be presented at the next committee meeting, and then the members of the committee will make their final selections." The meeting is adjourned.

Needs Not Addressed by the Thirteen Service Responses

The thirteen service responses listed in figure 9 describe a wide range of services and programs a library might provide to meet specific community needs. The list is intended to be as inclusive as possible. Although it is unlikely, it certainly is not impossible for a library planning committee to identify a need that cannot be effectively addressed by one of these service responses. In that event, the members of the planning committee may want to develop a unique service response. Workform F: Developing Your Own Service Response has been provided to help committee members who decide they wish to do this.

Consider the Effect of the Preliminary Service Responses on the Library

All libraries start the planning process from a different place, but they all have one thing in common: They are currently offering a variety of programs and services that fully use the staff, collection, facility, and technology resources available to them. In most instances, that means that any new programs and services are going to have an effect on the way things are being done now. This should go without saying, but it doesn't seem to, probably because a lot of libraries have developed plans in the past and then filed those plans away and ignored them. If this process is going to be different, library boards and managers must make a commitment to finding the resources required to provide new services and programs even if it means reallocating existing resources, and library staff will have to understand and accept that this is going to happen.

Each service response has specific resource requirements. As library board members and staff review the service responses, they will note that some are staff-intensive, some will have a significant effect on the library's collections, some have serious technology implications, and some will affect the way the library facilities are used. This is a key point and one that everyone involved in the planning process needs to keep in mind. The plan being developed isn't an end in itself: It is a blueprint the library will use to build a program of services. The plan will be useful only if it reflects the reality in which library managers allocate resources. Therefore, you will want to continue to remind everyone that the choices they are making are real and not theoretical.

Staff Review

By this point in the planning process, all of the staff know that the library is developing a new plan and that the planning committee has been meeting. Now it is time to involve the staff more deeply by asking them to review and comment on the preliminary service responses selected by the committee. That leads to the question of which staff members should be involved in the review process. In smaller libraries, it is both possible and desirable to involve all full-time staff members and any part-time staff members who want to be included. In large systems, this is not always feasible. Certainly, at a bare minimum all supervisors must be involved. If possible, all professional staff members should be involved, too, along with as many paraprofessional and clerical staff members as possible. After all, the final plan is going to affect everyone who works in the library. The earlier that staff have a chance to become a part of the planning process, the more likely they are to endorse the final product.

Regardless of which staff members are officially involved in the review of the preliminary service responses, any interested staff member should have access to the notes from the committee meetings (including the vision statements; the strengths, weaknesses, opportunities, and threats; and the final list of needs), the complete list of service responses and brief definitions from figure 9, the list of preliminary service responses recommended by the committee, and the full descriptions of those recommended service responses. There are several ways to do this:

post the information on the library intranet

print and distribute the information to each section and unit of the library, to be posted in the break room or circulated among the staff—or both

e-mail the information to all staff members who have e-mail addresses

share the information with all supervisors with the explicit understanding that each supervisor will take the responsibility for passing the information on to his or her staff

When all staff members have had a chance to review the work of the committee and the information about the recommended service responses, the library director or a designated senior staff member will hold a series of meetings to get the reaction of the staff to the committee's recommendations. The SWOT analysis process used earlier by the planning committee to determine the current conditions in the community in relation to the vision can be used again here. This time the SWOT analysis will be used to evaluate the effect of the preliminary service responses on the current services and programs of the library. The questions to ask are

What strengths does the library currently have that would support the services and programs in the recommended preliminary service responses?

What weaknesses does the library currently have that would have to be addressed before the library could implement the recommended preliminary service responses?

What new opportunities would the library have if the recommended preliminary service responses were implemented?

What threats to existing services or target audiences are posed by the recommended preliminary service responses?

It will be important to keep the meetings during which staff discuss the committee's recommendations as neutral and fact-based as possible. All change is hard, and some staff members may feel threatened by the mere suggestion that the library might provide new programs or make significant changes in existing programs. A few staff are going to be negative about any new ideas. The majority of the staff are going to have mixed feelings. On the one hand, if the committee has done its work well, the links between community needs and the recommended service responses will be clear to the staff and so will the benefits that will result from focusing on those service responses. On the other hand, most staff already feel overwhelmed by what they are currently being expected to produce, and the idea of more or different services may seem daunting.

The person who is leading the staff meetings will want to emphasize that any changes will be incremental and that, if people are to be asked to provide new services, appropriate training and the other necessary resources will be made available. It will also be useful to have the staff representative on the planning committee attend each meeting and make a short presentation about the process. That should remind staff that they, too, have been represented in the committee's deliberation.

The following true example from a midsized library that had completed the planning process underscores the importance of staff involvement in the selection of service responses. We'll call the library the Mytown Library.

The Mytown Library planning committee selected six preliminary service responses: General Information, Lifelong Learning (with an emphasis on services to both children and adults), Current Topics and Titles (with an emphasis on services to both children and adults), Information Literacy, Cultural Awareness, and Literacy (with an emphasis on adult literacy). The library director held a series of staff meetings that were open to anyone who wished to participate to discuss these priorities. The meetings were organized around the four questions in the library SWOT analysis listed previously (and available in a slightly different form on Workform G: SWOT Analysis of the Library).

From these meetings the director learned that the staff believed that the library was already doing a good job in the area of General Information and that they would be building on a strength if that were selected as a priority. Staff also believed that the library was doing a good job in meeting the adult public's needs in the areas of Current Topics and Titles and Lifelong Learning and that these were services the public valued highly. However, there was general agreement that the children's room had been focused primarily on Formal Learning Support for many years and that a shift in emphasis to Current Topics and Titles and Lifelong Learning was going to require new materials and extensive staff training. Interestingly, most staff (including some, but not all, of the people who worked in the children's area) strongly agreed with the members of the committee that such a shift in emphasis was long overdue.

The recommendation that the library select Information Literacy as a priority was the most difficult for the staff to discuss in a neutral manner. Many staff felt woefully inadequate when dealing with technology and were therefore threatened by the possibility of an increased emphasis on providing such services. The Cultural Awareness and Literacy priorities were both new to the library and didn't get a lot of attention. What did generate considerable debate, however, was the fact that Local History and Genealogy was not on the list of recommended service responses. The local history and genealogy services were heavily used and highly regarded in the community. Staff from all departments felt that it was a vital service with a vocal constituency, and they strongly recommended that the committee reconsider the Local History and Genealogy service response at their next meeting. At the end of the staff meetings, the director and her senior staff wrote a short report highlighting what they had heard. The report was distributed to all staff for review and comment, and staff agreed that it fairly reflected what they had said during the meetings.

This example is not unique. In many libraries, the staff discussion of library strengths and weaknesses and of the possible opportunities and threats that might result from changed priorities has been very positive. Certainly the library staff members who actually work with the public and are responsible for providing the frontline services of the library have a unique perspective and one that must be taken into consideration when service responses are selected. They often see more clearly than library managers the validity in what the planning committee members have recommended. They are also in a good position to point out potential pitfalls, as seen in the Mytown example.

Board Review

The library board or governing authority must also review and react to the preliminary service responses. In fact, this is one of the three approval points recommended in figure 4: Sample Time Line. Board members should receive the same packet of information that was made available to the staff and members of the planning committee: notes from the committee meetings (including the vision statements; the strengths, weaknesses, opportunities, and threats; and the final list of needs), the complete list of service responses and brief definitions from figure 9, the list of preliminary service responses recommended by the committee, and the full descriptions of those recommended service responses. In addition, they should receive a copy of the report of the reaction of the staff to the preliminary recommendations.

The library director, the senior staff member who led the staff meetings, or the board member who is serving as the official board representative on the planning committee can lead the discussion of the committee's recommendations. It often works well to have the director and the official board representative on the committee share the responsibility for walking the board through the committee's recommendations. If there are questions or concerns about the committee's recommendations, the board's representative on the committee should take the lead in describing the committee's process and rationale. He or she, after all, was on the committee to represent the board and to ensure that the lines of communication between the board and committee were open and clear.

In some ways, this meeting may be more challenging to manage than the staff meetings. The staff work with the public every day, and most of them have a real sense of what the public (or that portion of the public who currently use the library) value. The members of the board often see library services from a distance and are more likely to filter their perceptions through their own value structures and beliefs. Many board members became involved in the library in the first place because they valued books and reading and the traditional services that libraries have always offered. Some of them aren't comfortable with the increasing emphasis on technology in the delivery of information services and the other changes that are altering public libraries every day.

When the board members endorsed the library planning process, they understood intellectually that the people on the planning committee were likely to recommend changes in library services and programs.

During this meeting, they will be asked to deal with the reality of those recommendations, and not everyone will find that a comfortable experience. It can be hard to remember that suggestions for new or different programs do not automatically imply that current services or programs are bad or inadequate. It helps to remind the members of the board that such suggestions often reflect the changes in the community and in the tools available to libraries to meet community needs.

The emphasis in this planning process on designing library services to meet identified community needs is very useful here. If the committee has done its work well, the members of the board will see the clear relationship between the community vision, the needs identified by the committee, and the library service responses the committee is recommending. This keeps the discussion firmly focused on why the library should consider changing its service priorities and not on the more personal reactions to such changes.

It is not uncommon for board members to respond to the committee's recommendations in a somewhat different way from staff. Staff tend to think about how the proposed services will affect them and their current clients. The members of the board are often more inclined to consider the political ramifications of the proposed priorities. Let's return to the example from the Mytown Library.

> The Mytown planning committee had recommended that the emphasis in children's services be shifted from Formal Learning Support to Life-long Learning and Current Topics and Titles. Staff considered these recommendations from the point of view of the parents and children they talked to every day, and most felt that the recommendations reflected what the people wanted.
>
> The members of the Mytown Library Board, on the other hand, spent considerable time talking about the probable reaction of school officials and teachers to the proposed change in priorities. During their discussion they noted that the library had been providing classroom collections to teachers for a very long time, and if the committee's recommendations were adopted, that service would have to be considered carefully and might well be phased out. The board ultimately endorsed the proposed changes. However, they also decided that after the staff had identified the changes in current services that would be required because of the new priority in children's services, the board chair would discuss the changes and why they were being made with the superintendent of schools.
>
> One area in which the board and the staff were in complete agreement was the concern both groups felt over the absence of the Local History and Genealogy service response from the committee's proposed list of service responses. Local History and Genealogy was the highest priority for the board in a straw vote on service responses done at the board meeting prior to the meeting in which the board received the committee's recommendations. After a careful review of the vision

and needs that the committee members used to identify their preliminary recommendations, most board members had decided that Local History and Genealogy was probably not the most important service response for the library after all. However, they continued to be unanimous in their belief that it should be included somewhere on the final list of service responses.

After the board meeting, the discussion leader summarized the reactions of the board members and added that summary to the report of the staff reactions. This report was shared with the staff and board members and was used as the framework for the discussion of staff/board recommendations with the members of the committee during their next meeting.

Make Final Selections

Shortly after the meeting in which they selected preliminary service responses, the members of the committee should be sent the same packet of information made available to staff and board. At the next meeting of the committee, the only activities will be to discuss the service responses in more detail, to hear about the reaction of library staff and board members to the preliminary recommendations, and to make the final selection of service responses to be recommended to the library. Most committees are able to reach consensus on the final service responses to recommend fairly easily. However, in the event that the committee in your library has difficulty, the information in "Groups: Reaching Agreement" section of the Tool Kit may be useful. That section includes descriptions of a variety of ways to help groups make decisions, ranging from consensus building on one end of the spectrum to a forced-choice voting process on the other end of the spectrum.

To see how this part of the process worked in a real library, let's continue with the Mytown example started in the previous section.

The staff, you remember, had been strongly in favor of the committee's recommendations concerning General Information, Lifelong Learning, and Current Topics and Titles, although they acknowledged that the recommendations would lead to significant changes in the library's current services to children. Staff had been concerned about their ability to manage the Information Literacy service response, and they were upset about the fact that the committee had not included Local History and Genealogy in the list of proposed service responses. The members of the Mytown Library Board were also concerned that Local History and Genealogy was not on the list. Board members were sensitive to the possible political ramifications of shifting resources from supporting classroom collections to services more in keeping with Lifelong Learning and Current Topics and Titles.

The library director of the Mytown Library made a forty-five minute presentation to the committee during which she discussed all of the reactions she had received from staff and the board concerning the committee's recommended service responses. The committee members then discussed what they had learned about the preliminary service responses they had selected when they read the expanded descriptions of each of those service responses. Finally, the committee members looked again at the needs they identified during their preliminary meeting. When it came time to make the final selection of service responses, several members of the committee asked that the Local History and Genealogy service response be added to the list of items under consideration. After a little more discussion, the facilitator asked the members to vote for their top five choices. The vote was virtually unanimous. The committee not only agreed on which service responses to include on the list but also on the priority of each. The final service responses selected by the committee in priority order were Lifelong Learning (with an emphasis on children and adults), Current Topics and Titles (with an emphasis on children and adults), Information Literacy, General Information, and Local History and Genealogy.

In this library the process clearly worked. Committee members, board members, and staff members were able to work together to identify the best priorities for the library, and everyone involved felt that they had a say in the final decision.

Write the Library Mission Statement

The last activity in this task is to write the library mission statement. There has been a lot of discussion about library mission statements in the past decade and some very real disagreements about the function of a mission statement. In this process, a library mission statement is a marketing tool. Its purpose is to inform the community about the library's priorities in clear and easily understood terms.

Traditional library mission statements have tended to be global in nature and convoluted in structure:

> The Wordy Public Library is dedicated to meeting the educational, recreational, informational, and social needs of the citizens of Wordy. The library collects, organizes, preserves, and administers its resources and holdings for the use of all residents, adult, young adult, and juvenile, regardless of race or ethnic heritage. It promotes the use of library materials and services throughout the community, including to the schools, other government organizations, nonprofit organizations, and the business community. It cooperates in statewide and national resource sharing activities, such as interlibrary loan, and cooperates with other local groups and library agencies to further the best interests of the community in any way possible. It uses appropriate technologies to maintain and improve library operations and services.

Most of us would agree that the Wordy Public Library mission statement doesn't provide much information about the library's priorities. In fact, the mission might be paraphrased to read "The Wordy Public Library does everything for everyone all of the time." The mission is neither clearly written nor easily understood, as exemplified both by the use of library-specific terms like "interlibrary loan" and the inclusion of so many long, long, long lists. However, it is often easier to see what is wrong with someone else's mission statement than it is to write an effective mission statement for our own library.

A strong mission statement is a creative expression of the service responses the library has selected for the current planning cycle and is written in words that are meaningful to the people in the community. The easiest way to write a mission statement is to read through the descriptions of the library's service responses in Part Two of this book, noting key words or phrases that seem important to you. Then begin to draft a mission statement using those words and phrases. Remember, in this instance, less is more. Consider the following two mission statements, both of which would be appropriate for the Mytown Public Library's service responses of Lifelong Learning, Current Topics and Titles, Information Literacy, General Information, and Local History and Genealogy.

Mission Statement 1

The Mytown Public Library gives residents of all ages the means to continue to learn throughout their lives; to meet their recreational reading interests; to find, evaluate, and use information in a variety of formats; to get answers to their questions; and to better understand their personal heritage.

Mission Statement 2

Mytown residents will have access to innovative library services, delivered in an efficient and effective manner, that will

> assist everyone to continue to grow and learn throughout their lives
>
> provide the materials, programs, and services needed to meet their recreational needs
>
> develop their ability to find and use information in a variety of formats
>
> provide the information services needed to answer their questions
>
> enable people to explore their personal heritage

Both of these mission statements make the library's priorities clear, and both are phrased in terms that are easily understood. The only real difference is in the format, although the second statement does provide a little more information than the first. It is when you compare these two mission statements with the example from the Wordy Public Library that the true differences become apparent.

It is very difficult to write anything in a committee setting. Therefore, one staff person should be asked to develop a draft mission statement to be reviewed by as many people as seems advisable and then revised as needed. The final draft of the mission statement will, of course, be presented to the library board for its review and approval. However, the fact that the board will have already approved the service responses that serve as the foundation for the mission statement should make this review process relatively simple.

TASK 6: Write Goals and Objectives

If you look at the planning process in a certain way, it resembles a triangle resting on its point. The process starts at the large end of the triangle when you consider all of the possibilities to describe the ideal future for your community. Then you move on to identify community needs and select library service responses, and your options become fewer, and the triangle narrows. Figure 10 illustrates this process.

As you review figure 10, you will note that there are really only three parts of the process left to be completed to give you the information you need for your formal planning document. The first of these is to write the goals for the library plan, and the second is to write the objectives that will be used to measure the library's progress toward reaching its goals. These will be completed by library managers and staff in Task 6. The final part of the process, identifying activities, will be discussed in Tasks 7 and 8 in the next chapter.

It is normally best to ask one or two people to work together to draft goals and then distribute those goals for review and discussion. When the goals have been revised, one or two people will then draft objectives, which go through the same review and revision process.

Understand the Semantics of Planning

The literally hundreds of planning models in use in this country right now each define the terms "goal," "objective," and "activity" a little differently. This can make any planning process that includes people with experience using other planning models very confusing—and very frustrating. No one likes to be involved in a debate over the meaning of the terms used in planning, particularly because there is clearly no one globally correct answer. Fortunately, there is an easy way to deal with this problem: Simply remind people that the purpose of language is to communicate, and if all agree to use specific meanings for the planning terms

FIGURE 10
The Planning Process from General to Specific

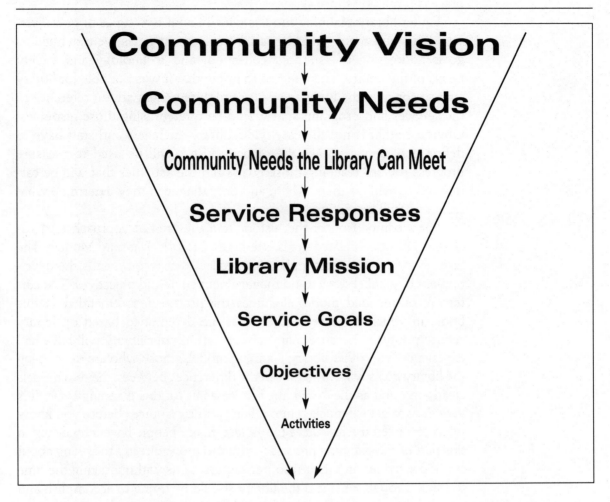

while involved in library planning, everyone will be able to use those terms to communicate effectively. In this process, following are the definitions being used:

Goal   The outcome your community (or a target population within your community) will receive because the library provides programs and services related to a specific service response

Objective   The way the library will measure its progress toward reaching a goal

Activities   The strategies or groupings of specific actions that the library will carry out to achieve its goals and objectives

Write Goals

The first, and perhaps the most important, thing to understand about the goals you will write for this plan is that they are *service* goals. Service goals are derived directly from the service responses you have selected, and they focus on the benefits the community will receive because the library is providing those services.

Earlier library planning models talked about two types of goals: service goals and management goals. Management goals were defined as goals addressing the staffing, collection, and technology and facility needs of the library. This seemed to imply that it was possible for library staff to consider the library's resource requirements without reference to the services and programs that would be offered using those resources. Obviously that is not the case. First, library managers and staff have to define their service goals, the objectives that will be used to measure progress toward reaching those goals, and the activities that will be carried out to achieve them. Then, and only then, can they determine what resources will be required.

For a comparison of the historic and the present approaches to addressing resource-related goals, see figure 11: Two Planning Models. The historic model illustrates a planning process that recommends the development of parallel service and management goals and objectives. The current recommended model illustrates the process recommended in this book, in which resource requirements are determined based on library service priorities. Because many of the staff in your library will have had experience with other library planning models, those who are developing the library goals will want to keep the differences between the two models clearly in mind as they write the service goals for this planning cycle. It is very easy to get sidetracked into talking about resources before you know what you need the resources for. In fact, many people have a tendency in this part of the planning process to want to move directly to talking about specific activities and their resource requirements without taking the time to think through what it is the library should be trying to accomplish and how progress toward those ends will be measured.

The second thing to keep in mind when writing library service goals is that the focus should be on the *community* and not the library. All library goals should begin by naming the audience targeted by the service described in the goal:

> The children in Anytown will have the resources they need to
> pursue their extracurricular interests.

This goal starts by identifying the target audience (the children in Anytown) and then goes on to describe the service the members of the target audience will receive (will have the resources they need) and purpose the service will serve (to meet their recreational needs). Not every goal has to target a segment of the community; some goals may address services for everyone in the community:

> All residents of Anytown will have the skills needed to find,
> evaluate, and use information in a variety of formats.

FIGURE 11
Two Planning Models

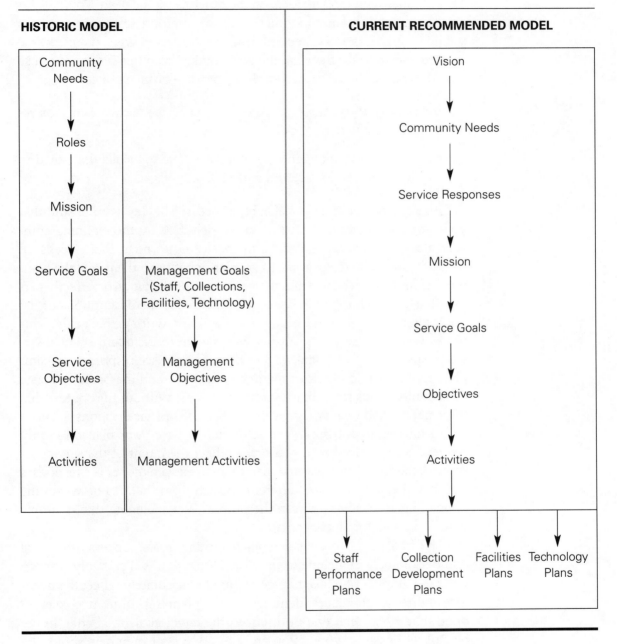

HISTORIC MODEL

Community Needs → Roles → Mission → Service Goals → Service Objectives → Activities

Management Goals (Staff, Collections, Facilities, Technology) → Management Objectives → Management Activities

CURRENT RECOMMENDED MODEL

Vision → Community Needs → Service Responses → Mission → Service Goals → Objectives → Activities → Staff Performance Plans, Collection Development Plans, Facilities Plans, Technology Plans

The third thing to keep in mind is that the goals you develop can be narrower in focus than the service response from which they are derived. In the case of some service responses, this narrowing of focus is almost inevitable. Look, for example, at the issues surrounding jobs and economic development. In some communities, a variety of jobs are available and too few workers have the skills required to fill the jobs. In other communities, there are too few jobs and, as a result, a high employment rate. In the communities with too few workers with the required skills, the community need would probably be career information and job training. In the communities with too few jobs, on the other hand, the need would be for economic development. In either case, the appropriate service response would be Business and Career Information. However, when it comes time to write the goals for the plan, the goal coming from this service response would focus on the key aspect of the response—business or career.

> *Business goal*   Workers in Anytown will have a choice of jobs requiring a variety of skills.

> *Career goal*   Workers in Anytown will have the skills they need to be employed locally and make a living wage.

As you can see, this is a flexible process. The key is to ensure that your goals accurately reflect the needs identified by the planning committee and the service responses they selected to meet those needs. In fact, you are likely to see a strong similarity between the needs the planning committee identified and the goals you write. It is also perfectly permissible—indeed it is often very helpful—to use the descriptions of the service responses themselves as the basis for writing the goals. This works well because you probably won't want to include the actual service responses in your final written plan. The service responses are simply a tool to help committee members, the staff, and the board translate community needs into library service priorities. Without the context that these people had when they reviewed them, the service responses can be ambiguous and confusing. It is far better to base your plan on clearly written, community-based goals that reflect the intent of the service responses the committee selected than to try to explain the service responses and to write goals that are different enough from them to be worth the effort. This is another point in the process when keeping things simple works out well for all concerned.

The final issue to consider when writing goals concerns the ideal number of goals to include in the plan. While you will certainly want to write the number of goals that are required to accurately reflect the priorities and target audiences identified by the planning committee, keep in mind that the general rule of thumb is the fewer goals the better. In the best of all possible worlds you and the other staff members should be able to easily remember and cite all of the goals in the plan. Let's say that the planning committee selected five service responses. If you write two goals for each of those service responses, you will have ten goals, which is three or four more than most people will remember. If you then identify two objectives for each goal, you will find yourself with twenty objectives before you have even started considering the activities that will be required to accomplish the goals and objectives. As you see, things can proliferate quickly.

Determine Measures of Progress for Each Goal

In the planning process described in this book, an *objective* is defined as "the way the library will measure its progress toward reaching a goal." Library managers have been grappling with issues surrounding measurement and evaluation for decades. The problem is certainly not lack of data. Library staff currently collect more data than they know what to do with, and through their automation systems, they could have access to even more data than they currently collect. Instead, the problem seems to be one of context. We aren't sure what the data we collect means, and we don't know how to use the data we have to make decisions, to judge our progress toward reaching our goals, or to illustrate to the public the difference the library makes to the community.

The librarians and consultants who wrote *Planning for Results* suggested that library managers provide a context by dividing the data they collect into three basic types of measures. The first is a measure of the number of people served by a service or program. You can count people in one of two ways: You can count a person every time he or she uses a service (total number of users), or you can count a person once no matter how often he or she uses a service (total number of individuals served). The second type of measure determines how well a given service met the needs of the people being served. This is done by asking the people receiving the service what they think in a survey, a focus group, or an interview. The third category of measures concentrates on the number of service units or service transactions that were provided by the library. These include the familiar circulation counts, number of reference questions asked and answered, number of programs presented, etc. Figure 12: Measuring Progress provides more information about each of these measures, including examples.

Library managers and staff can select from among these three types of measures the ones that seem most appropriate to use when measuring the progress being made toward each of the library's goals. Suggested measures in each category have been included in the information about each service response in Part Two of this book, and they provide an excellent starting place for the staff members responsible for developing objectives.

As you review the recommended measures for each of the library's service responses, keep in mind the need that the service response is supposed to be addressing. Sometimes that need can only be measured using one type of measure. For example, let's say the planning committee identified a need for young adults to make better decisions about their current activities and future lifestyle and selected the Lifelong Learning service response as the one most likely to address that need. The goal might read "Young adults in Anytown will have the information they need to make informed decisions." It won't be informative to count the number of young adults who use the library, because such a count doesn't

---

FIGURE 12
Measuring Progress

MEASURE 1

People Served

- Total number of users served

  What this measures: The total number of users who used a service during a given time period

  Example: If the same 20 children attend a story hour every week, at the end of the year the total number of children served through the story hour would be 1,040 (20 children times 52 weeks).

- Number of unique individuals who use the service

  What this measures: The total number of unique individuals who use the service during a given time period regardless of how many times they use the service

  Example: If the same 20 children attend a story hour every week, at the end of the year the total number of unique children served through the story hour would be 20.

MEASURE 2

How Well the Service Meets the Needs of the People Served

What this measures: The user's opinion about how well the library's service(s) met his or her needs; this opinion could be about the quality of the service, the value of the service, the user's satisfaction with the service, or the impact of the service

Example: This data is normally gathered through user surveys and expressed as a percentage of the number of people surveyed. "During FY___, at least ___% of the high school students who use the public library for homework assistance will indicate they found what they needed."

MEASURE 3

Total Units of Service Provided by the Library

What this measures: The number of actual library service transactions that were done to make progress toward a specific goal (all of the standard library outputs such as circulation, number of reference transactions, etc.)

Example: Most libraries collect these data to report annually to their state library agency. "By FY ____, the number of reference questions answered will have risen from ___ to ___."

---

provide any information about why they came to the library nor does it tell us if they found what they needed. It doesn't matter how many items the young adults check out or how many online searches they perform. Again, those numbers won't provide information about the extent to which the identified need is being addressed. The only valid measure of whether the library is meeting the need in this case is to ask the young adults if they think they are getting the information they need to make informed decisions.

Not all goals are that restrictive. You could use any of three types of measures for this goal: "The children in Anytown will have the resources they need to pursue their extracurricular interests."

Number of users   Number of children who attend library programs

How well the service meets the needs   Percent of grade school children who say they have used the public library to meet their recreational needs

Total units of service   Circulation of juvenile fiction; circulation of juvenile videotapes and audio books

When you have a choice of possible measures for a goal, it may be helpful to consider the following questions before making your selections:

Which of these measures is likely to be most meaningful or credible to the citizens of our community?

Do any of these measures give us data that is clearly more appropriate to use as a measure of progress toward meeting the need identified by the planning committee?

Do any of these measures use data we already collect?

If we don't currently collect the data in one or more of the measures, can we do so fairly easily and reasonably accurately?

Of these questions, the most interesting is the first. In *Measuring Program Outcomes: A Practical Approach,* United Way leaders point out:

> In growing numbers, service providers, governments, other funders, and the public are calling for clearer evidence that the resources they expend actually produce benefits for the people. . . . That is, they want better accountability for the use of resources.[3]

Often the public finds information about the number of people who use a service and how well those people thought the service met their needs to be more compelling than traditional library statistics about circulation and number of questions asked. Consider the following statements, for instance. Which of them do you think the people in your community would find most meaningful? Why?

40 percent of the grade school children in Anytown used the public library for recreational purposes last year

79 percent of the business people in Anytown who used the library's electronic business service said that the service met their need for quick, accurate information

Circulation of children's materials increased by 5 percent in the past year

The library answered 135,000 reference questions last year

The library answered 1.5 reference questions per capita

Write Objectives Incorporating Measures

Most of us consider measurement and evaluation to be two sides of the same coin, but in fact, that is not the case. While evaluation requires measurement, measurement alone does not constitute evaluation. Evaluation is the process of comparing a measure of performance against some predetermined standard or criterion to determine how well or poorly the service has been performed. In the preceding section, you looked at the three types of measures of performance that library planners are encouraged to use in this process. In this section, you will learn how to write objectives by adding to the measures you have selected the standards to be used to evaluate success or failure.

This is actually easier than it sounds, although most people don't believe that. Somehow, the whole idea of writing objectives has come to be perceived as a monumental, difficult, and time-consuming task that requires special skills and knowledge. In reality, writing objectives is a simple matter of putting together three elements in a single sentence. Every objective contains the same three elements:

- a measure

- a standard against which to compare that measure

- a date or time frame by which time the standard should be met

For example:

> The number of children enrolled in the summer reading program (the measure) will increase by 10 percent (the standard to determine success) each year (the time frame).

This really is as clear-cut as it appears to be. Consider this example:

> During FY____ (the date), at least 50 percent of the preschool children in Anytown (the standard to determine success) will participate in one or more library-sponsored programs (the measure).

Although the three elements appear in a different order in the examples, all three are included in the objective.

You have already selected the measures to use in your objectives. The next step is to decide upon the appropriate criteria to be used to determine how successful the library has been in making progress toward the goal and the time frame for that process. This is fairly straightforward if you have baseline and trend data in the area being measured. For instance, in the first example, library planners probably had access to the registration figures for the library's summer reading program from the previous five or ten years. Those figures provide a baseline from which to project future growth. This does not mean that they should project a growth that was similar to the preceding years. If this is an area of priority for the library, and it must be because it is being included in the library's plan, then it is very probable that the library will be working toward greater growth in the future than in the past. Therefore, even though growth may have held steady at 5 to 6 percent in the past, by writing this objective the library now may be making a commitment to do what is necessary to increase that growth rate to 10 percent. Whatever the desired increase, the staff writing the objective have the security of knowing exactly what the current conditions are and being able to judge fairly accurately what will be required to achieve that increase.

It is more difficult to establish the criteria to determine the progress being made toward a goal if the library has never before collected the data required by the measure to be used. In the case of the goal "Young adults in Anytown will have the information they need to make informed decisions," as stated previously the only suitable measure is to ask young adults whether the library helped them to do this. However, how can the library set the criterion for success? As this data has almost certainly never been collected before, no one has any real idea what percent of the young adults in the community currently use the library for this reason.

The tendency of library managers at this point is to decide not to establish any standard for success during the first year of the planning cycle but to collect the baseline data needed to make an informed projection in year two of the cycle. This is certainly the safest solution, but it is not particularly helpful to the staff who will actually have to translate the library goals and objectives into services and programs and then decide what resources will be required to provide those services and programs. Staff might very well make one set of recommendations if the criterion for success is that 5 percent of the young adults in the community will say they use the library for information to make decisions and a very different set of recommendations if the criterion for success is that 40 percent of the teenagers in town say they use the library for such information.

The truth is that the people who write the goals have some idea about what will constitute success. In the absence of any other data, those people's ideas about the desired outcome could be used as the criterion against which to measure the progress the library is making toward reaching a goal. Because you will be regularly monitoring the progress being made toward all of your goals, if you find that your preliminary projections were unrealistic, you can modify them. A more detailed discussion of the monitoring process is given in Task 12: Monitor Implementation.

The key point to keep in mind when deciding on the standards to be used to determine success or failure is that you want the plan to set expectations that are credible and fair. You want to create a plan that will actually cause the library to stretch a bit. If you are afraid to take any risks at all, you are likely to set the criteria for success so low that they will be achieved with little or no additional effort. In that event, it is difficult to see what has been gained by going through this planning process at all.

Workform H: Writing Objectives can be used as a template by the people writing objectives. When the draft of the objectives has been reviewed by the staff and revised as needed, it should be distributed, along with the final goals, to all staff members who will be participating in the identification of activities in the next task.

NOTES

1. Charles R. McClure and others, *Planning and Role-Setting for Public Libraries: A Manual of Options and Procedures* (Chicago: American Library Assn., 1987), xii.

2. Ethel Himmel and William James Wilson, *Planning for Results: A Public Library Transformation Process* (Chicago: American Library Assn., 1998), 54.

3. United Way, *Measuring Program Outcomes: A Practical Approach* (Alexandria, Va.: United Way of America, 1996), 4.

Chapter 4

BUILD
Assembling
the Future

MILESTONES

By the time you finish this chapter you will know how to

- involve library staff members in the identification of activities that will result in the library's making progress toward reaching its goals and objectives

- help the staff understand the difference between efficiency and effectiveness

- identify the most important resources that will be required for each possible activity

- select the activities for the current year

- explain the gap analysis process to the board and staff

- use the gap analysis process to determine the staff, collections, facilities, and technology requirements for the selected activities

In the *build* step library planners continue to move from the general to the specific. It is in this step that staff finally get to talk about the actual services and programs the library will offer during the next two or three years. During this step, too, library managers will begin to identify the resources that will be required to accomplish the selected activities. These pragmatic tasks will conclude the preliminary phase of the planning process and will provide all the remaining information required to prepare the written planning document.

The identification of activities often makes the planning process seem real to staff for the first time. It is one thing for a busy paraprofessional in the children's section of the library to glance through documents containing vision statements, service responses, goals, or even objectives. It is a completely different thing for that staff member to suddenly understand that the actual programs and services she is going to be expected to provide over the next two or three years may be quite different from the ones being offered now. This is frequently the point at which staff members, some of whom have heretofore appeared to be completely uninterested in the planning process, start asking questions and expressing concerns, to the intense frustration of library managers who have been trying hard to keep staff involved in the process at every step of the way.

It may help to remember that people normally only respond to communications they believe affect them in some way. For whatever reason, most frontline staff feel fairly far removed from the development of the library mission or the creation of library goals. However, those same staff take a lot of pride in the services they provide and the programs they manage. When the planning process begins to shine a spotlight on the daily operations of the library and it becomes clear to staff that real changes are being seriously considered, the message hits home. For this reason, it important to involve as many staff members as you can in the identification of possible activities.

Because some staff members may not have been paying as much attention as you had hoped during the early steps of the planning process,

DO encourage staff to be creative when identifying possible activities

DO continually remind everyone involved that the planning will affect the way the library's current resources are allocated

DO involve staff at all levels in the resource allocation process

DON'T assume you can obtain new resources to accomplish all of the new things in your plan

DON'T collect more data than you need to make resource allocation decisions

DON'T underestimate the effect the plan will have on the "way we've always done things here"

you will probably have to prepare a summary describing the process used to identify the goals and objectives in the library plan before moving on to the tasks in this step. In this summary, you might want to point out that the selected service responses, and the goals and objectives based on them, do not always reflect new services. In fact, they probably represent many, if not all, of the services your library currently provides. What the planning process has done is provide a mechanism for staff to review the current library programs and services in relation to clearly articulated community needs. Although this review will almost certainly lead to some new programs or services, it will far more often result in increased or decreased emphasis on programs or services currently being provided.

This is an important distinction to make. If staff enter into the identification of activities believing that the only purpose is to identify new programs and services, they are likely to be a little resistant. After all, the prospect of adding a lot of new programs and services is fairly unattractive. Staff should be encouraged to consider the identification of activities as a way of looking at new choices and evaluating the effectiveness of current activities with the intent of building on strengths and providing more effective services.

It will be important to remind staff that the library board and the library managers are fully committed to finding the resources required to implement any new activities by reallocating existing resources and, when possible, by obtaining new resources. The acknowledgment that no one expects the staff to continually do more and more work is very reassuring, and it needs to be repeated regularly. However, be careful to combine that reassurance with a continual reminder that the resources for most changes will have to come from reallocation, which in turn means that people will be doing different things or doing what they are doing now in different ways.

This raises an interesting question that is often debated when discussing the allocation of library resources. The question is a version of the classic "chicken and egg" debate. Which comes first, a decision about the level of resources that will be made available to accomplish a specific outcome or the identification of the activities that will be required to accomplish that outcome? Proponents of the belief that the first step should be the decision about the level of resources that will be available to accomplish an outcome say that allocation of library resources should reflect priorities, and, therefore, outcomes that are more important should automatically receive a greater proportion of the available resources than outcomes that are less important. They add that staff are likely to identify very different activities if they know they will have access to significant resources than they would identify if they thought they were operating with a leaner budget.

On the other hand, proponents of the belief that the first step must be the identification of activities say that the issues surrounding resource allocation are too complex to be able to make global allocation decisions based solely on outcomes. Some outcomes can be achieved by allocating significant collection resources but minimal staff resources. Others will require significant staff resources but will have little or no impact on the collection or the facility. Yet others will require considerable technology support. In view of these differences, it doesn't seem too useful to make a blanket decision that a particular outcome is so important that it will receive a flat 10 percent of the library resources.

The people who support this point of view acknowledge the danger inherent in asking staff to identify activities without knowing what resources will be available. However, they suggest that the way to address that problem is to encourage staff to be as creative as possible and not to worry about funding when considering possible activities. The resulting activities can then be evaluated using several criteria, including the resources each will require. This will help ensure that final activities selected to accomplish the library's goals and objectives will make balanced use of all available library resources.

This book recommends that resource allocation decisions begin with the identification of activities, so the two tasks you will complete in the *build* step are

> TASK 7
> Identify preliminary activities

> TASK 8
> Determine resource requirements

TASK 7: Identify Preliminary Activities

Activities are defined as the strategies or groupings of specific actions that the library will carry out to achieve its goals and objectives. Staff tend to find the identification of activities the most interesting task in the whole planning process, probably because these decisions are real and concrete. It also is a task that encourages staff to think creatively, to use their imaginations, and to consider the "what-ifs" that they are normally too busy to think about. The vast majority of people who work in libraries like their jobs and care a great deal about the services they provide and the clients they serve. This task builds on that caring and commitment.

Consider the Possibilities

Before you can begin the task of identifying activities, you will have to decide which staff members you want to involve and how you plan to involve them. In the best of all possible worlds, every interested staff member would have an opportunity to participate in this process. As Joseph and Jimmie Boyette, who reviewed the work of top management consultants and innovators in *The Guru Guide,* pointed out, people do not resist their own ideas. The Boyettes go on to say that "people who participate in deciding what and how things will change [are] not only more likely to support the change, but also actually changed themselves by the mere act of participation."[1] Following are several possible ways to involve staff:

Subject specialists   Assign each goal and the objectives that support it to the section of library that is currently providing the bulk of the services in the area addressed by the goal. For instance, assign the staff in the children's department to identify possible activities for all goals that target children. The benefit of this approach is that the staff members with the most expertise in a given area will be responsible for identifying the activities in that area. There are, however, two possible drawbacks. The first is that by restricting the discussion of future services to the people who are currently providing the services under review, there is a good chance that you will simply perpetuate the status quo. The second drawback is even more basic: Not all goals can be as neatly assigned as those focused on, for instance, children's services. Some goals may address services provided by several units or departments. Others may focus on new target audiences or services that are currently not provided by the library.

Library units   Assign the members of each library unit to work together to select the goals and objectives that seem most relevant or interesting to them and then to identify possible activities for the selected goals and objectives. The most important benefit of this approach is that it includes all library staff members in the process. One obvious drawback is that the members of each unit will self-select the goals and objectives they want to discuss, and some goals may not be selected. A second possible difficulty with this approach, although it is more subtle than the first, is potentially more serious: The quality of the recommendations from each work unit will depend on the way the unit manager presents the process and facilitates the selection of activities. In real life, that almost always results in very uneven recommendations.

Cross-functional teams   Appoint cross-functional teams that include staff with various job classifications from several units within the library. Assign each team to develop possible activities for one of the goals and the objectives that support that goal. The chief benefit of this approach is the broad exchange of ideas that occurs when a judiciously selected group of people with different points of view considers the options for accomplishing a goal. However, it is important that appointments to cross-functional teams be carefully considered so that each team has an appropriate balance of skills and knowledge, and this can be a time-consuming process. Also, if your library has never used cross-functional teams before, it will probably take some time for the team members to become comfortable enough with each other and their roles to begin productive deliberations.

Open meetings   Hold a series of open meetings, each one focused on a specific goal and the objectives that support that goal. If you work in a medium-sized library, one meeting per goal will probably be sufficient. If you work in a large library, consider scheduling two meetings at two different times of day to address each goal. For instance, you might have the first meeting to discuss goal 1 from 8:00 to 9:00 and the second meeting to discuss goal 1 on a different day from 4:00 to 5:00. The most obvious benefit to this approach is that everyone who wants to can participate in the process. Staff members can self-select the goal or goals that interest them, which will open up the discussions to new points of view. Another benefit comes from having the same people facilitate each meeting. This ensures that everyone involved has the same experience and helps maintain a consistent quality of recommendation. The major drawback is time. It is difficult to schedule these meetings at times that are convenient for staff, and it is even more difficult to release public services staff from the desks to attend the meetings. A second drawback may be the meeting facilitator. As noted earlier, it is important that these meetings be facilitated by the same people, which can pose scheduling problems, particularly if you end up with two meetings per goal. The skills of the facilitators are also an issue. If your facilitators are not skilled or do not understand the process, the quality of recommendations will be still be consistent—just not necessarily consistently *high*.

A second question to consider before you begin to identify possible activities is what technique the staff involved (whoever they are) will use to identify possible activities. The variety of ways in which groups can work together to identify choices range from small group discussions to a nominal group process to full-scale brainstorming activities. Each of these techniques has strengths and weaknesses, and no one technique is right for all libraries. This, like so much of the planning process, will depend on local conditions. If you need more information about these techniques, see "Groups: Identifying Options" in the Tool Kit section of this book.

The Anytown Public Library reviewed all of the options open to it and decided to hold a series of open meetings to identify possible activities for each goal. Part 5 of the Anytown planning experience illustrates how it organized and managed those meetings.

THE ANYTOWN PLANNING EXPERIENCE

PART 5 Considering the Possibilities

The director and senior staff members meet and review the options for identifying activities. They decide that the benefits of holding open meetings outweigh the very real scheduling problems that are likely to result from those meetings. The library director and one of the unit managers agree to facilitate the open meetings. They will work together for most meetings, but, in the event that one of them is unavailable, the second will be able to work alone. The group decides that one meeting for each of the library's eight goals will be sufficient, although there is a strong minority opinion that thinks two meetings for each goal would be better. The final decision is based on logistics: The thought of managing sixteen meetings in a two- to four-week time frame is simply overwhelming. Even the thought of managing eight meetings within that time is somewhat staggering. The times and places for the meetings are selected, and a staff member is assigned to write the memo announcing the meetings. Each member of the staff has already received a copy of the goals and objectives and a short description of the planning committee's work to date.

After the memo describing the activity identification process has been distributed, the library director meets with all of the library unit managers to answer questions and underscore the importance of this activity. She asks the managers to strongly encourage their staff to attend one or more of the meetings and makes it clear that she expects the managers to juggle desk schedules as needed. Members of the technical services staff have agreed to help cover the public desks, and the managers are encouraged to work with the head of technical services to schedule that staff.

The library director and unit director who are facilitating the open meetings meet to review and discuss the goals and objectives to be sure that they both understand them. [They also review "Groups: Identifying Options" in the Tool Kit section of this book and discuss each option.] They decide to use brainstorming as the way of identifying possible activities in the open meetings because that is the quickest way to generate ideas in a large, disparate group. They discuss the role that each of them will play in the meetings that they facilitate as a team and consider how they want the meeting room arranged and what equipment they will need. They decide not to use tables in the room because it is easier just to move chairs into small discussion groups. The only equipment they need is an easel with a full pad of newsprint, markers, and masking tape to hang the sheets on the wall. As they discuss logistics, it occurs to the director that they probably should have extra copies of the goal and objectives under review available at each meeting because not everyone will remember to bring those documents. Finally, they discuss refreshments and decide that they will provide coffee and tea for all of the meetings but will not provide food.

At least thirty minutes before the first meeting, the two facilitators check the meeting room to make sure it is arranged as they requested and that the coffee and tea are set up and ready to go. As people come into the room, they are asked to sign in. The facilitators point out that there are extra copies of the goal and objectives under review available for those who need them.

One of the facilitators starts the meeting by introducing herself and her cofacilitator. She then asks everyone in the room to briefly introduce himself or herself and say where in the library they work. The other facilitator then reads aloud the goal and objectives under review and asks if anyone has any questions. After dealing with questions, the facilitator tells the group they are here to suggest ways that the library could make progress toward achieving this goal and these objectives. The facilitator strongly encourages the group to "think big" and not to worry about practicality; that will come later. She explains that for right now they should consider all of the possibilities, no matter how visionary. The facilitator presents the rules of brainstorming [from "Groups: Identifying Options" in the Tool Kit], writing them on the newsprint as she goes. This part of the meeting takes about ten minutes.

The facilitators count the participants attending the meeting and discover that there are thirty-seven people in the room. They want to split into smaller groups of about five members each, so they determine they will have seven groups. Participants count off, one to seven, to form the groups.

The small groups are given fifteen minutes to generate ideas using the brainstorming techniques. At the end of the time, one of the facilitators tells the groups that the recommendations from the groups will be taken in a round-robin process; each group will present one recommendation at a time until all groups have presented all of their recommendations. Groups are encouraged to present recommendations that may be similar to other recommendations, although they should not present the same recommendation more than once. As the groups report, one of the facilitators records the recommendations on the newsprint, and each completed sheet of newsprint is posted on the wall. This part of the process takes about twenty-five minutes.

During the last ten minutes of the meeting, one of the facilitators asks the members of the group if the reporting process generated other ideas. If so, those ideas are also recorded. The facilitators promise that the members of the group will receive a transcript of their recommendations within the next day or two. The facilitator then describes the process that will be used to review the recommendations and make the final selections. [See Review the Suggested Activities and Make Preliminary Selections following.] The facilitators then thank the participants for their creative work and adjourn the meeting.

Immediately after the meeting the recommendations are entered into a word-processing program. The list of participants is also entered into the program. Then the newsprint sheets are taken down and discarded, and the room is prepared for the next meeting. The list of attendees and the list of recommendations are sent to all staff members within two days of the meeting.

When all of the meetings have been held for all the goals and all of the staff suggestions have been made, someone will have to compile those recommendations into two lists. Each activity will be recorded on both lists. One list should arrange the suggested activities by goal. The second list should be organized by the focus of the activity. That focus might be a specific resource requirement (all suggestions for Web-based activities), the type of program (all adult programs), the target audience (activities targeting new immigrants), or a combination of these along with any others that seem appropriate. The groupings will be a judgment call by the person or persons compiling the list. Regardless of how the activities on the second list are grouped, each activity should also include an indication of the goal to which it was originally attached. Figure 13: Sample Activity Compilation provides an example of what these lists might look like.

FIGURE 13
Sample Activity Compilation

ACTIVITIES BY GOAL	ACTIVITIES BY FOCUS
GOAL 1: All children in Anytown will enter school ready to learn.	**Web-Based Activities**
1. Develop a parenting home page with links to parenting sites on the WWW	1. Develop a parenting home page with links to parenting sites on the WWW (Goal 1)
2. Present storytime programs at all publicly funded day-care centers	2. Develop a Web page focused on services to the business community (Goal 3)
3. Work with day-care centers to develop programs that will encourage parents to bring their children to the library	3. Allow users to ask question via e-mail; post most interesting questions and answers on library home page (making any changes needed to protect the user) (Goal 4)
4. Develop a newborn packet to be given to new mothers that includes information on the importance of reading to preschool children, a free book, and an application for a library card; publish the packet in both English and Spanish	4. Add a reference page to the library home page linking it to various reference sites on the WWW (Goal 4)
5. Present story programs in the library	5. Create electronic tutorials in English and Spanish on how to use the library's online catalog and make them available from the library home page (Goal 5)
6. Add a read-to-me program to the summer reading program	6. Provide links to "how-to-use the Internet" tutorials from the library's home page (Goal 5)
7. Present a series of parenting programs for the parents of preschool children	7. Work with the junior high schools to develop a homework help Web page (Goal 6)
8. Work with social services agencies to identify mothers of at-risk children, and develop and deliver reading-readiness programs and services to those mothers and their children	8. Complete the indexing of local newspapers and make the index available through the library Web page (Goal 8)

Review the Suggested Activities

The review of the suggested activities begins by deciding who will be involved in the review process. In this instance, a smaller group (five or six people) is probably better than a larger group. It is difficult to analyze information and reach decisions in a crowd. The real question is the composition of the committee and there are only three choices: the library director and senior managers; the library director (or a designee) and selected senior and middle managers; or the library director (or a designee) and staff selected from all classifications. Each library director will have to make this decision based on his or her management style, the expectations and interest level of the staff, and other local conditions.

There are two questions as you and your colleagues begin to review the activities that have been suggested by the staff. The most important is "Which of these activities are the most likely to accomplish the outcomes described in the goal and objectives?" However, all too often, the first and only question that is asked is "Do we have the resources required to accomplish this activity?" These two questions reflect two very different concerns. The first question focuses on effectiveness. The second looks at efficiency. The difference between effectiveness and efficiency is simple:

Effectiveness = *doing the right thing*
Efficiency = *doing the thing right*

This difference can easily be lost in the discussions about the various activities the library might select. Many public librarians have operated with fewer resources than they wanted or knew they could use for a long time. The lack of resources has become even more serious as client demands escalate and the tools used to meet those demands change rapidly, leading to a tendency among library managers to think poor. Any activity that would require more resources than are currently available or that would require significant reallocation of resources is automatically discounted as "an interesting idea but, of course, impossible."

This kind of thinking presents several problems. It not only reinforces the status quo, but it also leads to the selection of activities that are relatively inexpensive over those activities that would clearly be more effective in meeting the library's identified goals and objectives. As a result, many public libraries continue to be textbook examples of the 80/20 rule. A hundred years ago Vilfredo Pareto, an Italian economist and sociologist, formulated the 80/20 rule:

In most endeavors 80 percent of your results come from 20 percent of your efforts.

In other words, 80 percent of your efforts are being dissipated on activities that are not producing the results that you have identified as important.

The truth is that an activity that takes only a few resources but does not help the library make progress toward meeting its goals and objectives is far more expensive than an activity that requires significant resources but does contribute to meeting the library's desired outcomes. This can be a hard message to sell to library staff who feel that they never have enough resources for the jobs they have been hired to do. However, the time and energy invested in delivering this message and making sure that staff understand it will pay huge dividends. The planning process described in this book provides an excellent opportunity to help library staff members think more about effectiveness.

Effectiveness

As you consider the suggested activities, you will want to make your first selections based on the potential effectiveness of each activity. If you decide an activity is *unlikely* to be effective, you will do one of two things with it: If it is not an activity the library is currently implementing, you will simply delete it from the list of activities under consideration. There is no point in continuing to consider activities that you don't think will get you where you want to be, no matter how attractive those activities may be. If, however, the ineffective activity is something that is currently being done by the library, you will move it to a list of activities to be reconsidered and phased out later in the process. You certainly don't want to continue to allocate resources to activities that don't help you meet your new goals and objectives.

You might use two criteria to evaluate the effectiveness of an activity: The first criterion is the relation of the activity to the target audience. Not all activities will actually meet the needs of the target audience under review. An activity that focuses on school age children is not particularly relevant to the goal of helping preschool children enter school ready to learn. By the same token, an activity that calls for providing preschool story programs in the library on Tuesday and Thursday mornings will not be at all relevant to children who are in day care, and in many communities the vast majority of preschool children are in day care.

The second criterion to consider is the relation of the activity to the intended outcome. This is not quite as clear-cut as the first criterion. Goals describe outcomes in general terms. Objectives, because they define how the library will measure success, describe outcomes much more specifically. You will usually apply this second criterion to the objectives of the goal under review. Let's say the goal under consideration is "Small business owners in Anytown will have the information they need to make informed decisions." The objectives for this goal might include "By FY___, 70 percent of the small business owners in Anytown will say that the library provides fast, easy access to business information." The activity "increase the number of items in the library's print business collection" is not likely to make a significant contribution toward the outcome described in that objective. The criterion of measure in the objective is the *perception* of the business owners that they have fast and easy access to information. That is far more likely to result from activities such as "provide dial-in access to business databases" or "fax requested articles directly to the business person's site" than an activity that requires a visit to the library. Workform I: Analyzing Activities—Effectiveness is a tool to use in your review of the activities.

Efficiency

Once you have narrowed your list of activities to those that you think are likely to be effective in helping to meet the library's goals and objectives, you are ready to evaluate the activities to decide which will be the most efficient to implement. However, we still are not ready to ask the question, "Do we have the resources required to implement this activity?" Before we can do that, we have to determine what resources are likely to be required to accomplish each activity. Library resources can be divided into four categories:

- staff (all classifications, full- and part-time)
- collections (in all formats, including electronic)
- technology (specifically, the technological infrastructure required to support the library services and programs)
- facilities (including furnishings and equipment)

Task 8 provides further guidance on determining resource requirements. As you consider each of the activities that remain on the list, you will want to think about both the types and levels of resources required to accomplish it. You might rank the resource requirements using the following scale (also used in Workform J: Analyzing Activities—Efficiency):

- critical resource to accomplish activity
- important resource to accomplish activity
- resource will be affected by the activity but not significantly
- resource will not be affected by the activity

When you have ranked all of the activities remaining on your list, put the number of the goal that is being addressed in parentheses at the end of each activity. Then sort the activities again, this time by type of resource required. List together all of the activities for which staffing would be a critical or important resource. Then list all of the activities for which collections would be a critical or important resource. Continue by grouping those that require technology and those that require facility resources. Now consider the activities again, this time in terms of selecting activities that make a balanced use of library resources.

Intangibles

Finally, consider the intangibles. This is where your professional judgment and experience come into play. Which of the activities under review

> are likely to excite the public
>
> will generate interest from your funders
>
> have a real chance of success
>
> reflect new ideas and which build on the experiences of other libraries
>
> provide a base for services you think will be needed during the next planning cycle
>
> support the status quo instead of looking to the future
>
> seem designed to avoid risk
>
> are a little boring

This discussion of the intangibles is just as important as the review of the effectiveness and efficiency of the suggested activities. It is at this point in the review of activities that you and your colleagues will use your creativity and your vision to fine-tune the plan to reflect the unique conditions in your community and in your library.

Select the Preliminary Activities

When you are through with your review of all of the suggested activities, you should end up with a group of possible activities that would be effective in meeting one or more of the goals in the plan. You will have identified general types of resources that would be required to accomplish each of those activities and rearranged them by type of resource required. Finally, you will have reviewed the possible activities to identify those that are likely to be of most interest to the people in your community. Some of the possible activities on your list will be long-term activities that will occur throughout the three to five years of the plan. Others will be short-term activities that will be completed during the first year of the planning cycle.

Based on all of this data, you will make the preliminary selection of activities. As you make your selections, first consider which activities will result in making progress toward more than one goal. In one library that completed this process, the activities for every goal included a number of Web-based services, all of which required that the library significantly enhance its Web presence. In a much smaller library, a review of the activities indicated that progress toward a number of different goals could be made if the library provided better access to the resources it currently owned by completing a retrospective conversion project and providing an online catalog.

The next aspect to consider is the balance of resources required. There is no point in selecting a dozen activities that require significant staff resources and one activity that requires significant collections resources. As you debate the strengths and weaknesses of the activities, the ultimate criterion will be intangible: Of these activities, which seem to be the best fit for your library and your community? When you are through with this process, you should have a list of activities that you think will result in making real progress toward the goals and objectives in the library plan.

This is an exciting point in the planning process because for the first time you can really begin to see how the plan will affect the day-to-day operations of the library. Now you have the information you need to compare your current activities with what you are considering doing in the future, and you will find that some current activities are not on the list of proposed activities. This is a sign that those activities may not support your new priorities and should be carefully reviewed. Don't forget, it is as important to use this process to help to decide which activities to reduce or eliminate as it is to use the process to identify new activities.

You also need to remember that the list of activities is still only a *preliminary* list. You really haven't looked yet at the specific resource requirements for each activity. It is one thing to say the activity "Provide children's programming in Spanish, Laotian, and Russian" is staff-intensive. It is another thing to actually identify the staffing requirements for that activity and figure out how, or if, you can meet them. You will be looking at the resource allocation implications of your choices in considerably greater detail in the next task. You may well have to make some modifications in your activities when you have more information about the resource requirements for each.

You will, of course, want to keep the staff who were involved in identifying possible activities informed about the status of their recommendations. The best way to do that is to distribute to all staff members the list of preliminary activities along with brief notes about why each was tentatively selected. Then you might hold two or three more open meetings to explain the review process and how the choices were made. Another option would be to explain the process and rationale for the selections at a meeting of unit managers and ask them to pass the information on to their staff members. However, inevitably, this will lead to the front-line staff receiving mixed messages. See "Library Communication" in the Tool Kit for more information on how to communicate effectively within your library.

TASK 8: Determine Resource Requirements

This book is intended to be used in conjunction with *Managing for Results: Effective Resource Allocation for Public Libraries,* which was published by the Public Library Association in 2000, and much of the information in this task comes from that book. *Managing for Results* identified a number of resource allocation challenges facing public library managers. Of those challenges, the most relevant to the selection and review of preliminary activities is that in today's environment managers must make hard choices. These choices are made even more difficult because they don't come with guarantees.

As you have no doubt already noted, when you were reviewing activities, most of your choices weren't between clearly wonderful activities and clearly terrible activities. Instead you were selecting from among an array of activities that were fairly equal in terms of effectiveness. When you made your preliminary selections, some potentially exciting and effective activities were left off the list for a variety of reasons. This is not a new frustration for library managers. We have never had the resources to do everything for everyone all of the time, although there are days when it seems that only that will satisfy our vociferous public and our equally opinionated staff. Making choices has always been difficult, and it is becoming more difficult as the number of options open to libraries increases. However, while choosing is difficult, not choosing is dangerous.

Library managers who are unable to select from among equal but competing priorities end up doing nothing new or different. As Karen Hyman said in her witty and all too accurate article "Customer Service and the Rule of 1965":

> The Rule of 1965 defines anything the library did prior to 1965 as basic; everything else is extra. For decades, libraries have dealt with change by setting limits to marginalize what we do to ensure that library services are sometimes good but rarely essential to any but the neediest or most determined. Often these limits hang around forever, well beyond the growing pains or economic imperative.[2]

Libraries are just like other public and private organizations—they must adapt to their changing environments to survive. Libraries that follow the "Rule of 1965" are rapidly becoming dinosaurs and facing extinction.

It would be easier for library managers to make choices if they could have some assurance that all of the decisions they make are the right decisions. Unfortunately, there are no guarantees. Certainly, decisions based on the kind of planning process described in this book are more likely to be good choices than decisions made without the benefit of planning, but all the decisions you have made to this point in the planning process deal with possibilities and intentions. As soon as you start dealing with implementation—with reality—things will change. You may find that a resource you counted on will not be available or that an activity that seemed like such a great idea just doesn't work. A developer might announce that he is creating a subdivision just for retirees and plans to advertise it nationally, which will lead to a big increase in the number of seniors in your community, thereby changing the needs in your community.

The best decision-making model for library managers is often "estimate, implement, check, and adjust" and then "check and adjust" again regularly. In this task you will be checking the preliminary activities you selected in the previous task to determine if you can actually find the resources needed to implement them. If not, you will have to adjust the list of activities to be accomplished during this planning cycle to reflect the reality in which you will be operating.

Complete the Gap Analysis Process

The process for determining what resources will be required to accomplish specific activities is called *gap analysis*. The gap analysis process was introduced in the original *Planning for Results* and was refined and expanded in *Managing for Results*. In fact, a case could be made to support the premise that *Managing for Results* was written primarily to provide library managers with the tools they needed to complete the gap analysis process.

The gap analysis process has six elements, the first two of which you have already completed. The remaining four elements will be completed during this task.

1. Determine the activity to be reviewed.
2. Identify the resources that will be required (critical or important) to implement the activity.
3. Determine the type and amount of each required resource that is currently being allocated to implement the activity under review.
4. Determine the type and amount of each required resource that will be needed to implement the activity under review.
5. Compare what you currently have with what you will need, to see if you have a gap that needs to be filled or a surplus that can be allocated to other activities.
6. Develop a plan for filling the gap or reallocating the surplus.

Workform K: Gap Analysis will help you think through these elements and provide you with a place to record your responses.

The gap analysis process itself is clear and easy to understand. It is just a detailed and explicit listing of the reasoning process that most of us go through when we consider resources in our private and work lives. The difficulty comes not from the analytical process, but from the content. How do you know what resources are currently being allocated to a given activity? Even more challenging, how can you figure out what resources will be required to implement an activity? The problem, of course, is that most of us haven't thought about our current resource allocation in terms of activities or outcomes. Instead, we define our resources by type (staff, collection, facilities, technology), by building (branch, main library), by department (audiovisual, fine arts, business), or by general audience (juvenile, teen, adult).

Implicit in the gap analysis process is a programmatic approach to budgeting. This is in keeping with the trends in local governments. Many city and county governments are moving to program budgets in response to public pressure to be more outcome-oriented. However, program budgeting is very much at odds with the traditional ways that library managers have developed their budgets. Most libraries operate with a line-item budget, and when they receive X percent increase they normally divide it among the library units based on some local formula. Any new or expanded services are expected to be funded with new resources. There has rarely been any effort to review the library's base budget, and the resources that make up that base have only been reallocated in dire emergencies. As a result, in many libraries the data required to determine what resources are being allocated to specific activities simply does not exist. See Task 11 for more information about library budgeting and developing program budgets.

Data Gathering

Managing for Results presents a detailed discussion of the issues to consider when allocating each of the four main library resources (staff, collection, facilities, and technology). It also includes a selection of fifty-six workforms to help you gather the data you need to make informed resource allocation decisions. Don't be concerned about the fact that the book includes fifty-six workforms; there is no reason to even consider completing all of them. *Managing for Results* makes that point very clearly:

> It is extremely unlikely that any library will ever collect all of the data described in this book or use all of the workforms included here, nor is it easy to think of a situation in which that would be desirable. . . . *The underlying assumption in this book is that you will gather only the information you plan to use for a specific purpose in the immediate future.*[3]

As you and your colleagues work through the gap analysis process, you will probably want to start by reviewing the major allocation issues for each resource. Then you will review all of the workforms in *Managing for Results* to select those that will help you determine what specific resources are currently being allocated for the activity under review and identify the resources that will be required to implement the activity at the level needed to accomplish the intended outcome.

The workforms in *Managing for Results* provide the means to consider five different aspects of the library's resources in relation to the activity under review: capacity, utilization, access, and age or condition. (The latter two aspects, of course, do not apply to staff as a resource.)

Capacity   The ability to perform or produce something or the maximum amount of something that can be produced

Utilization   The application or employment of something for a purpose

Access   A means of approaching or making use of something

Age   The length of time something has existed

Condition   The existing circumstances or physical description of something

As you can see in figure 14: Approaches to Data Collection in *Managing for Results,* you will have a number of ways to measure most aspects for most types of resources. Each item listed in columns 2 through 5

FIGURE 14

Approaches to Data Collection in *Managing for Results*

	STAFF	COLLECTION	FACILITIES	TECHNOLOGY
CAPACITY	Abilities Training needs Hours available	Number of volumes Number of titles	Materials storage Equipment and furniture Space	Workstations and terminals Equipment, software, and telecommunications Printers
UTILIZATION	Abilities Public service indicators Analysis of an activity	Circulation In-library use Off-site use	Materials storage Equipment and furniture Space	Workstations and terminals Printers
ACCESS		Document delivery Materials availability Electronic text availability	Space	Printers Adaptive technologies
AGE/ CONDITION		Copyright date Coverage Timeliness Worn/damaged	Equipment and furniture	Workstations and terminals Equipment, software, and telecommunications Printers

refers to one or more workforms in *Managing for Results.* The trick will be to select from among the aspects those that seem most relevant to the activity under review.

A brief overview of each of the four resource chapters in *Managing for Results* is included in the following sections to help you and your colleagues get started. This is intended as an introduction to the main themes of that book and not as a replacement for them.

Staff Resources

Staff costs account for more than 50 percent of the total annual expenditures of most public libraries and would account for even more if fringe benefits were factored in.[4] However, a lot of library managers aren't exactly sure how much time staff spend on specific tasks nor can they directly link most staff activities to the library's goals and objectives. In the absence of that information, too many staffing decisions are based on an uneasy compromise between manager and front-line staff expectations and feelings. Given that the most consistent feeling that many staff members have is that they are being overwhelmed by too much work, it is not all that easy to consider adding new services and programs. That is why it is so important to base your staffing decisions on current, valid data. It is only when you have such data that you can credibly decide what staff activities are effective and should be continued or expanded and what staff activities are no longer making significant contributions to meeting the library's goals and objectives and therefore should be discontinued and replaced by other more effective activities.

When deciding what data you will need to make decisions about the staff required to implement an activity, consider five main issues:

1. What activities should be performed and when and where should they be performed?
2. What abilities are needed to accomplish the selected activities?
3. How many staff are needed in relation to patron use and staff workloads?
4. How are staff members currently using their time?
5. Where can the staff time be found to accomplish the library's priorities?

The workforms in *Managing for Results* listed in figure 15 can be used to help you gather the data you need to answer these questions.

Collection Resources

Most librarians agree that the collection represents the heart of the library, the central reason for the library's existence. There has always been far less agreement on how to shape that collection. Historically, there have been debates about the relative importance of the children's

FIGURE 15

Managing for Results Staffing Workforms Summary

Workform	Title	Purpose
OVERVIEW		
S1	Staff Functions Related to a Service Response/Priority	To determine the staff functions that will be affected by the library's service priorities
ACTIVITIES AND ABILITIES		
S2	Activities Involved in a Service Response/Priority	To determine the characteristics of the specific activities necessary to provide one service priority
S3	Staff Abilities Required for a Service Response/Priority Activity	To pinpoint the specific staff abilities needed for one activity related to a service priority
S4	Checklist of Abilities for Activities	To clarify when, where, and how abilities for a service priority are to be utilized
S5	Analysis of Training Needs and Costs for a Service Response/Priority	To help assess the real costs of training staff to acquire desired abilities
CAPACITY, UTILIZATION, AND PRODUCTIVITY		
S6	Estimate of Productive Work Hours Available	To calculate the hours of expected work by staff category
S7	Comparison of Public Service Indicators	To compare activity levels among public service units/teams
S8	Analysis of an Activity	To analyze the sequence of tasks involved in performing an activity
OBSERVATIONS AND TIME		
S9	Daily Direct-Observation Log	To collect data on staff activities by structured observations
S10	Unit/Team/Library Observation Summary	To show the number and variety of activities performed by various staff categories during one day
S11	Staff-Activity Analysis	To illustrate the congruence of how a staff member spends time and the tasks important to the job assignment
S12	Daily Time/Activity Log	To collect information about staff activities during one day
S13	Activity Log Summary	To categorize and summarize activities performed by one employee in one day
S14	Unit/Team/Library Activity Summary	To summarize time spent on many activities
ESTIMATING THE COSTS/VALUE OF ACTIVITIES		
S15	Conversion of Capacity to Cost	To calculate compensation costs for different time periods
S16	Estimate of the Cost/Value of Individual Staff Activities	To analyze time and money spent for individual activities
S17	Estimate of the Cost/Value of Unit/Team/Library Activities	To analyze time and money spent for unit activities
S18	Estimate of the Cost/Value of a Service Response/Priority	To calculate the anticipated or actual costs of

Sandra Nelson, Ellen Altman, and Diane Mayo, *Managing for Results: Effective Resource Allocation for Public Libraries* (Chicago: American Library Assn., 2000), 32–3.

collection and the adult collection, the appropriate collections for the central library and the branch libraries, the appropriate amount of money to spend on fiction best-sellers, the value of paperbacks, the number of reference materials needed, and the proportion of the budget to spend on videotapes and audio books, just to name a few. More recently, the debates have focused on the appropriate balance between print and electronic resources and the effect that providing public access to the Internet is having on collection development decisions. These debates are often intense, and many librarians have strong philosophical beliefs about the issues under discussion. This can make a rational, data-based approach to the allocation of collection resources difficult. No one ever convinced a true believer to change his or her mind with data.

The situation is complicated by the volatile nature of the collection development environment in which we are operating. It seems as if new information technologies are being introduced every day. The Internet continues to grow at an astounding rate, and more and more Americans have access to the Internet at home or at work. The mainstream publishing industry is in a state of transition, and an increasing number of small, independent presses are publishing only on the Web. At the time of writing, the E-book was still being used by relatively few people, but that is likely to change quickly—no one is sure how that will affect public libraries. Library staff members who are making collection development decisions need to be flexible and open to new ideas. They need to understand the library's goals and objectives and how the collections can be shaped to support those outcomes. Most importantly, they need to base their decisions on accurate information about current collection use and projected trends in collection use.

Consider four questions when deciding what collection data you will need to make informed decisions about resources required to implement a collection-intensive activity:

1. How can the collection requirements for service priorities be determined?
2. What needs to be done to evaluate the library's current collections?
3. How should the library address the question of format?
4. What resources are required to develop collections that support the library service priorities?

The collection workforms in *Managing for Results* listed in figure 16 can be used to help you gather the data you need to answer these questions.

Facility Resources

When library staff begin to plan for a new building, the first thing they do is write a building plan describing the programs and services they intend to

FIGURE 16
Managing for Results Collection Workforms Summary

Workform	Title	Purpose
		OVERVIEW
C1	What's important	To determine the data needed to complete the gap analysis process
		SIZE
C2	Volumes—Print and Media	To record information about the number of volumes in the collections that support a specific activity
C3	Titles—Print and Media	To record information about the number of titles in the collections that support a specific activity
C4	Titles—Electronic	To record information about the number of electronic titles in the collections that support a specific activity
		UTILIZATION
C5	Circulation—Print and Media	To record information about the circulation of print and media items that support a specific activity
C6	In-Library Use—Print and Media	To record information about the in-library use of print and media materials that support a specific activity
C7	In-Library Use—Electronic	To record information about in-library use of electronic resources that support a specific activity
C8	Off-Site Use—Electronic	To record information about the off-site use of electronic resources that support a specific activity
		ACCESS
C9	Document Delivery	To record information about the number of days it takes users to get materials that support specific activities when those materials are not available at the time the user visits the library
C10	Materials Availability	To record information about the success users have in obtaining materials that support a specific activity when they come to the library
C11	Electronic Text Availability	To record information about the level of access provided to electronic resources that support a specific activity
		AGE
C12	Copyright—Print	To record information about the age of the print titles in the collections that support a specific activity
C13	Copyright—Media	To record information about the age of the media titles in the collections that support a specific activity
C14	Periodicals—Print and Microform	To record information about the coverage of the print and microform periodical titles that support a specific activity
C15	Periodicals—Electronic	To record information about the coverage and the timeliness of the electronic periodical titles that support a specific activity
		CONDITION
C16	Worn or Damaged—Print	To record information about the condition of print items in the collections that support a specific activity
C17	Worn or Damaged—Media	To record information about the condition of media items in the collections that support a specific activity

Sandra Nelson, Ellen Altman, and Diane Mayo, *Managing for Results: Effective Resource Allocation for Public Libraries* (Chicago: American Library Assn., 2000), 114–15.

offer at the new facility. The architect uses the building plan as the basis for decisions about space allocation and utilization. In most cases, this results in a new library building that is spacious and functional. However, as time goes by, things begin to change. The community grows and changes, and community needs evolve. Library staff develop new programs and services to meet the changing needs. Library use goes up. Increasing dependence on technology of all types places new stresses on the facility. The building, once the ideal space for providing library services to the community, gradually becomes more and more crowded and less and less functional.

For most staff, the only possible solution seems to be a new building, but that is often not an option. Community leaders expect the library to use a building for at least thirty years, if not forever. There is no question that our programs and services and the tools we use to deliver them are going to change significantly in that thirty-year period. That suggests that we are going to have to do more with reconfiguring our existing facilities to support new services and programs than we have done in the past.

Five issues to consider as you decide what data you will need to determine the facility resources that will be required to implement your activities are

1. What is the capacity of the library's facilities to support the library service priorities?
2. How are the existing facilities being utilized?
3. What is the condition of the existing facilities?
4. What effect will technology have on the facilities?
5. How can the existing facilities be changed to better support service priorities?

The workforms in *Managing for Results* listed in figure 17 will help you gather, organize, and analyze the data you need to answer these questions.

Technology Resources

For centuries library managers dealt with three major areas of resources: staff, collections, and facilities. Equipment was traditionally considered to be a subset of facility resources. It is only since the mid-1980s that most library managers have begun to consider technology as a resource category separate from facilities. In this planning model, the term *technology* refers to hardware, operating and networking software, telecommunications services, electrical circuits, and data cabling or wiring. Electronic information resources (online databases, CD-ROM information products, etc.) are considered a part of the library's collection.

In one way, this is the easiest category of resources to allocate. Technology resources have been a constantly moving target for most libraries, and there is no ingrained sense of "we have always done it this way" to get in the way of making changes in allocations. On the other

FIGURE 17
Managing for Results Facility Workforms Summary

Workform	Title	Purpose
OVERVIEW		
F1	What's Important?	To determine what data is needed to complete the gap analysis process
CAPACITY		
F2	Materials Storage	To assess the storage space available to house materials to support intended activities
F3	Equipment and Furniture	To inventory the equipment and furniture the library has to support intended activities and to indicate the condition of the furniture and equipment
F4	Space	To assess the capacity of the spaces in the library that support specific activities
UTILIZATION		
F5	Space	To assess the utilization of spaces in the library that support specific activities
TECHNOLOGY		
F6	Facility Requirements	To assess the impact of technology on the library's facilities used for an activity

Sandra Nelson, Ellen Altman, and Diane Mayo, *Managing for Results: Effective Resource Allocation for Public Libraries* (Chicago: American Library Assn., 2000), 197.

hand, technology resources are managed differently from the other resources discussed in this task. Monies for staff, collections, and facilities tend to be clustered into individual budget categories. Money for technology is generally spread throughout the library's budget. Hardware is often considered a capital outlay, electrical circuits and data cabling are usually included in the facility budget, and telecommunications costs are frequently lumped with other telephone costs. This makes it difficult for library managers to stay aware of the full impact of technology on the library's budget. It also makes it difficult to accurately assess the technology resources needed to implement the selected activities.

The following five questions can help you and your colleagues decide what data you need to collect to make informed decisions about the allocation of technology resources:

1. How can technology needs be defined based on service priorities?
2. How can the types of technology that a library needs be identified?
3. What is the current capacity, utilization, and condition of the library's technology?

4. What technology will be required to meet current and anticipated needs?

5. How can required capacity be converted to cost estimates?

The workforms in *Managing for Results* listed in figure 18 will help you collect and organize the data you need.

Prepare a Preliminary Budget for Each Proposed Activity

The gap analysis process helps you determine what it is going to take to accomplish the activities you are considering. As you collect data, you will begin to get a picture of the staffing, collection, facility, and technology resources that will be required. One of the best ways to track and analyze the data you are collecting is to prepare a preliminary budget for each activity under review. This will allow you to compare the costs for each activity before you make your final activity decisions. It will also ensure that everyone understands the resource commitments that will be required to accomplish the outcomes in your plan.

If you work in one of the relatively few libraries that currently uses a program budget, you have the process in place to develop activity budgets. However, if your library currently has a line-item budget or some other type of budget, you may find Workform L: Activity Budget helpful. It provides a template for an activity budget that is self-explanatory and easy to use. In fact, Workform L looks a lot like a simplified version of the line-item budget you are probably using now. The difference is that instead of including all costs in each line, you will be recording only the costs associated with the specific activity under review in that line. For example, instead of including all of the staffing costs for a unit or the library as a whole in the *salary* line, you will just record the salary costs that will be required to accomplish the specific activity you are considering. There are also places on the template to record projected costs for the activity in the areas of administration, collections, technology, and facilities.

This is a new approach for many managers. Some of the activity costs are relatively easy to estimate; others will require considerably more effort. If you or a colleague has trouble making a projection in one or more areas, it may help to go back to the appropriate section of *Managing for Results* to review the discussion of the issue or to select an instrument to collect the data you need to help clarify your thinking. It will require a reasonable amount of work to develop these preliminary activity budgets; however, that work will pay big dividends.

When you select your final activities you will do so with a fairly clear idea of what will be required to accomplish those activities. Based on that information, you can begin to think about where you will get the

FIGURE 18

Managing for Results Technology Workforms Summary

Workform	Title	Purpose
	NEEDS ESTIMATE	
T1	Equipment, Software, and Dial Capacity	To estimate the technological capacity needed to support a planned activity
T2	Printers	To estimate how many and what types of printers are needed to support a planned activity
T3	Summary of Equipment, Printers, Software, and Dial Capacity	To summarize the capacity of technology needed to support a specific activity in each library unit
T4	Leased Lines	To determine the leased line capacity needed to support a specific activity
T5	Summary of Needs Estimates: Leased Lines	To summarize the leased line capacity needed in each library unit
	CAPACITY AVAILABLE	
T6	Workstation and Terminal Functions	To record information on the number of single and multifunction workstations and terminals in each library unit
T7	Workstation and Terminal Condition	To record information on the condition of the workstations and terminals in each library unit
T8	Equipment, Software, and Telecommunications	To record information about the equipment, software, and telecommunications capacity in each library unit
	UTILIZATION	
T9	Utilization: Observation	To collect utilization data through observation
T10	Utilization: Public Services Sign-Up Analysis	To analyze utilization data obtained from sign-up sheets in library units that allow users to reserve a specific time to use equipment or to sign up on a first-come, first-served basis
T11	Utilization: Summary	To summarize the utilization data gathered using Workforms T9 and T10
	COMPARISON OF CAPACITY REQUIRED TO UNUSED CAPACITY	
T12	Comparison of Capacity Required to Unused Capacity Available	To compare the capacity needed with the capacity available in each library unit
	ADDITIONAL EQUIPMENT AND LINES NEEDED	
T13	Technology Needed	To determine the number of additional devices to be purchased to reach needed capacity in each library unit
T14	Leased-Line Capacity Needed	To determine the additional leased line capacity to be acquired to reach needed capacity in each library unit
T15	Costs of Needed Technology	To translate the number and types of devices needed and the dial and leased line telecommunications capacity required into estimated costs

Sandra Nelson, Ellen Altman, and Diane Mayo, *Managing for Results: Effective Resource Allocation for Public Libraries* (Chicago: American Library Assn., 2000), 235–6.

resources you need. You really have only two choices: to reallocate existing resources or to obtain new funding. Both have limitations. You can't reallocate more than you currently have—and, in truth, you probably can't reallocate anywhere near *all* of what you currently have. By the same token, you probably shouldn't rely on getting large amounts of new funds unless there are special circumstances that will affect your library (a new building, a new tax levy, etc.). The reality check provided by the preliminary activity budgets will help ensure that you don't make commitments that will be impossible to keep.

When all of the preliminary activity budgets have been completed, ask one person to merge them into a single budget and then reformat that budget to match the library's regular budget. This may not be as straightforward as you might wish, particularly if your library currently uses a line-item budget. However, this is a critical step in the review process. You have to be able to compare the total resources that will be required to accomplish your plan with the resources currently available. Based on that comparison you can decide which of the activities can be accomplished by reallocating resources and which will require new resources. If you find that it will take twelve full-time staff to accomplish all of the activities under consideration and you currently have fourteen full-time staff, you are not going to be able to implement those activities simply by reallocating current staff. Furthermore, it is unlikely that you will get significant staff increases during the three years of the planning cycle. Instead, you will have to select from among those staff-intensive activities the ones that seem to you to have the potential for being most effective and efficient.

The more you and your staff know about what it costs to provide activities, the more efficiently and effectively you can manage the library. The more you understand about the links between resources and outcomes, the more clearly you can explain those links to staff, board members, library funders, library supporters, and others in your community.

Select Final Activities

When you have completed the preliminary activity budgets, you will have the information you need to select the final list of activities that the library will implement during the new planning cycle. It is very unlikely that you will have all of the resources you need to fully implement all of the activities on your final list. However, you will have a fairly good idea of what resources will be required, and you will have made some initial decisions about where to find the resources you need. The information in Task 11: Allocate or Reallocate Resources will help you decide how to actually reallocate your resources and how you might obtain the new resources you need.

The activities you have selected are inevitably going to change some of the services and programs that the library offers. It is also likely that your decisions will result in shifts in actual resources within the resource categories. For instance, you may decide to allocate more money for children's fiction, which will mean that there is less money available for other types of materials. You may also shift resources between categories, if that is permitted by the fiscal regulations in your community. For example, you may decide that it is critical to enhance the library's technology infrastructure and that to fund those enhancements you will use a combination of monies currently allocated for collections and staff. Don't ever forget that these changes are going to be hard for everyone involved. It is important to keep everyone involved and aware not only of the decisions being made but of *why* those decisions were made.

There is no such thing as a *final* decision, and that is certainly true in the case of the activities you select. The environment is always changing, and the library must continually adapt to those changes. The most effective approach for all library staff—managers and front-line employees alike—to take during times of rapid change is the model suggested at the beginning of this task: estimate, implement, check, and adjust. It isn't enough to identify what activities are most likely to meet your outcomes and the resources that will probably be needed to implement those activities. You will need to involve all staff in continually monitoring the status of the activities and recommending adjustments that will make them even more effective and efficient.

NOTES

1. Joseph Boyette and Jimmie Boyette. *The Guru Guide: The Best Ideas of Top Management Thinkers* (New York: Wiley and Sons, 1998), 69.

2. Karen Hyman, "Customer Service and the Rule of 1965," *American Libraries* 30, no. 9 (Oct. 1999): 54.

3. Sandra Nelson, Ellen Altman, and Diane Mayo, *Managing for Results: Effective Resource Allocation for Public Libraries* (Chicago: American Library Assn., 2000), 6.

4. Public Library Data Service, *Statistical Report* (Chicago: American Library Assn., 1998), 41.

Chapter 5

COMMUNICATE
Informing the Stakeholders

MILESTONES

By the time you finish this chapter you will know how to

- write the basic library plan

- present the draft of the basic plan to the staff and the members of the planning committee for review and comment

- submit the final draft of the basic plan to the library board or your local government for review and approval

- review your public relations plan to ensure that all appropriate audiences have been identified

- select the portions of the basic plan that need to be included in communications to each target audience

- determine the formats and languages in which the plan should be published

During the *communicate* step you will decide on the types of written and electronic planning reports you will produce to disseminate the results of your planning efforts throughout the library and the community. In the past, libraries tended to produce a single library plan that was nicely printed and neatly bound. It was often quite detailed and included not only the mission, goals, objectives, and activities for the planning cycle but also extensive background data about the library and the community. It was not uncommon for these planning documents to be forty or fifty pages long. A library had a specific number of copies of the plan printed and distributed to the members of the library board, to local government leaders, and to the various units of the library. Then, typically, the planning documents were filed or put on a bookshelf somewhere and referred to once or twice a year (if that). This is not the approach that is being recommended here.

Everyone involved—the planning committee, the staff, and the board—has invested a lot of time and energy in the planning process. That time and energy will have been wasted unless the results are integrated into the ongoing operations of the library and disseminated widely throughout the library and the community. For these two things to happen there must be an accurate record of the planning process used by your library and the decisions that were made during the process. That record becomes the library's basic plan. This basic plan serves two primary purposes: First, it provides a way to ensure that everyone involved in the planning process to this point is informed about and in agreement with the decisions that have been made. Second, as the official planning document approved by the library's governing authority, it provides the authorization needed to begin implementation.

As important as these two purposes are, they are just the beginning points in the *communication* step. There is no such thing as a one-document-meets-all-needs library plan any more than there are really one-size-fits-all stockings or exercise programs that work for everyone. Once the basic plan has been approved, the information it contains will be used to develop a variety of communication tools, each tailored to meet the needs

---

DO consider tailoring the presentation of your plan for specific groups

DO keep any print or electronic publications of the plan attractive and easy to read

DO be sure that each staff member has a print copy of the final plan

DON'T use library jargon or acronyms when writing your plan

DON'T assume the plan will be approved exactly as presented to your board or local government

DON'T think of the publication of the plan as the last step in the planning process

and interests of a specific audience. This focus on a variety of audiences is very important. Most librarians and library supporters agree that we all need to do a better job of "telling the library story" to make people more aware of the library's mission and services. What is sometimes overlooked in our enthusiasm for reaching out into the community is that there are multiple audiences that need to be informed, both internal and external. It may be even more critical to the success of the plan to reach the internal audience, the staff, than it is to reach the public. Certainly, if the staff doesn't buy into the plan, it will be very difficult to implement.

A lot has been written about the public's changing perception of libraries. Representatives from the Benton Foundation have been talking to people across the country about libraries since the mid-1990s, and what they have heard suggests that Americans need help in understanding the future course of libraries.[1] Planning efforts, like this one, provide you with a perfect opportunity to tell the people in your community about the library, to emphasize the fact that the library's service priorities were selected to meet community needs *as defined by community residents,* and to sell your new programs and services. Marketing experts say that a good marketing plan includes six elements: self-assessment, market definition, product planning, product creation, selling, and evaluation. Thus far in this planning process you have addressed all of those elements except selling. In the *communication* step you will learn to sell your new services and programs, and the two tasks that you will accomplish to do that are

> TASK 9
> Write the basic library plan and obtain approval
>
> TASK 10
> Communicate the results of the planning process

TASK 9: Write the Basic Plan and Obtain Approval

Few activities are more frustrating than trying to write anything in a group setting. The discussions inevitably become focused on style and not substance, and because we each have different writing styles, there are no clear-cut right or wrong answers. Group writing activities take an inordinate amount of time and rarely produce the best product. Therefore, the responsibility for writing the basic plan should be assigned to a single staff member, preferably a staff member with strong writing skills and a clear understanding of the library's planning process. This staff member should be given the time needed to write the draft plan within an acceptable time frame, either through reassignment of some duties or adjustments in some deadlines.

Note the emphasis on producing the draft with an acceptable time frame. If you have followed the suggested schedule in figure 4: Sample Time Line, you will be ready to write the draft of the plan between three and four months after you began the planning process. There is a tendency to reach this point and think that the real planning process is over and that there is no need to rush on to the final *communicate* and *implement* steps; nothing could be farther from the truth. Your planning efforts have probably generated a reasonable amount of interest in the community and have certainly generated a lot of discussion within the library. They have a certain momentum. To take advantage of that momentum, you will want to be able to present the draft of the basic plan to the staff and members of the planning committee for review and comment within two or three weeks after selecting the activities.

Draft the Basic Plan

The primary audience for the basic plan is the library's governing authority. The main purpose of the basic plan is to receive the endorsement and approval of that governing authority to move forward with the implementation of the plan. There are also two secondary audiences for the basic plan: the members of the planning committee and the library staff. In the case of these audiences, the purpose is to create an official record of the work of the various people involved in the planning process and to be sure that everyone agrees that the record is accurate and complete. You will want the basic plan to be clear, concise, credible, logical, and persuasive.

A *clear plan* is one that is easy to read and understand. The language in the plan is simple and familiar to the reader. The layout is uncluttered and makes good use of white spaces. A clear plan never uses library jargon or acronyms.

A *concise plan* uses the fewest possible words and sentences and avoids redundancy. It is short and to the point.

A *credible plan* is both accurate and believable. It is particularly important that the members of the planning committee and the staff are able to easily identify their recommendations in the basic plan. The credibility of the plan will be undermined if it has numerous spelling or grammatical errors. You can't trust the spelling and grammar checkers in your word processing software to catch all errors. Someone who is good at proofreading will need to read carefully and correct all versions of the plan before they are printed and distributed.

A *logical plan* has been arranged in an orderly pattern that makes sense to the reader. When appropriate, supporting documentation is provided to validate specific decisions. For instance, the identified community needs can be used to support or validate the library's priorities.

A *persuasive plan* convinces people to take certain actions. You want to motivate the members of your governing authority to approve the plan. You also want to motivate the members of the planning committee to become library advocates and spread the word about the plan to the community. In addition, you want to persuade the library staff that the planning effort has been inclusive and successful and that the outcomes described in the plan are appropriate and realistic.

As you can see, writing the basic plan is not going to be all that easy to do. The following list of recommended sections to include in the plan can provide a useful starting point.

Title page   This should be attractive, easy to read, and dated.

Table of contents   Although optional, a table of contents is only necessary if your basic plan is longer than ten pages.

Executive summary   This is a one-page synopsis of the basic plan that includes, at a minimum, the mission and the goals. This is the only part of the basic plan that everyone is sure to read, so it is important that it be clear and concise and that it is easy for the reader to see the library's priorities for the planning cycle.

Introduction   An introduction provides a brief description of the planning process used. It includes the names of the planning committee members and the groups that they represent.

Community needs section   Here you include a brief summary of the community vision, current conditions, and community needs. This may be included as a part of the introduction if you wish.

Mission statement   The mission statement reflects the selected service responses in your plan; therefore, there is no need to list the service responses separately. Besides, the two- or three-word title of each service response isn't particularly informative for people who have not been introduced to the concept of service responses and have not read the longer descriptions of the service responses.

Goals and objectives   All goals and objectives should be listed, but you will have to decide the best order in which to list them. There are at least two good choices: You could list them in priority order; that is, list all of the goals that relate to the highest service priority first followed by goals that support the second highest priority, etc. Another option is to cluster the goals by service target audience and then list them by priority. The decision you make will be based on local conditions and preferences.

Selected activities   Although optional, selected activities can be included to highlight new and interesting services. Including these specific examples can make the plan more credible and more persuasive. You don't want to include all of the activities in your basic plan so you can keep the plan flexible and respond easily to new opportunities throughout the life of the plan. (The activities you do not include in the basic plan will not be lost or forgotten. As you will see in Task 11, those activities will be incorporated into the annual work plans of each library staff member. In Task 12 you will be encouraged to review and revise the activities that support the library's outcomes annually and make changes as needed.)

Review the Draft of the Basic Plan

Before the draft of the basic plan is ready to be submitted to the library's governing authority for approval, it should be reviewed by the staff and by the members of the planning committee. If the library's governing authority is a city or county and you also have an advisory library board, include that advisory board in the review process too. It is very important that the draft version of the basic plan distributed for review be clearly marked *DRAFT* and that reviewers be encouraged to consider all aspects of the plan in their review: its content, organization and formatting, and style of writing. You will have to decide whether everyone should review the draft of the plan simultaneously or if you want to have the staff review and comment on it before it is sent to the planning committee for review—or vice versa. Unless the reviewers identify serious problems with the draft of the plan, a single review by each group will be sufficient.

Staff

There are a variety of ways to disseminate the draft of the basic plan to the staff for review. If your library has an intranet, the draft can be posted there, and staff can be notified in a memo from the director that it is available for review and comment. If you don't have an intranet, the draft of the plan will probably have to be photocopied and distributed to the staff. In the ideal world, every staff member would receive a copy of the plan and be given an opportunity to comment. In the real world, this is expensive and cumbersome for very large libraries. Another option would be to distribute copies of the draft to each unit supervisor and make it clear to those supervisors that they are to circulate the draft among their staff members and encourage them to comment. However the plan is disseminated, the deadline for responses should be clear, and all comments and suggested revisions should be made in writing and include the name and unit of the person making the recommendation.

Setting the deadline by which the comments and suggested revisions must be received will be a judgment call. A lot will depend on how you disseminate the draft. If you post it on the library intranet, it is not unreasonable to expect staff to review the plan and comment within ten days. If you expect supervisors to circulate the draft among their staff, it will take at least two and perhaps three weeks for everyone to see the plan. You want to move the process along as expeditiously as possible, but you also want to make sure that staff feel that they had a fair chance to react to the plan before it was made final.

Planning Committee

The members of the planning committee will attend one last committee meeting to discuss the draft of the basic plan and suggest revisions. The meeting probably won't take long and could easily be scheduled from 11:00 to 1:00 and include lunch. Remember that committee members will need as much advance notice as possible to get the meeting on their schedules. They will also need to receive a copy of the draft of the basic plan no less than one week prior to the meeting. Given the mail, that means that the drafts will have to be mailed at least ten days before the meeting.

Submit the Final Draft of the Basic Plan to the Approving Authority

The library director, the person responsible for writing the basic plan, and any others that the director might decide to include will meet after the staff and planning committee review processes to assess the reactions to the draft. They will consider the recommended revisions and decide how to handle each. Then the person responsible for writing the plan will incorporate all of the agreed-upon changes into the plan and produce the final draft of the basic plan.

Once this final draft is completed, it is ready to be submitted to the library's governing authority for review and approval. Some libraries have had the final draft of their plans professionally printed before they were sent to the governing authority for review and approval so they would present a professional-looking document. In several cases, the actual result was that the members of the governing authority were offended because they thought that the library was taking their approval for granted. Obviously, you want to avoid this kind of misunderstanding. You can create a professional, attractive, and easily read final draft of your plan using word processing software. Clearly mark the document *FINAL DRAFT*, photocopy it, and it is ready to deliver to the members of the governing authority.

The next question is the best way to deliver the plan to the members of the governing authority. The answer depends on your governing authority. If you report to an authority board, you will work with the board chair and the board representative on the planning committee to decide how to manage the review process. The easiest thing to do is to mail each member a copy of the final draft of the plan along with the notice of the meeting during which it will be reviewed. Allow at least ten days prior to the meeting for members to review it. If you report to a city department head or a city or county executive, it may be more effective to make an appointment to deliver the final draft in person.

During the review process, it will be important to remind the members of your governing authority that they have seen pieces of the draft of the plan before: Earlier in the process they reviewed the planning committee's community vision statements, their assessment of current conditions, and the community needs they identified. The members of the governing authority formally approved the service responses that form the framework for the plan during Task 5 of this process. Therefore, there shouldn't be any big surprises in the library's priorities for the next planning cycle.

There may be some discussion of the objectives that the library intends to use to measure progress toward reaching the goals, and some members of the governing authority might be interested in more details about the activities. However, if you have kept the members of the governing authority informed and involved in the process all along, the approval process should be relatively straightforward. If there are any serious concerns raised about the plan, the board member or members who served on the planning committee should be given the first opportunity to respond. After all, the primary reason board members were appointed to the board was to ensure that the lines of communication would be open and clear between the two groups.

TASK 10: Communicate the Results of the Planning Process

In Task 2 you and your colleagues developed a communication plan to ensure that everyone involved—staff, board, funders, and community members—would be kept informed about the major decisions that were made during the planning process. One of the many benefits that result from a planning process like this one is that you end up with the information needed to develop an effective ongoing public relations program as well. You have identified your customers, defined what you want to accomplish, determined how you will measure your success, and decided on the services and programs (products) you will offer. Now you need to be sure that your customers use the services you have so carefully designed. That means that you have to continue to get your message out.

Define Who and Why

As noted earlier, you have both internal and external audiences, and if your plan is going to be successfully implemented, you must communicate effectively with both. To do that you need to decide what you want to occur as a result of your communications with each audience you identify. Typically, communications are intended to inform an audience about something or to persuade them to do something. In the case of staff, a communication might be intended to direct the staff to do something.

Internal Audiences

A number of different internal audiences need to be considered when communicating the results of the planning process including senior managers, unit managers, professional staff, paraprofessional staff, clerical staff, janitorial staff, part-time staff, and volunteers. The members of the library board could also be considered an internal audience, as could the leadership of the library Friends group or foundation. It is likely that you will want different results from your communications with each of these groups. For example, you might be communicating with library supervisors to direct them to begin to incorporate the first year's activities into their work programs. You might be communicating with part-time employees who work primarily in the evening to inform them about the plan and to help them understand the library's priorities. Your communications to the leaders of the foundation will probably focus on persuading them to support some of the services and programs in the plan financially.

External Audiences

Many more external audiences than internal audiences exist, and choosing from among them can be difficult. However, general messages written to appeal to everyone often fail to interest anyone. Your primary external audiences have been defined by the goals in the library plan. Consider the following goals, used as examples in chapter 3.

> The children in Anytown will have the resources they need to meet their recreational needs.
>
> Workers in Anytown will have the skills they need to be employed locally and make a living wage.
>
> Young adults in Anytown will have the information they need to make informed decisions.

In each case the audience is clear. Of course, not all of your goals are targeted to specific groups. Some of them are more general in nature: "All residents of Anytown will have the skills needed to find, evaluate, and use information in a variety of formats." With these more general goals, you will have to develop multiple communications targeted to segments of the target population. The segments you target will be defined by the objectives and activities you have selected to support the goal. Regardless of the audience, external communications usually have two main purposes: to persuade people to *use* the services and programs of the library and to persuade people to *support* the services and programs of the library.

Match the Communication to the Audience

In *The TELL IT! Manual,* Amy Owen pointed out that the central question in "telling the story" is "Who needs to know what?" She suggested several rules for deciding, two of which have particular applicability to deciding how to disseminate information about your plan.

> *Rule 1: The more important the individual, the less they want to know.*[2]
>
> Most library managers already know all there is to know about rule 1. Important people have limited time and limited patience. They respond well to very brief, succinct summaries, and they tend to ignore anything longer than a brief paragraph or two. It is likely that these people are going to read the executive summary of the basic plan and nothing else. Therefore, it is very important that that section of the plan be well written.

> *Rule 2: Tailor the message to the individual or group.*[3]
>
> This rule gets to the heart of effective communication. Every one of your target audiences has a different interest and a different need. As Owen points out, politicians prefer anecdotes about how services affect real people. Staff, on the other hand, are primarily interested in how the topic under discussion will affect their jobs—they want the details. Teens aren't interested in programs for tots or seniors; they will respond best to communications that talk about them and their interests in their terms.

Formats and Languages

Matching the communication to the audience is not just a matter of selecting the right content. It is also important to select the right format and the right language. The widespread public access to the Internet offers a new avenue for communicating the library's message. Other effective communications media include printed documents, public presentations, newspaper articles, media spots, etc. Print is usually the least expensive medium, and it can be very effective. A number of libraries have developed a one-page trifold summary of their basic plan to be distributed throughout the community, and these have worked well. Additional trifold publications could be developed to highlight the services and programs for specific target audiences that are included in the plan.

There are two issues to consider with language. The first, obviously, is the native language of the people with whom you are trying to communicate. Communities are becoming more diverse, and library managers can't assume that information published in English will meet the needs of non-English-speaking residents. If you decide to publish a part or all of your plan in a language other than English, be very sure that you have a good translator and then have the draft checked by a number of people who write the language fluently before it is printed. There are horror stories of librarians who published documents in a language other than English, thinking they said one thing only to discover—too late—that the message was quite different.

Actually, there are also instances in which English language communications have turned out to be open to more than one interpretation. That illustrates the second issue with language: People use and respond to words very differently. This is particularly true if you plan to use written communications. Teens have a different vocabulary than seniors, and each group would probably be turned off by a communication addressed to the other. It is always a good idea to have a variety of people, including representatives of the target audience, check and recheck any document before it is published.

Don't Expect to Accomplish Your Purpose with a Single Message

You often see the same commercial over and over again on television or in your local newspaper and hear the same ads on the radio throughout the day because repetition is necessary to get through to the consumer. On May 3, 1999, Ned Potter reported on *ABC Nightly News* that the average office worker must sift through 30 e-mails, 22 voice mails, 18 pieces of regular mail, 15 faxes, and 11 Post-it notes every day.[4] That is a lot of information, and it certainly makes it clear why it is so important that any message you send from the library must be clear, concise, focused, and *repeated*.

NOTES

1. Andrew Blau, "Telling the World You Are Better—What Is the Customers' Frame of Reference" (presentation at the opening session for trustees, American Library Association Conference, Chicago, 26 June 1999).

2. Amy Owen, "Let People Know What Happened: Telling the Story," in *The TELL IT! Manual: The Complete Program for Evaluating Library Performance* (Chicago: American Library Assn., 1996), 30–1.

3. Owen, 30–1.

4. Ned Potter, *Information Overload: How to Deal with Too Much Data.* Available: http://more.abcnews.go.com/sections/tech/closerlook/infooverload990503.html on 3/2/00.

Chapter 6

IMPLEMENT Moving into the Future

MILESTONES

By the time you finish this chapter you will know how to

- allocate or reallocate the resources required to implement the activities in the plan

- integrate the activities in the plan into the ongoing operations of the library

- monitor the progress the library is making toward achieving the goals and objectives in the plan

- adjust the plan as needed when circumstances change or planning assumptions prove to be invalid

- develop activities for the second and third years of the current planning cycle

- use what you have learned in this planning cycle in your next planning process

Up to this point in this process the emphasis has been on planning. In the *implement* step the focus shifts to doing. This is a new emphasis in public library planning models. Earlier models focused almost exclusively on creating the plan and paid little or no attention to the activities required to put the plan into practice. *A Planning Process for Libraries* allocated a little more than a page to implementation issues. *Planning and Role-Setting for Public Libraries* moved directly from writing the plan to evaluating the effect of the plan on library services and programs during and after the planning cycle. *Planning for Results* placed a lot of emphasis on determining the resources required to accomplish the outcomes in the plan, but it didn't address integrating the activities from the plan into the ongoing operation of the library.

The assumption in all of these books seemed to be that library managers needed a lot of help to define their priorities, write their goals, and select their activities, but once that was done, librarians would have no problem implementing the decisions. In too many libraries, that assumption turned out to be false. The experience this library manager describes has been all too common:

> Unfortunately the implementation of a long-range plan has had little effect on our day-to-day operations. Activities are seen as extras and rarely get carried out the way they were intended to.[1]

The shift from planning to implementing can be tricky. You certainly want to acknowledge all of the hard work that has gone into developing the library's plan and to celebrate the successful completion and approval of the basic planning document. However, you don't want to imply that the planning process is complete. This can be a difficult distinction to make. There is a natural tendency for staff to look at the final planning document and say, "Thank goodness that's over. Now we can get back to

DO	encourage your staff to think of the library plan as the blueprint they are using to build better library services
DO	remember that the key to effective resource allocation is to estimate, implement, check, and adjust
DO	monitor the progress being made toward achieving the goals and objectives in the plan at least once a month
DON'T	assume that staff will automatically integrate the activities in the new plan into their daily routines
DON'T	hesitate to make changes in the plan when circumstances change
DON'T	wait more than three years before beginning a new planning cycle

our real work." Of course, the work that staff members want to return to is usually the work they were doing before the planning process started, partially because change is hard and resistance to change is natural. An even larger part has to do with inertia. Newton's Law of Inertia says, "An object at rest or in a state of uniform motion tends to remain in that state unless acted upon by some outside force." This is as true of people as it is of inanimate objects. It takes considerably more energy to learn something new, do something unfamiliar, or stop doing something than it does to continue to do what you have always done before.

Another challenge that library managers face when implementing a new library plan is that of denial. Even though you have been talking about the effect of the plan on the library's resources since the review of the preliminary service responses and even though you spent considerable time and energy identifying the resource allocation implications of the activities in the plan, most staff—and some managers—still believe that all new services will be supported with new resources. That, of course, is impossible. No library is going to receive an ever-increasing appropriation to add new services while continuing to offer all of its current services unchanged. In fact, in today's tax-resistant climate, there is considerable pressure on library managers to add new services with little or no additional resources. This unpalatable truth is not something many of us want to acknowledge.

Not only are staff members resistant to change but some library board members may find that there is a big difference between making an intellectual commitment to change and making the difficult resource adjustments required to accomplish the change. The public, too, will react to any changes in library services or programs—and not always positively. No matter how narrow the audience for a service or how little used the service is, the chances are good that someone will complain if it is altered or eliminated. What that means is that any changes in publicly funded services are ultimately political changes and, therefore, have the potential to be controversial.

Most library managers are well aware of this. It is one of the main reasons that some managers avoid making hard resource allocation choices among competing priorities. Instead they provide minimal support to all priorities, virtually guaranteeing that all library services will be, at best, mediocre. The payback for these managers has been few complaints; however, the price has often been high. People don't get excited about inadequate or mediocre services, and they don't support those services politically or economically. There is some evidence that the price may be even higher in the future. The public now expects public-sector managers to be as accountable for outcomes as private-sector managers are. That accountability is being measured in two ways: responsiveness to changing needs and fiscal responsibility. This planning process has given you the tools you need to excel in both areas.

The two tasks you need to accomplish the *implement* step are

TASK 11
Allocate or reallocate resources

TASK 12
Monitor implementation

TASK 11: Allocate or Reallocate Resources

Task 8 included an overview of the information in *Managing for Results: Effective Resource Allocation for Public Libraries.* In that task library managers were encouraged to use the information and workforms in *Managing for Results* to develop preliminary activity budgets that identified the resources required to accomplish the activities being considered. Then the managers used that information to select the activities for at least the first year of the planning cycle. Now we are going to move from identifying what resources will be needed to accomplish the activities in your plan to actually finding and deploying the required resources.

Although you will be allocating or reallocating resources in the areas of staff, collections, facilities, and technology, your most important decisions will be those that affect staff responsibilities. It takes people to make things happen. The old adage "if everyone is responsible, then no one is responsible" is absolutely true. Activities will not be implemented unless one person is made responsible for each. Therefore, the starting point for this task will be the assignment of a specific staff member to be responsible for managing the implementation of each activity in your plan.

Consider a number of questions when you make these assignments:

Who has the skills required to manage the implementation of the activity?

Is training available that could help the person strengthen his or her skills?

Who is interested in the services or programs addressed by the activity?

Who is responsible for providing similar services or programs now?

What will be the effect of a new assignment on the person's current responsibilities?

What is the person doing now that can be discontinued, streamlined, or reassigned?

That last question bears repeating: What is the person doing now that can be discontinued, streamlined, or reassigned? This is the question that you and all of the people responsible for implementing the activities in the plan will have to address again and again. The selection of the person to be responsible for managing the implementation of each activity is just the first of many staffing decisions that will have to be made. Every activity, regardless of the primary resource required, will also require some staff, and everyone currently working in the library believes they are working to capacity. A lot of them also believe that they don't have the collection, facility, or technology resources they need to do their jobs well. All of this means that staff interest in the resource allocation part of the planning process is anything but academic. They know that the resource decisions that are going to be made will have a big effect on their work environment—for better or for worse.

Managers in every organization in this country—profit, nonprofit, and government—are facing the same challenges. A wide variety of excellent print and electronic resources are available to help library managers become *change* managers. While this was being written, a search of books on Amazon.com using the key words "change management" resulted in a list of 1,893 books. A similar search using the search engine Google returned 83,200 hits. Although many of the authors of these books and Web sites take different approaches to change management, there is general agreement on some basic guidelines. Most experts believe that communication—up, down, and throughout the organization—is the key to successfully managing organizational change. Communication is such a critical component of the success of your planning efforts at every step of the planning process that a section on "Library Communication" has been included in the Tool Kit.

Most experts also stress that successful organizational change efforts must be based on clearly identified priorities, on goals that focus on meeting the customer's needs, and on performance measures that provide a mechanism for accountability. The good news for you, your colleagues, the library staff, and the library board is that the planning process you just completed provides the perfect foundation for organizational change. These additional change-management guidelines will help you build on that foundation to effectively integrate your plan into the ongoing operation of the library:

> Involve staff at every step of the process. The more that staff have to do with designing the changes, the more comfortable they will feel with them.
>
> Don't get so involved in the process of change that you lose track of the reasons for changes. Always know why you are making changes, and always include the reasons when discussing changes with staff, the board, and the public.
>
> Acknowledge the emotional reactions that we all have when faced with change. Some change experts suggest that people dealing

with change go through much the same process as people dealing with grief: shock, denial, anger, guilt, depression, acceptance, and growth. These are strong emotions, and they won't just go away if you ignore them.

Acknowledge the contributions made by the services and programs that are being phased out. A decision to change the priority of a service based on new community needs in no way diminishes the value of that service in the past. Celebrate your achievements, and link your past successes at meeting community needs with your current efforts to continue to do so.

Don't expect change to be quick. It took a long time to establish your current organizational norms, and it will take a long time to change them. Furthermore, the larger your library is, the longer it will take to change things. It is much like the difference between trying to turn an ocean liner (remember the *Titanic*) and turning a canoe.

Stay focused on the end result. Your plan is intended to improve the library's service to the people of your community.

Don't expect to control the change process. No one person can control organizational change. What you and other library managers can do is understand the change process and manage it.

Find the Needed Resources

Your basic plan may have been reviewed and discussed by all interested parties and approved by your governing authority, but at this point the plan is still just words on paper. It will remain words on paper until it is fully integrated into the library budget because the truth is that no matter what a library's planning documents might say, the budget defines the library's actual priorities.

Start by reviewing the preliminary activity budgets with the people assigned to implement those activities. Be sure that they understand how the budget figures were determined and agree that the figures seem valid. Make whatever adjustments seem appropriate, but remember that significant increases in the resources to be allocated to one activity will probably affect the resources available for other activities. When you have completed the review of activity budgets, you will know exactly what resources will be required to implement your plan. In chapter 4 you were encouraged to tell the staff that the library board and the library managers were fully committed to finding the required resources through reallocation of existing resources or acquiring new resources if possible. Now is the time for you to deliver on that promise.

Reallocation Issues

If your library is typical, reallocation is going to provide more of the needed resources than new funding, and so we return again to the question of what activities can be discontinued, streamlined, or reassigned. Staff are justifiably skeptical about plans to reallocate their time. While long-time staff members can give example after example of new programs that the library initiated over the years, they are often hard-pressed to think of examples of programs that have been discontinued. Many staff are afraid that instead of being assigned to A and B *instead of* X and Y, they will be assigned to A and B *in addition to* X and Y. This is the equivalent of the football practice of "piling on" in which one player tackles another and then five or six more players join the tackle, leaving the poor player who was tackled first at the bottom of a heavy pile. Football teams are discouraged from piling on by an immediate penalty. Library managers who pile on assignments also pay a price in low staff morale, increased turnover, reduced quality of work, and lack of trust in the administration. However, because this price is one that is paid over time, it is harder for some managers to make a direct link between cause and effect.

Another side to this discussion of reallocating staff time needs to be mentioned too. Sometimes the problem with doing A and B instead of X and Y isn't because managers won't make hard choices but because staff don't want to quit doing things that they enjoy or believe are more valuable than the alternatives. Staff reactions can range from refusing to use the computer to do something because "it's faster to do it by hand" to continuing to surreptitiously clip items for the supposedly closed vertical file to resenting the need to help people access electronic resources because it takes time and energy away from providing "real" reference services.

A classic example of staff fighting to maintain the status quo occurred in a large library system that completed the planning process in the late 1980s. As a result of the community needs assessment, the library plan shifted priorities from preschool services, particularly those offered in the library on week days, to services for school-age children, specifically fourth, fifth, and sixth graders. During the preliminary discussions of the resources required to implement this change, the managers agreed that it could be accomplished by reassigning the current staff who were providing children's services. Some of the children's librarians were appalled by the new focus of youth services. The library's youth services program had traditionally emphasized in-library preschool programs, and many of the staff were wonderfully skilled storytellers who loved their jobs and the children they served. The children's staff met with the library management team to request that they be allowed to continue to do their traditional story programs in addition to the new activities that resulted from the plan (a sort of reverse piling on). The managers deserve a great deal of credit for saying no firmly and clearly. Staff only work so many hours every day, and the work they do during those hours has to contribute to meeting library priorities.

You gathered some of the information you need to begin to reallocate staff during Tasks 7 and 8. In Task 7, you divided the list of suggested activities into two groups, one that included the activities that supported the goals and objectives of the library plan and one that did not. Now you and your colleagues need to review that second list and identify other current activities that do not directly support the new library priorities. The workforms included in the staffing chapter in *Managing for Results* will help you identify these activities. In Task 8 you did the preliminary work needed to identify the staff resources that will be required to accomplish the activities that support the library priorities. Now you will need to look at the staff resources currently allocated to the activities that do not support the library's priorities and consider which of those resources should be reallocated.

You will go through a similar process to identify the collection, facility, and technology resources that could be reallocated to support the priorities in the plan, and in each case, you will find that you have to address staff concerns about the proposed changes. In many libraries, collection development responsibilities are distributed among staff, and each staff member has a specific budget to purchase materials, money that is often considered "my money for materials." Needless to say, taking some of "my money" away and giving it to someone else, for whatever reason, is not likely to be well received. The same reactions can be expected to changes in the spaces in which people work and the equipment they use. Remember, the more you can involve staff in the resource allocation decisions being made, the more likely they are to support those decisions. Staff will also feel better if it is possible to fund new activities with a mix of reallocated and new resources.

New Resources

At one time library managers could count on an automatic inflationary increase of 3 percent to 5 percent each year. Those were the good old days, and they are gone forever. Today's library managers and supporters have to fight for every new tax dollar they receive and compete against other strong candidates for grants and donations. There is also an increasing emphasis on performance measures and results from both public and private funders. Consider these comments from local, state, federal, and foundation sources.

> Why does the city need this service? How do these expenditures benefit the citizens of Hendersonville?—City Council, Hendersonville, Tennessee[2]

The Priorities 2000 Task Force will look at zero-based and performance-based budgeting models to replace baseline budgeting, which uses the prior budget as the foundation each succeeding budget is built upon.—Minnesota House Republican Caucus Priorities Task Force 2000[3]

The focus of the budget is moving away from seeking more, more, more. The process must be transformed to focus on what managers produce and citizens get for their money—results, performance, value, quality, and customer service.—Office of the Vice President, Al Gore[4]

Kingsley House has been more successful in maintaining funding and getting supplemental funding because we are able to demonstrate the impact of the dollars. Corporations are quite impressed with our ability to show impact—the effect on kids and our ability to keep adults out of a nursing home.—Executive Director of Kingsley House and New Orleans Day Nursery Association[5]

Although the four quotations come from very different sources, they share a remarkable commonality of theme: outcomes matter. Library managers and supporters who are seeking new resources would be well advised to echo that theme in their requests. Fortunately, just as this planning process has provided you with the foundation you need to successfully reallocate resources, so has it provided you with the information you need to obtain new resources. You have identified priorities based on community needs, you have targeted specific audiences, and you have developed performance measures. You know what outcomes you are trying to reach, and you know that those outcomes are important to the decision makers in your community because they helped you identify them.

Now you need to decide what to ask for in your request for new funding and from whom you should request that funding. These two decisions are interconnected and will be based on the answers to the following questions:

Is there a link between the outcomes in the plan and the priorities of any of the agencies or individuals that might provide funding?

This is the first question to ask and the most important. Elected officials, grant funders, and private donors are always more willing to support programs that further their goals. For example, if one of your goals is to help preschool children enter school ready to succeed and your state library agency offers grants to support that kind of program, it makes sense to apply for such a grant. However, you want to be careful not to request resources in areas that are not priorities in your plan just because money is available in that area. If there is nothing in your plan about preschool services, you definitely do not want to apply for that grant. There is no such thing as free money, and it takes time and energy to manage grant funds, not to mention the fact that the granting agency normally expects you to continue programs with local resources when the grant ends.

Does the item you are considering require a one-time allocation or ongoing funding?

Examples of one-time allocations include the funds to renovate a portion of the library to use as a teen center or a cyber-reference area. Resources that require ongoing funding typically include staffing (including any staffing required for that renovated teen center or cyber-reference area), although libraries certainly do hire contract employees to do special projects. Some resource requests include both a one-time allocation and an ongoing appropriation. For instance, a library might ask for a large sum of money to update and expand the collection of preschool materials plus an annual sum to maintain the collection at the new level. Tax dollars are usually the only source of ongoing funding available to libraries, although that may change as more libraries establish foundations. One-time allocations can come from either tax dollars or grants and donations.

Can the item you are considering be funded by reallocating resources, or must it be funded from new resources?

You can accomplish a lot of the priorities in your plan by reallocating your resources, but some things are simply too expensive—in time or money—to fund that way. The definition of "too expensive" will be different in every library, and you need to be careful not to overuse it. Funders are not sympathetic to requests that imply that everything the library is doing now is absolutely essential and that new resources must be allocated to meet all new needs. There is another danger here, too, particularly if you are dealing with your government funders. If you tell them that a program is too expensive to fund through reallocation and the funders don't allocate the new resources you request, you can't turn around and find the resources internally for the program. If you do, you ruin your credibility for any future funding requests.

Does the item you are considering support a new service, or will it be used to expand an existing service?

In general it will probably be easier to get new resources for new services. This is particularly true for grant funding, which is often intended as seed money to initiate programs or services. However, even government funders may be more inclined to provide money for new services and expect library managers to reallocate current resources to expand existing programs.

Given the earlier emphasis on the difficulties that some staff have dealing with the reallocation of resources, it may be comforting to know that organizational changes funded with new resources are generally easier for everyone. The new resources usually mean that staff don't have to change much about the way they personally do business. New staff will implement the new service, or new dollars will fund the additional materials needed, or a building expansion will provide the space needed for the new program. Staff may well be affected by these new resources but not as intensely as they would be affected by reallocations of resources in the same areas. Furthermore, most library staff genuinely care about the library's services and the people who use those services. Staff are more willing to deal with changes that are supported with increases in funding because those increases represent a validation of their work and acknowledgment of the importance of the library.

Integrate Activities into Ongoing Operations

Your final activity budgets identify the number of staffing hours and the costs for any materials resources, technology support, or facilities adjustments that will be required to implement the activity. At the beginning of this task you were encouraged to develop a new library budget that reflected all of these costs. Now you need to complete the process of integrating the activities you have selected to accomplish your priorities into the ongoing operations of the library.

Staff Performance Plans

The place to start integrating activities into library operations is with staffing requirements. Remember, nothing gets done unless someone is assigned to do it and has the skills needed to do it right. The workforms in the staffing chapter of *Managing for Results* (see figure 15 in Task 8) provide the data you need. The *Managing for Results* Workform S3 helps you decide what abilities are needed to accomplish the activity; Workform S4 provides information on when, what, and how those abilities will be used; and Workform S5 takes you through a process to determine the staff training that will be required to accomplish each activity and the cost of that training. Based on the information you gather using those three workforms, you can review and revise the library position descriptions to reflect the new responsibilities and skills required for each. You can also develop a comprehensive training plan to ensure that staff have the skills they need.

After all of the position descriptions are updated and the training plan is in place, you are ready to incorporate the activities for the new planning cycle into each employee's annual performance plan. As Patricia Belcastro points out in *Evaluating Library Staff: A Performance Appraisal System*:

> The key to successful implementation of this performance appraisal system is the managers' ability to communicate to the staff their expectations for performance. For the employee to perceive any evaluation as fair, the employer must first clearly state what is expected of the employee.[6]

Libraries use a variety of employee performance plans. In some libraries the annual performance plan is a city or county generic checklist of activities. In other libraries, each employee develops annual goals and objectives that are used at the end of the year to evaluate employee performance. Obviously, it is going to be easier to incorporate the activities into the second type of performance plan, but managers in libraries that use generic checklists can also make new assignments using the "other duties" part of the checklist to attach a list of desired outcomes for the coming year.

The revision of employee performance plans is one process that must start at the top and then spread throughout the library. The first performance plan that should be changed is the library director's. The director's performance plan should make it clear that the board/governing authority holds the director responsible for making progress toward the outcomes described in the plan. This is not to say that the director should be expected to achieve 100 percent of the objectives in the plan. That is unrealistic and discourages any kind of risk-taking. Rather, the board should set a reasonable standard to meet, perhaps that at least 80 percent of the objectives in the plan will be met during the planning cycle. Obviously, if unforeseen circumstances arise (a recession, a fire or flood, a huge influx of new residents, or whatever), the board and director will have to revise the plan to reflect the new reality.

Next, the director should meet with senior managers to revise their performance plans to incorporate the new priorities and to be sure that managers have the skills and information needed to revise the performance plans of the people who report to them. The senior managers, in turn, will work with unit managers to revise their performance plans and provide the coaching they need to work with front-line staff. Finally, the unit managers will meet with each of their employees to discuss the implications of the library's new plan on the unit and to specifically tell each employee what she or he will be responsible for accomplishing during the coming year.

All staff, from the director down, are likely to find this process challenging. "Change is hard" has been a recurring theme throughout this book, as has the fact that the closer change hits to home the harder it is. An employee's performance plan is as close to home as it gets, and managers at all levels should be prepared to deal with the staff anxieties that this process will inevitably produce. As managers work with staff to revise their performance plans, they can explain that everyone in the library—including the director—is going through this same process, and that everyone—including the director—is a little nervous about the new assignments. This is when having a comprehensive training plan will be invaluable. Managers will be able to provide specific and detailed assurance to staff that they will get the training they need to continue to provide the same high-quality service to the public they always have.

Other Resources

Once you have integrated the activities from the plan into employee performance plans, making the other resource adjustments needed is going to seem relatively simple and straightforward. It is always easier to deal with things than with people. The budgets for each activity provide the information you need to revise the materials allocation formulas you use to reflect the library's changing priorities. The activity budgets also include the information you need to make adjustments in the way library facilities are apportioned and in the technological infrastructure that supports the library's services. The staff who will be responsible for making the changes have been informed as a part of the performance planning process described. When those changes are completed, you and all of your colleagues will be in a position to help the community move toward the ideal future that was described at the beginning of this planning process. You will exemplify the first two characteristics of library excellence that are the foundation of this process:

> Excellence must be defined locally—it results when library services match community needs, interests, and priorities.

> Excellence is possible for both small and large libraries—it rests more on commitment than on unlimited resources.[7]

TASK 12: Monitor Implementation

It takes strong leaders, effective managers, and caring and committed staff members to accomplish what you will have accomplished. You can and should congratulate yourselves for a job well done! Then you need to remember the third characteristic of library excellence:

> Excellence is a moving target—even when achieved, excellence must be continually maintained.[8]

The plan that you are implementing is based on hard work and lots of data, but it is still just a plan. Conditions change all of the time, both internally and externally, and the libraries that thrive in this environment are those that put into place processes and procedures to continually monitor and adjust services and programs. The best way to do that is to follow the rule for effective resource allocation described earlier: *estimate, implement, check,* and *adjust.* Your plan describes your estimates, and you have done everything you need to do to *implement* the plan. That leaves *check* and *adjust.*

Monitor Implementation and Make Interim Adjustments as Needed

The goals in your plan identify the outcomes you are trying to achieve. Each objective defines the way you intend to measure progress toward reaching the outcome, a standard against which to compare that measure, and a date or time frame by which time the standard should be met. It is likely that the library already collects a lot of the data needed to determine if the objectives are being met. If there are objectives that include data elements that are not currently being collected, you will need to design appropriate data-collection instruments and make arrangements to have the needed data collected.

In the past, some libraries have waited until the end of the time frame for the objective to determine whether the objective was achieved. This is fine if everything goes according to plan; however, if for any reason there is a problem in reaching the standard described in the objective, it doesn't do you much good to discover that after the fact. It makes a lot more sense to gather interim data and to establish an ongoing review of the progress being made. You already have the mechanisms in place to support this review: employees' performance plans, regularly scheduled management meetings, regularly scheduled staff meetings, and the reports you make to your governing authority.

The performance plans discussed in the previous task are the most effective monitoring tools you have. Managers should meet with employees several times each year to discuss the progress the employees are making toward meeting the expectations described in their performance plans. If any employee is not meeting those expectations, the manager and the employee should work together to identify the problem. It may be that the employee hasn't received all the training needed; that the collection, facility, or technological resources required have not been made available; or that the original estimates about the level of those resources that would be required were not accurate. Of course, it might also be because the employee in question is having trouble adjusting to the changes in his or her responsibilities. When the manager and employee have agreed on the reasons the employee is not meeting expectations, they should develop a plan for addressing those reasons.

The employee performance appraisal process provides a micro view of the implementation of the plan. You will also need a macro view of progress being made toward implementing the plan to be able to make the adjustments that will be needed. This macro view comes from incorporating a review of the objectives into your regularly scheduled management meetings, staff meetings, and reports to your governing authority. You are working toward a point when it will be second nature for the library staff and board members to use the outcomes described in the plan as the logical justification for all resource allocation decisions. That will happen only if the library director and library manager make the plan the focus for their decision making and make the fact that they are doing so explicitly clear to staff and board members through regular reports.

Review and Revise Activities

Most library plans cover a period of three to five years, and inevitably a lot will change during the life of the plan. The process recommended in this book results in a flexible plan that can be easily adapted to meet new conditions. The goals and objectives in this process describe the outcomes the community will receive from the library and how progress toward reaching those outcomes will be measured. The goals and objectives are likely to remain valid throughout the life of the plan because they do not include any information on how the outcomes will be achieved. It is the *how* that is being most affected by rapid changes in the information industry. All of the detailed *how* information is included in the activities and, because they are not a part of the official planning document, they can be updated as often as necessary.

At a minimum, activities should be reviewed and revised annually. If your plan includes activities that span several years or activities that will not be started until the second or third year of the planning cycle, it will be worth the time to record the assumptions upon which those activities were based. That information will be valuable when you review the activities during the course of the planning cycle. For example, let's say in the mid-1990s a library developed a plan that included this activity: "Create a CD-ROM network to provide information to people in the business community by XX (a date three years into the planning cycle)." This activity was based on three assumptions:

The only cost-effective way to provide user access to electronic data is through CD-ROM technology.

Most of the business databases that are appropriate for the business people in the community are available only on CD-ROM.

The library is developing a CD-ROM network for other services, and the business services could be incorporated into the network without significant increases in the technological infrastructure.

Now let's fast-forward three years. The Internet has changed everything. The library is in the process of establishing a Web site and has just started providing public access to the World Wide Web. The library is also negotiating with several online information vendors to provide access to their databases through the library Web site. Clearly in this new environment, none of the assumptions upon which the activity was based are still valid, and there is no point in blindly implementing the activity just because it seemed like a good idea three years ago. By the same token, there is no point in negating all of the work that went into the development of the goal and objective the activity supported just because things have changed and the activity in question is no longer the best way to achieve the outcome in the plan. The obvious answer is to change the activity to use the best tools available to make progress toward the goal and meet the objective.

And Then It Starts Again . . .

You and your colleagues will be able to keep the library plan relevant to the community by adding new activities and redesigning ongoing activities for several years, but ultimately you are going to reach the point when tinkering with the activities is not enough to make the plan an effective management tool. That is when you begin this process again. You will follow the same steps and complete the same tasks. However, you won't be starting from the same place. The library and the people who work there will have been changed by the successful creation and implementation of your plan. Furthermore, this time you will have inertia on your side. Remember, it takes far less energy to continue a successful planning effort than it does to start one the first time.

NOTES

1. Annabel K. Stephens, *Assessing the Public Library Planning Processes* (Norwood, N.J.: Ablex), 111.

2. *Hendersonville Free Press*, 6 May 1992.

3. Christopher Sprung, *House Republicans Turn from Taxes to Spending.* Available: http://www.legal-ledger.com/archive/727house.htm on 3/2/00.

4. Office of the Vice President, *Mission Driven, Results Oriented Budgeting: Accompanying Report of the National Performance Review,* September 1993. Available: www.npr.gov/library/nprrpt/annrpt/sysrpt93/mission.html on 3/2/00.

5. United Way, *Measuring Program Outcomes: A Practical Approach* (Alexandria, Va.: United Way of America, 1996), xvi.

6. Patricia Belcastro, *Evaluating Library Staff: A Performance Appraisal System* (American Library Assn., 1998), 2.

7. Charles R. McClure and others, *Planning and Role-Setting for Public Libraries: A Manual of Options and Procedures* (Chicago: American Library Assn., 1987), 1.

8. McClure, 1.

Part Two

Public Library Service Responses

The "Public Library Service Responses" contains a wealth of information about how public libraries can serve their communities, valuable suggestions about how libraries can evaluate services, and a look at the critical resources libraries may need if they wish to excel at a specific service.

The New Planning for Results stresses the importance of the connection between community needs and library services. It guides libraries in their efforts to design an overall program of service that is both dynamic and relevant. Exercise some caution if you are using this part of *The New Planning for Results* outside the context of the PLA planning process. Service responses should not be selected in a vacuum. A library shouldn't choose to offer a particular service simply because that's what the library has done in the past or because the library board, director, or staff is comfortable providing it. The selection of service responses should be firmly rooted in an awareness of what the people of the community served want and need.

What exactly is a service response? How does a service response differ from the eight library roles introduced in *Planning and Role Setting for Public Libraries* in 1987? In simple terms, *a service response is what a library does for, or offers to, the public in an effort to meet a set of well-defined community needs.* Roles are broadly defined categories of service; they describe what the library does in a very general way. Service responses, on the other hand, are very distinct ways that libraries serve the public. They represent the gathering and deployment of specific critical resources to produce a specific public benefit or result.

This process provides thirteen service responses:

- Basic Literacy
- Business and Career Information
- Commons
- Community Referral
- Consumer Information
- Cultural Awareness
- Current Topics and Titles
- Formal Learning Support
- General Information
- Government Information
- Information Literacy
- Lifelong Learning
- Local History and Genealogy.

This is by no means an exhaustive list of the possible ways libraries can meet the needs of their communities; it simply captures most of the primary services that libraries offer. Because communities differ, however, the ways libraries implement these services differ as well. The Business and Career Information service offered at one library may vary significantly from the Business and Career Information service offered by another library. The differences are perfectly appropriate if they result from a tailoring of services to address local needs.

The service responses that follow aren't intended to make libraries more alike. Quite the contrary, the descriptions and the examples offered are provided to help library planners see the many possibilities that exist for matching their services to the unique needs of their communities. The service responses are a starting, not an ending, point.

Each of the service response descriptions that follow is organized in the same way. Following is a description of the various sections you'll find repeated under each service response.

Example of Needs Addressed by This Service Response

This section states the type of need the service response is designed to address. It helps you make the connection between the needs you've identified in your community and the services the library should provide.

What the Library Does and Provides

A general description of what a typical library providing this service offers to its community is found in this section. The phrase "the library will" is used to indicate what is typically required to achieve excellence in providing a specific service. The *wills* point out the key characteristics common to most libraries that excel at the service. The phrase "the library may" is used to indicate desirable enhancements offered by some libraries that serve to underscore the high priority they place on a given service.

Some Possible Components

This section lists *some* of the kinds of things libraries do as a part of carrying out a particular service response. Many more ideas could be added; however, you'll find that these lists can be helpful as you try to visualize what a new service might be like in your community. Use this list to expand your thinking about some of the options available to your library as it attempts to match community needs and services.

Target Audiences and Service Aspects

Common ways that libraries narrow the focus of the services they provide are addressed in this section. One is by targeting a service to reach a specific population. Another is by concentrating on a certain aspect of the service. For example, one library might choose to design a service aimed at helping community college students meet their formal educational goals, while another could decide to provide homework help for children in grades 3 through 5. A third library might concentrate on supporting the reading readiness curriculum of area preschools. While all three libraries are offering the Formal Learning Support service response, it's obvious that the services at the libraries would be quite different.

In the same vein, one library might emphasize helping genealogists trace their family history, while another could stress access to information about local or regional history. Local History and Genealogy have been linked in the service responses because they share some critical resources. The same is true of Business and Career Information service. A library could decide to separate them, to emphasize just one aspect rather than both. Libraries often find this kind of targeting enables them to have a significant impact on a segment of the population at a much lower cost than they would incur if they offered the service to everyone in the community.

Resource Allocation Issues to Consider

This section gives you an idea of the resources that are or may be required to achieve excellence in a particular service area. Remember that the idea behind selecting service responses is the identification of service priorities. This section contains specific information about what your library probably needs in the way of staff, collections, facilities, and technology if you choose to emphasize a particular service. This component is included because *The New Planning for Results* is built around the idea that a library can have a greater impact on its community if it does a few things well than if it does many things less well.

For example, the Resource Allocation component addresses the following types of questions:

What are the desirable characteristics of staff who provide services that support the Lifelong Learning service response?

What kind of collection does a library need to do an excellent job of providing the Government Information service?

What are the special facilities needs associated with high-quality Formal Learning Support?

What sort of technology does the library need to offer exceptional Community Referral service?

It's important to note that you should use this section to figure out what you need to carry out a service response rather than to determine whether you should do it. If a service is critically important to the people in your community, you should be looking for ways to offer the service rather than finding reasons for *not* offering it. You may eventually come to the conclusion that your library simply doesn't have the resources to perform a service well, even if it reallocates them from other services. But don't reject a service out of hand before exploring reallocation, finding new sources of revenue, partnering with other community organizations, targeting service to a specific population, or concentrating on a single aspect of the service.

While issues such as adequate electrical and computer network wiring and compliance with the Americans with Disabilities Act Guidelines (ADAG) have not been included in each service response, make sure you consider them as you think about what you'll need to carry out a given service at a high level. For example, if you've selected a service response that involves the heavy use of library meeting facilities, it probably isn't adequate for your library to simply have rest rooms that are accessible somewhere in the library; accessible rest rooms should be located in close proximity to the meeting rooms. Along the same lines, if you select a service that entails the heavy use of computerized databases, special attention needs to be given to the adequacy of your library's electrical and computer network wiring, adaptive technologies, and appropriate adjustable workstation furnishings.

Possible Measures to Consider When Developing Objectives

Information about how your library can evaluate its performance in carrying out a service is discussed in this category. This information should help you develop high-quality objectives to measure your library's progress toward its goals.

Stories

This section provides stories about libraries offering the service. The stories are included for two reasons. First, they demonstrate the fact that no two successful libraries are exactly alike. The libraries included in "Public

Library Service Responses" have truly customized their services to fit their communities. Second, it is hoped that the stories will stimulate creativity, that seeing what other libraries have done will encourage you to experiment and innovate.

Chapter 3: Design: Inventing the Future of *The New Planning for Results* includes a procedure to help libraries build their own service responses. While you should carefully consider adapting one of the service responses that are included in *The New Planning for Results* before you jump right into developing your own, if your community has specific needs that aren't adequately addressed by adopting and adapting the thirteen service responses, try building your own unique responses.

Basic Literacy

Example of Needs Addressed by This Service Response

A library that offers Basic Literacy service addresses the need to read and to perform other essential daily tasks.

What the Library Does and Provides

The library will provide a learning environment, specialized materials, and access to trained tutors to help people reach their personal literacy goals.

The library may provide specially designed facilities and access to instructional technologies that enhance the effectiveness of tutoring efforts. Library staff, or highly trained volunteers, may be used to provide the tutoring.

Some Possible Components of Basic Literacy Service

- English as a second language (ESL) programs
- Family literacy programs
- Tutoring or tutorial materials and exam preparation guides
- Programs teaching functional math skills

- Use of instructional media/tutoring software
- Small meeting spaces for tutors and learners to meet

Target Audiences and Service Aspects

Target Audiences

A library offering Basic Literacy service may choose to serve the general public or to target a specific population such as recent immigrants or parents of preschoolers. Efforts may be focused on individuals or may involve other family members.

Service Aspects

Literacy training may concentrate on improving general reading comprehension or it could focus on providing assistance needed to accomplish a specific goal, such as attaining a General Education Development (GED) diploma.

Resource Allocation Issues to Consider

Staff

Staff providing Basic Literacy services should be encouraged to complete a literacy volunteer training program. Library staff members need to be aware of the challenges and the problems faced by adult new readers, individuals learning English as a second language, and other learners enrolled in the literacy program. Formal education in reading instruction and educational methods is desirable. Staff providing this service should have strong community networking and communication skills. All volunteer and paid tutors used in the program should have completed a comprehensive training program for literacy volunteers.

Collection and Information Resources

The library providing Basic Literacy service should have materials and resources such as workbooks and controlled-vocabulary texts specifically designed for use in literacy programs. The library may choose to offer computer software intended to supplement the interaction between learners and their tutors. A supplemental collection of high-interest/low-vocabulary materials may also be provided.

Facilities

Libraries providing Basic Literacy service need to provide quiet and relatively private areas for tutoring. Small study rooms (for two people) are ideal. Classroom space may be provided. Storage space for materials used by tutors on a regular basis is desirable.

Technology

Computer-based and computer-assisted literacy training opportunities should be considered by all libraries providing Basic Literacy service. Multimedia computers and software designed to encourage independent learning may be provided.

Possible Measures to Consider When Developing Objectives

People Served

Total number of users served (measures the total number of users who used a service during a given time period):

- Number of people who used computer-based literacy programs
- Number of people who attended English as a second language classes
- Number of people who attended tutoring sessions
- Number of people who used computer-based basic mathematics skills programs

Number of unique individuals who used the service (measures the total number of unique individuals who used the service during a given time period, regardless of how many times they used the service):

- Number of students enrolled in literacy classes
- Number of people who obtained a GED diploma through library literacy programs

How Well the Service Met the Needs of People Served

- Percent of people who participated in library literacy programs who indicated on a survey that the program helped them meet their personal learning goals

- Percent of people who participated in library literacy programs who indicated on a survey that the program was offered at convenient times and locations
- Percent of people interested in enrolling in library literacy programs who indicated on a survey that they were placed in a class or assigned a tutor in a timely manner

Total Units of Service Delivered

- Circulation of literacy-related materials
- Number of literacy volunteer hours
- Number of tutoring sessions held

Basic Literacy Stories

Broward County Library System

(Fort Lauderdale, Fla. Service Population: 1,378,000)

The Broward County Library approaches literacy as a continuum of learning. All of the branches and main library have high/low materials and basic literacy materials. However, the program is enriched by the active outreach program that extends into the community to find potential students and to help them identify the program, educational level, and type of classes they need to learn. Nine different library programs target the learning needs of people of different ages. Preschool children discover the joys of reading and learning through the Magic Circle program, while the young adult program, Young Sisters and Brothers, teaches study skills, life skills, and positive values as it highlights keys to success. More than 1,000 adults have participated in the Each One Teach One program that offers basic literacy tutoring. The Story Tree is a literature appreciation program for adults that encourages participants, who don't have to be able to read when they begin, to discuss literature and to write family stories.

The Collier City Learning Library Branch offers the full complement of literacy programs to families and students. This is also where training and workshops are provided for library staff and volunteers who work in the various literacy programs. In developing new programs and approaches, the library emphasizes programs that can be duplicated so that other groups and libraries across the country can use them in their own literacy efforts.

The great success of these programs comes from a combination of a significant commitment of library resources (for example, fifteen staff members work as programmers in literacy areas); extensive partnering with schools, community organizations, and government agencies; and a network of library-trained literacy volunteers. Literacy volunteers at the library have their own Friends of Literacy organization and publish a newsletter.

Hancock County Library System
(Bay St. Louis, Miss. Service Population: 37,000)

The Hancock County Library System's beautiful headquarters facility in Bay St. Louis, Mississippi, may not look much like a school from the outside, but it's the alma mater for scores of students aged seventeen to seventy-one, who have received their General Education Development (GED) diplomas through a program offered at the library. The library uses the phrase "Literacy is lifelong learning" as a theme for its literacy efforts.

A volunteer corps of more than sixty volunteers, working with a full-time literacy coordinator, offers a variety of literacy services in addition to the GED preparation program. The Hancock Library System's family literacy program involves both independent and joint programs for three- and four-year-olds and their parents or adult caregivers. The library also offers English as a second language classes, basic skills tutoring, and computer skills instruction. The literacy efforts of the library have been so successful that the Waveland Branch has recently been converted into a multidimensional family literacy center, renamed the Waveland Library Literacy Center by Waveland city officials.

Business and Career Information

Example of Needs Addressed by This Service Response

A library that offers Business and Career Information services addresses a need for information related to business, careers, work, entrepreneurship, personal finances, and obtaining employment.

What the Library Does and Provides

The library will provide expert personal assistance, specialized electronic and print resources, and services of interest to the business community, to investors, to individuals who are seeking employment or who are dealing with a changing work environment, and to individuals who are contemplating a career move or change. Library users will be able to access a significant amount of information without visiting the library by using the telephone, fax, e-mail, or other electronic delivery systems.

The library may provide computers, printers, and other office equipment for public use; may offer special programs on business and career topics; and may offer specialized facilities for business meetings and for career counseling. The library may also create business and career resources or may locate and organize related information on a Web page.

Some Possible Components of Business and Career Information Service

- Career guidance counseling
- Job placement service
- Public use computer equipment for preparing résumés
- Copy or business services center
- Programs on investing, entrepreneurship, writing résumés, or job interviewing skills
- World Wide Web links to business, investment, bid and procurement, and job placement Internet sites

Target Audiences and Service Aspects

Target Audiences

Services may be designed to meet the special needs of entrepreneurs, small-business owners, and individuals seeking or facing a change in career or employment.

Service Aspects

The library selecting Business and Career Information service may offer both of these related services or may choose to concentrate on either the business or career aspect. A library might focus on a specific component of one of these two areas such as providing investment information or college financial aid information.

Resource Allocation Issues to Consider

Staff

Staff providing Business and Career Information service need to develop and maintain a good knowledge of business, financial, career, and employment topics. Formal coursework in economics or business administration or work experience in related areas is desirable, as is education or experience in guidance or career counseling. Staff should be highly skilled in using a variety of computer search engines to access resources on the Internet and other online sources.

Collection and Information Resources

Business and career information changes constantly, and new, up-to-date, reliable resources need to be sought continuously. Libraries concentrating on specific aspects of this service, such as providing assistance in job hunting, personal investment, or entrepreneurship, will need different specialized tools. Libraries need to consider the purchase of multiple copies of high-demand items such as materials on résumé writing, occupational guides, and civil service or placement exam manuals.

Facilities

While some libraries provide a separate business and career information desk, this service is often provided from the same physical space as other reference and information services. Typically, a great deal of space and furnishings is shared. Meeting room space for programming is important but may also be shared with other services. Since many business and career information resources tend to be noncirculating, adequate table space should be provided to support in-house use of materials.

Technology

Communications technologies are particularly important for the business aspect of this service response. The library needs a high-quality telephone system and the capability of sending and receiving faxes at the business information service desk. Copying facilities should be adequate to meet heavy demand. Libraries may want to consider a business services center including color copying equipment, copiers that collate, binding machines, etc. Libraries should consider offering videoconferencing facilities. Public-use computers and printers loaded with a standard suite of office productivity software are important for both business and career service. The availability of telephones (including data transmission capability) and fax machines is highly desirable, as is the availability of personal e-mail accounts through the library.

Possible Measures to Consider When Developing Objectives

People Served

Total number of users served (measures the total number of users who used a service during a given time period):

- Number of people who attended a business program

- Number of people who attended a career program
- Number of people who used library computer programs to create résumés.

Number of unique individuals who used the service (measures the total number of unique individuals who used the service during a given time period, regardless of how many times they used the service):

- Number of small-business owners who indicated on a survey that they used the library for business-related information
- Number of students who indicated on a survey that they used the library for career-related information
- Number of unique individuals who participated in library-sponsored job skills assessment programs

How Well the Service Met the Needs of People Served

- Percent of people using investment materials who indicated on a survey that the materials met their needs
- Percent of people using the career reference center materials who indicated on a survey that the materials met their needs
- Percent of people using business reference service who indicated on a survey that the information that met their needs was provided to them in a timely manner

Total Units of Service Delivered

- Circulation of business materials
- Circulation of career materials
- Number of times the library's business Web page was accessed
- Number of business and career reference questions answered
- Number of consultations with small-business owners to ascertain their business information needs

Business and Career Information Stories

Milwaukee Public Library
(Milwaukee, Wisc. Service Population: 623,000)

The Milwaukee Public Library places extensive emphasis on both the business and employment aspects of this service. The focal point of business information activity is the Central Library in downtown Milwaukee, while activity in neighborhood libraries is expanding. Job and career services are emphasized at three of the library's twelve branch locations.

Career and Job Information Centers located at the Atkinson, Center Street, and Tippecanoe branch libraries offer one-stop shopping for job seekers. Books and videotapes on résumé writing are available for viewing in close proximity to public-use computers and printers. Extensive job listings are available in the large selection of local, regional, and out-of-town newspapers as well as in periodicals and through the employment-related Internet sites identified by the library. Materials on starting small businesses provide a tie to the more extensive business resources that are located downtown.

The Milwaukee Public Library extensively markets its business resources through brochures, programs, and special events. Business Breakfast Seminars at Central Library proved so successful that the series was expanded to neighborhood libraries as well. These outreach efforts highlight the library's comprehensive standards, patents, trademark, military specifications, and government statistics collections and provide information about how both print and electronic resources can be used for practical purposes such as developing a business plan. The library provides electronic access to more than 1,000 trade and business journals.

Montrose Library District
(Montrose, Colo. Service Population: 90,000)

The public library is the best place to go in Montrose, Colorado, if you're interested in making money! This community, located on Colorado's Western Slope, has experienced a significant inflow of population by recent retirees and émigrés from cities throughout the United States in search of the area's rugged natural beauty, reasonable cost of living, and the "good life." In response, the Montrose Library District has developed a Business Resource Center at the library and has designed new services targeted at entrepreneurs and retired investors.

Much of the library's success in these areas has been built on partnerships. The library works closely with the community's active Senior Corps of Retired Executives (SCORE) group, and the library and SCORE depend on each other as they work with would-be entrepreneurs and with fledgling businesses. The community's established businesses contributed much of the funding used to create the Business Resource Center, responding to the library's message that by pooling funds the community could possess a valuable economic development resource. In addition to funding for the Resource Center, individual businesses purchase specific materials. For example, a local investment firm donated the funds used to purchase ValueLine.

Commons

Example of Needs Addressed
by This Service Response

A library that provides a Commons environment helps address the need of people to meet and interact with others in their community and to participate in public discourse about community issues.

What the Library Does and Provides

The library will provide public space for meeting and gathering that is recognized as inviting, neutral, and safe by all individuals and groups in the community.

The library may provide a variety of meeting and gathering spaces including large meeting rooms, small group meeting and study rooms, and open public spaces that invite conversation and discussion. The library may provide electronic means of assembling, such as videoconferencing facilities.

Some Possible Components
of Commons Service

- Large, medium, and small meeting room spaces
- Community events bulletin board or kiosk

- E-mail accounts for the public (or information about free e-mail service)
- Coffee shop or restaurant in the library
- Videoconferencing facilities
- Automated room scheduling

Target Audiences and Service Aspects

Target Audiences

A library could target a particular group for special attention, such as young adults or older adults.

Service Aspects

The library could concentrate on a particular aspect of the service, such as providing community meeting room space if it partnered with another organization or agency to provide community-based programming on a regular and ongoing basis.

Resource Allocation Issues to Consider

Staff

Staff involved in providing Commons service need to develop and maintain a good working knowledge of the community. Both good people skills and good management skills are required. A good knowledge of audiovisual equipment is necessary, as are good public relations skills. It is important to consider the amount of maintenance assistance required to handle frequent meeting room setup and cleaning. Libraries with multiple facilities may need an events or meeting facilities coordinator.

Collection and Information Resources

Many resources are important in that they are often the drawing point that brings people into the library.

Facilities

Commons is the idea of the library as an important public place in the community. Meeting spaces of various sizes designed for a variety of purposes are critically important to this service. Meeting rooms should be designed to allow for their use after library hours without compromising the security of the rest of the facility. Kitchenette and catering staging space should be provided adjoining large meeting rooms. Innovative approaches to creating unique environments such as coffee bars should also be considered. Parking available at or near the library should be adequate to handle the traffic generated by full capacity meeting room use in addition to parking required to support other library use.

Technology

Traditional audiovisual technologies such as videocassette recorders, televisions, overhead projectors, and microphones are heavily used in a library providing a Commons environment. Video projection and videoconferencing facilities should be considered. Meeting room facilities should be equipped with adaptive technologies to help the visually and hearing-impaired fully participate in meetings.

Possible Measures to Consider When Developing Objectives

People Served

Total number of users served (measures the total number of users who used a service during a given time period):

- Number of people who attended programs in library meeting rooms
- Number of people who attended exhibitions in the library gallery
- Number of people who attended videoconference programs in the library

How Well the Service Met the Needs of People Served

- Percent of organizations using library meeting rooms that indicated on a survey that the spaces, equipment, etc., met their needs
- Percent of individuals attending events in library meeting rooms who rated the event as satisfactory or excellent
- Percent of individuals who used the automated room reservation service who rated the service as satisfactory or excellent

Total Units of Service Delivered

- Number of meetings or events presented by staff
- Number of meetings or events offered by other organizations or groups
- Number of community organizations that used library meeting rooms

Commons Stories

Detroit Lakes Public Library
(Detroit Lakes, Minn. Service Population: 12,000)

The Detroit Lakes Public Library likes to think of itself as the "intersection of the community." Approximately 1,200 people attend the nearly 200 meetings and conferences that take place in the library's two meeting rooms (one with video teleconferencing capability) and four conference and study rooms each month. Library-sponsored programs are interspersed with heavy use of library facilities by community groups, businesses, and individuals.

An ongoing series of library-sponsored programs called the Great Minds Appreciation Discussion Circle (funded in part by the Minnesota Humanities Commission) explores topics ranging from "Is Civility in Politics Possible?" to "Does Poetry Matter?" This series has an intergenerational flavor as young people of junior high school age and older are encouraged to participate along with adults. Some years ago the library initiated a one-day nonreligious, nonpolitical community holiday called Mid-summer Celebration. This annual celebration includes music, dancing, a Swedish maypole, craft demonstrations, foods, and arts.

Public Libraries of Saginaw
(Saginaw, Mich. Service Population: 137,920)

The public library in Saginaw, Michigan, has people talking. People aren't just talking about the library, they're doing something even more important—talking to each other! The library has a long tradition of community involvement with organizations such as the school district, local academic institutions, and the local chamber of commerce, but recently it has put a new "spin" on cooperation with the formation of Saginaw Partners in Networking (SPIN). SPIN creates an electronic *community commons.*

The library has been the major force in organizing Saginaw's new electronic community network. Bringing organizations as diverse as the

Catholic Diocese of Saginaw, the Michigan Employment Security Commission, the Mid-Michigan Hispanic Business Association, and St. Mary's Medical Center together with more traditional educational and governmental partners has had the effect of redefining the word "community." United in their efforts to develop SPIN, more than sixty organizations in the community have learned more about each other, the Internet, and Web pages.

The library, already seen as the local Internet expert, has provided that expertise to the entire community. At the same time, the library has enhanced its position as the community agency that collects, organizes, maintains, and disseminates community information.

Sump Memorial Library
(Papillion, Nebr. Service Population: 14,900)

When the new Sump Memorial Library opened in December 1996, Papillion, Nebraska, gained much-needed public meeting and gathering space. The 23,000-square-foot building includes one large meeting room (which can hold up to 100 people and can be subdivided), a children's story and activity room (for up to twenty-five children doing crafts), two conference rooms (for eight to ten people), four small study and tutoring rooms, and a computer laboratory with sixteen computer workstations. The building's meeting room facilities have been in constant demand since the building opened, despite the fact that the library did little to advertise its availability.

The Sump Memorial Library is the site of noncredit community college courses, investment club meetings, neighborhood association meetings, support group meetings, and a multitude of other events. The library is also starting to become a popular meeting place for statewide meetings. It has recently hosted events sponsored by the Nebraska Council of Estate Planning Attorneys, the Nebraska Library Commission, and the Nebraska Library Association.

The library has a full-time information systems manager who teaches classes on using the Internet and creating World Wide Web home pages. The computer lab is open to the public for personal computing needs when library-sponsored classes are not in session. While the library sponsors its own programming in addition to the computer and Internet training—notably a wide variety of children's activities and storytimes—the majority of the meeting room use is by community organizations.

Community Referral

Example of Needs Addressed by This Service Response

A library that offers Community Referral addresses the need for information related to services provided by community agencies and organizations.

What the Library Does and Provides

The library will establish ongoing relationships with community organizations and local governmental agencies. The library will develop and maintain or will facilitate the development and maintenance of a database of available services and the qualifications for receiving those services. The library will provide easy, convenient, confidential access to the information in a variety of ways such as walk-in service, toll-free telephone service, or Internet access.

The library may provide intake and assessment forms from referral agencies, and library staff may conduct initial interviews or provide follow-up with clients and agencies to determine whether services were provided that met the individual's need.

Some Possible Components of Community Referral Service

- Community information database
- Twenty-four-hour information and referral line

- Dial-in access to community resource files
- Electronic access to community resource files through computer kiosks in public places such as malls, post offices, and schools
- Counseling and follow-up tracking service
- Three-way telephone capabilities to link users with service agencies or to provide for translating between library staff and customers

Target Audiences and Service Aspects

Target Audiences

The library offering Community Referral service could target its service to a segment of the population by providing high-level referral service only to agencies assisting young people, to the unemployed, or to groups that speak certain languages.

Service Aspects

The library could focus on a single aspect or on several aspects of the service through partnerships with other organizations or agencies. For example, the library might build and maintain the community database while another organization provides staff to handle in-person and telephone contacts as well as counseling. Another approach would be to concentrate on a particular type of community referral service, e.g., child-care providers, services for seniors and retirees, etc.

Resource Allocation Issues to Consider

Staff

Staff providing Community Referral service need to develop and maintain a good working knowledge of the community the library serves and extensive knowledge of community agencies and their services. Staff also need excellent computer skills and experience working with computer databases. A social work or counseling background is an asset. Clerical staff to do data entry may be required if the library is maintaining a large community information database. The ability to communicate in multiple languages, including American Sign Language, is highly desirable.

Collection and Information Resources

To a large extent, Community Referral service depends on information resources created or maintained by the library. Quickly changing information rather than the static information found in monographs is most important to the service. Some directories of services are used; however, this information rapidly becomes out-of-date. Information should be available in the languages spoken by people in the library's service area.

Facilities

The provision of Community Referral service sometimes involves the exchange of confidential information. Facilities should be designed to allow for some degree of privacy between the user and the library staff. The facilities requirements for this service response are minimal, with the exception of adequate electrical and network wiring to support the computers needed to host the community resources database if the library is providing access by telephone or through a dial-in service.

Technology

The value of a community resources database can be magnified if the information is made available to the public without having to visit the library. Providing dial-in or World Wide Web access to the information can be very helpful to potential users who are unable to use the library during normal business hours. A computer large enough and fast enough to host the database and a computer network capable of distributing the database throughout the community are desirable. Some computers should be equipped with adaptive technologies that allow visually and hearing-impaired people to access resources.

Possible Measures to Consider When Developing Objectives

People Served

Total number of users served (measures the total number of users who used a service during a given time period):

- Number of people who used community referral services
- Number of people successfully referred to a community agency
- Number of people who received information about local services

How Well the Service Met the Needs of People Served

- Percent of people who used the community referral service who indicated on a survey that the service was provided in the language of their choice
- Percent of people who used the community referral service who indicated on a survey that they received the information they needed
- Percent of people who used the community referral service who indicated on a survey that the service they received was satisfactory or excellent

Total Units of Service Delivered

- Number of times the community referral Web page was accessed
- Number of community referral questions answered
- Number of presentations by library staff describing community referral services
- Number of different brochures or flyers produced by the library as part of community referral service
- Number of agencies receiving updated information from the library

Community Referral Stories

Kootenai-Shoshone Area Libraries
(Hayden, Idaho. Service Population: 55,000)

The Kootenai-Shoshone Area Libraries have been providing some form of information and referral service for many years using a traditional all-paper system. Knowing that there was a better way, the library decided to do more than simply computerize its records. The library decided to advocate for a new system that would improve the quality, quantity, and accessibility of important community information as well. The result of the library's partnering with the Kootenai Medical Center, North Idaho College, Coeur d'Alene Public Library, Post Falls Public Library, and a host of other community organizations was the development of North Idaho Communities Online (NICON).

The library's community resource files concentrate on services to high school and community college students, the elderly, newcomers to the area, and area residents with low incomes. The addition of the Medical Center Library and the North Idaho College Library to the system means that the public now has access to additional health, consumer, and educational resources that were unavailable in the past. In addition, this wealth of local community information is available both through the Internet and through the NICON free-net nearly twenty-four hours each day. Users of the system from five northern Idaho counties can receive free NICON e-mail accounts that enable them to communicate with the libraries and in many cases with the service agencies quickly and without cost.

Spartanburg County Public Library
(Spartanburg, S.C. Service Population: 240,000)

The status of information about community services in the Spartanburg, South Carolina, area was fairly typical in the late 1980s when a group called the Spartanburg Consensus Project approached the library about taking on the role of gathering, organizing, and disseminating community service information electronically. The library, the United Way, the board of education, and many other community groups all maintained some information and provided some level of public access to their resources. The Consensus Project, a group of community leaders and public officials, recognized that the public would be well served if the collection and distribution of this important information was more coordinated. These community leaders also recognized that the library had information professionals who could do this job well.

Building on the fact that the library already had a library automation system from a vendor that also offered an information and referral module, the library applied for and received a Library Services and Construction Act grant to cover some of the initial start-up costs of the project. Now, a number of years later, the size of the database has grown to more than 4,000 records, and dial-in use, which averaged about five or six a day when the system was established, now routinely exceeds 100 daily. The library also generates a printed *Directory of Clubs, Organizations, and Services* from the computerized database each year.

Berkeley Public Library
(Berkeley, Calif. Service Population: 104,900)

If you need to know where to turn for help or if you need information about an organization in Berkeley, California, all you need to do is look in the BIN, the Berkeley Information Network, a database of more than 3,600 local organizations that has been in operation since 1980.

BIN includes information about nonprofit organizations, clubs, government agencies, and other neighborhood and community groups. Extensive subject indexing allows BIN users to locate information on local museums, services for people with disabilities, recycling, legal aid, schools, and emergency medical and dental services. Information contained in the database is collected, compiled, edited, entered, and indexed by library staff.

The library makes it easy to access the BIN. Library users can get the information themselves through the online public access catalog. Direct telephone help is also available whenever the library is open, and computer dial-in service is available twenty-four hours per day. Telnet Internet access is also provided.

Consumer Information

Example of Needs Addressed by This Service Response

A library that provides Consumer Information service addresses the need for information to make informed consumer decisions and helps residents become more self-sufficient.

What the Library Does and Provides

The library will provide expert assistance and specialized electronic and print resources to individuals who are interested in becoming more knowledgeable consumers and to individuals who need to make important consumer decisions. The library will offer resources that include critical reviews of products and services and wholesale price guides for durable goods. The library will also offer access to information on maintaining and repairing consumer goods.

The library may provide programs on topics such as health, nutrition, child care, and consumer affairs. The library may offer practical pamphlets, booklets, and electronic access to resources produced by cooperative extension agencies, governmental entities, and consumer advocacy organizations. The library may also create its own consumer resources such as informational brochures, or it may locate and organize consumer-related information on a Web page.

Some Possible Components
of Consumer Information Service

- Special programs on health, legal, or consumer topics
- Library Web page on consumer issues
- Library-produced publications and flyers on consumer topics
- Consumer complaint hotline
- Teletext service on consumer topics
- Consumer affairs bulletin board

Target Audiences and Service Aspects

Target Audiences

The library could focus its efforts on serving target populations such as teen-age mothers or seniors on fixed incomes.

Service Aspects

The library offering Consumer Information service could narrow its emphasis to a specific topic such as health information. It could focus on providing information needed to repair and maintain durable goods such as automobiles and washing machines.

Resource Allocation Issues to Consider

Staff

Staff involved in providing Consumer Information service need to develop and maintain a good knowledge of consumer, health, nutrition, and legal topics. They need to be highly skilled in database searching and should be familiar with a variety of computer search engines to access resources on the Internet.

Collection and Information Resources

Some aspects of Consumer Information service demand up-to-date reviews of consumer goods found in periodicals and from online sources. Other aspects of the service call for maintaining significant retrospective collections of repair manuals. Web sites, newsletters, and other publications from governmental agencies, universities, and nonprofit organizations also contain valuable consumer information.

Facilities

Facilities for providing Consumer Information service should be designed to allow for some degree of privacy between the user and the library staff. Consumer Information service is often provided from the same physical space as other reference and information services. Typically, a great deal of space and furnishings is shared. Adequate table space for use of noncirculating materials is essential. Meeting room space for programming is important but may also be shared with other services. Display racks should be provided for distribution of brochures and other free consumer publications.

Technology

A great deal of consumer information is available from online sources. Libraries offering this service need to provide physical space that can accommodate computers and printers. A copy machine or machines should be provided in close proximity to print resources. Standard programming tools such as an overhead projector, screen, and video playback and projection equipment should be available in the library's meeting facilities.

Possible Measures to Consider When Developing Objectives

People Served

Total number of users served (measures the total number of users who used a service during a given time period):

- Number of people who attended consumer information programs

Number of unique individuals who used the service (measures the total number of unique individuals who used the service during a given time period, regardless of how many times they used the service):

- Number of unique people who receive the library's consumer information newsletter

How Well the Service Met the Needs of People Served

- Percent of people who used consumer information materials who indicated on a survey that the materials were useful to them
- Percent of people who used consumer information reference materials who indicated on a survey that the materials met their needs
- Percent of people who used consumer information services who indicated on a survey that the information was provided in a timely manner
- Percent of people attending consumer information programs who indicated on a survey that the program was satisfactory or excellent

Total Units of Service Delivered

- Circulation of consumer information materials
- Number of times the consumer information Web page was accessed
- Number of unique consumer book lists produced
- Number of consumer information reference questions answered
- Number of calls received on the library-sponsored teletext consumer information line

Consumer Information Stories

Ann Arbor District Library

(Ann Arbor, Mich. Service Population: 137,000)

Whether you're interested in the health benefits of citrus fruits or you're concerned that the new car you just bought is a lemon, the Ann Arbor District Library has just the information you need. The information may be in a reference book, in a magazine, in a pamphlet, or on the Internet, but chances are good that you'll find what you want quickly and easily because this library's consumer information resources are organized with the customer in mind!

The Ann Arbor Library has traditionally maintained a consumer information table at the Main Library and at each of its three branch locations. In fact, the approach of gathering reference resources on particular topics together on large index tables has been used over the years with college resources, investment resources, and a number of other topical areas as well. When the library began designing its outstanding World Wide Web page, it decided to build on its success in creating topical interest centers. Whether you're using the library's consumer resources in person or you're accessing them on the Internet, you'll find information grouped in the same way. The Ann Arbor Web page has a consumer information page that contains resources for evaluating products, consumer protection information, health information resources, and so on.

Just because many resources are now available electronically doesn't mean that the library has forgotten the value of its print resources. Each subsection of the consumer Web page is divided into several sections. The check-out section describes books and other resources that can be found at the library, the second section provides a link to electronic resources such as periodical indexes, and the third section links the user to related World Wide Web sites.

Plainedge Public Library
(Massapequa, N.Y. Service Population: 20,000)

Most people think about getting information from the library off the shelf, over the desk, or on the telephone. In recent years, delivery by fax and over the Internet has been added to the delivery mechanisms used routinely by libraries. However, if you ask most Plainedge (N.Y.) School District residents how they received the most recent consumer information from the library they'd point to their mailbox! The Plainedge Public Library has been sending a variety of library and consumer information newsletters and publications directly to the 6,250 households in the Plainedge School District for nearly twenty years.

After conducting a number of community surveys and reviewing demographic projections for the community in 1976, the library was concerned with the potential impact that a decline in the numbers of two major categories of users, young children and at-home mothers, would have on library use. In their effort to develop new audiences for library services, the idea of providing consumer information through newsletters mailed directly to area residents was born.

The library mails three different library publications that contain some consumer information content. The *Library Newsletter,* mailed six times a year, contains one or two pages of consumer bulletins on a variety of general interest topics. *The Community Courier,* started because the school district doesn't have a local newspaper, is mailed quarterly and generally includes energy and ecology bulletins in addition to other information of importance to the community. The third publication, *News for the Consumer,* is distributed six to seventeen times each year, depending on funding. *News for the Consumer* provides four to twelve pages of information on topics such as health, money management, and nutrition. Library staff compile the content for these publications primarily from public domain materials and government documents; however, they often secure permission and occasionally pay royalties to reprint copyrighted articles.

Chula Vista Public Library
(Chula Vista, Calif. Service Population: 153,000)

Most people would probably associate the words "health," "baby," and "mom" with a health-care clinic, but for Hispanic women in Chula Vista, California, the words are connected to an exciting new service available through the public library. The Virtual Reference Network program provides multimedia health resources in Spanish at workstations in the library and over the World Wide Web.

The program, which targeted Hispanic women with lower reading skills in English and Spanish, was initially called Healthy Baby/Healthy Mom. It provided a presentation that combined video, images, and sound in Spanish and English narration to overcome the need for print literacy. A subsequent development included migrating to an online, collaboratively built database with local content available via the World Wide Web. While women and their health needs continue to be a primary focus, jobs and education have also been added.

Cultural Awareness

Example of Needs Addressed by This Service Response

A library that offers Cultural Awareness service helps satisfy the desire of community residents to gain an understanding of their own cultural heritage and the cultural heritage of others.

What the Library Does and Provides

The library will provide in-depth collections of materials and resources in many formats and will offer programs and special displays that reflect the cultural heritage of populations in the library service area.

The library staff may be multilingual. Print materials, media materials, the library's online catalog, other electronic resources, and cultural programming may be offered in the languages spoken or read by the residents of the community. The library may also offer resources and services that promote awareness of cultures in addition to those represented in the community.

Some Possible Components of Cultural Awareness Service

- Ethnic resource centers
- Library catalog, publications, and collections in several languages

- Lectures and book discussion groups
- Performance and exhibit space
- Cultural fairs and exhibits
- Dramatic, musical, and dance performances
- Diversity and cultural sensitivity forums

Target Audiences and Service Aspects

Target Audiences

Cultural Awareness service could be provided for all people in the community or could be targeted at specific age groups such as seniors or children in the intermediate grades.

Service Aspects

A library might concentrate on reflecting a particular culture represented in the community or it could focus on the literature or performing arts of a culture or cultures.

Resource Allocation Issues to Consider

Staff

Staff providing Cultural Awareness service need to develop and maintain a knowledge of and sensitivity to various cultures, especially those represented in the community the library serves. Staff should specifically have a good background in literature and in the arts. The ability to understand and speak languages spoken in the community is crucial, as are good public relations and organizational skills. Staff need a good working knowledge of audiovisual equipment. It is also important to consider the amount of maintenance assistance required to handle frequent meeting room setup and cleaning.

Collection and Information Resources

The collection and information resources supporting Cultural Awareness service usually include offerings in many formats and languages. The history, traditions, prominent historical and contemporary figures, and issues related to specific cultural groups should be a focus of in-depth collections. In addition to maintaining a collection of print materials representing the literature of a culture, materials such as video and audio recordings that capture performance arts are usually included. Libraries may also collect visual arts such as paintings and sculpture or may make these art forms available as computer images. Highly desirable are World Wide Web access and links to cultural sites in English, in other languages, and within and outside the United States.

Facilities

Performance and display space is critical for libraries providing Cultural Awareness service. Meeting rooms, a gallery, or display space should be provided. Good acoustics and a raised stage for performances are assets. Multilingual signage is an important consideration if the library serves a significant non-English-speaking population or users for whom English is a second language. Facilities that allow for public participation in arts and crafts projects should also be available. Parking available at or near the library should be adequate to handle the traffic generated by full-capacity meeting room use, in addition to parking required to support other library use.

Technology

A full range of technologies used by performers should be provided. A high-quality sound system capable of accepting a variety of inputs and video display or projection equipment are essential. Theatrical lighting and videotaping and editing equipment may also be provided. Since many cultural resources are available on CD-ROM and from the Internet, the library should supply multimedia computers capable of sound and of displaying high-resolution graphics. Meeting room facilities should be equipped with adaptive technologies to help the visually and hearing-impaired as well as non-English-speaking populations fully participate in meetings and activities.

Possible Measures to Consider When Developing Objectives

People Served

Total number of users served (measures the total number of users who used a service during a given time period):

- Number of people who attended cultural awareness programs
- Number of people who attended cultural awareness exhibits

Number of unique individuals who used the service (measures the total number of unique individuals who used the service during a given time period, regardless of how many times they used the service):

- Number of unique individuals who participated in the cultural awareness book discussion group

How Well the Service Met the Needs of People Served

- Percent of people who used cultural awareness materials who indicated on a survey that the materials were useful to them
- Percent of people who used cultural awareness services who indicated on a survey that the information was provided in a timely manner
- Percent of people who attended cultural awareness programs who indicated on a survey that the program was satisfactory or excellent

Total Units of Service Delivered

- Circulation of materials from designated cultural awareness collections
- Number of times the cultural awareness Web page was accessed
- Number of unique cultural awareness book lists produced
- Number of cultural awareness displays created
- Number of cultural awareness programs presented
- Number of languages in which library brochures are produced

Cultural Awareness Stories

Queens Borough Public Library
(Jamaica, N.Y. Service Population: 1,950,000)

The Queens Borough Public Library serves what may be the most ethnically diverse population in the nation. More than 40 percent of the adults in Queens speak a language other than English, and the library maintains book collections in no fewer than thirty languages. Many of the residents of Queens are recent immigrants from Asia, Africa, Europe, Latin America, and the Caribbean. The library's New Americans Program (NAP) seeks to engage these new residents by providing programs celebrating the arts and literature of their homelands. Music, dance, story telling, and puppetry are just a few of the art forms that are highlighted.

The library believes that its cultural awareness services and especially its programming serve a dual purpose. First, they make new residents feel welcomed by the library, and therefore more likely to use other services. Second, the programming presents other Queens residents with the opportunity to learn more about their new neighbors through cultural events. The New Americans Program always tries to attract an audience that includes about 60 percent of the featured ethnic or cultural group and 40 percent from the balance of the Queens community.

The New Americans Program also has a coping skills component. Lectures and workshops in the language of the target audience are held on topics ranging from stress management to child care, from how to start a business to learning about diabetes.

L. E. Phillips Memorial Public Library
(Eau Claire, Wisc. Service Population: 90,500)

People learn about their world and its people in numerous ways. The L. E. Phillips Memorial Public Library provides a gateway to the world through the exploration of literature, history, arts, and poetry for residents of the Eau Claire, Wisconsin, area. Over the last twenty years, the library has offered hundreds of opportunities for discovery, including lecture series, film series, exhibits, discussion groups, and a variety of other humanities programs for people of all ages. Care is taken to provide collection resources to support these programs.

The library was one of nineteen pilot sites for the American Library Association's (ALA) Writers Live at the Library series. This series included writers' workshops and readings by notable regional authors. Participants in other programs have explored the one entitled Genius of Toni Morrison; they've looked at the portrayal of Native Americans in the cinema; and viewed the Voices and Visions program on modern American poets. Junior and senior high school students have been exposed to literature and the arts through special readings, workshops, and programs designed with this specific audience in mind.

The L. E. Phillips Library is constantly writing and receiving grants from a variety of sources including the Wisconsin Humanities Council; the National Endowment for the Humanities (NEH) and the Lila Wallace–Readers Digest Fund through the Public Programs office of the American Library Association; and the Lannan Foundation. The library collaborates with many other organizations to make its humanities programming a reality. Discussion leaders are often recruited from the faculty of the University of Wisconsin–Eau Claire, and many programs are jointly sponsored by the Eau Claire Community Alliance, which includes the library, the university, the public schools in the area, and the Chippewa Valley Museum.

Current Topics and Titles

Example of Needs Addressed by This Service Response

A library that provides Current Topics and Titles helps to fulfill community residents' appetite for information about popular cultural and social trends and their desire for satisfying recreational experiences.

What the Library Does and Provides

The library will provide a current collection with sufficient copies of titles in high demand to ensure customer requests are met quickly. Materials will be offered in the formats and in the languages people want and will be selected primarily on the basis of local demand. The library's collections will be organized in ways that make items easy to find and will be merchandised to the public through the use of displays and display shelving. Staff knowledgeable of the content of best-selling titles and the style of popular authors and performers will offer expert guidance to the public. The library will monitor prepublication review sources and publisher advertising campaigns to anticipate public demand. The library may track personal appearances, media appearances, publicity tours of authors, and the schedules and media reviews of artists' performances for the same reason. The library may offer programs such as book talks, book signings, performances, and exhibits that promote current and forthcoming releases.

Some Possible Components of Current Topics and Titles Service

- Book talks
- Author book signings
- Readers' advisory services
- Preview stations for videos and recordings
- Display shelving
- Drive-through check-out or return

Target Audiences and Service Aspects

Target Audiences

Current Topics and Titles can be targeted to the general adult public as well as to other age groups such as young adults or children.

Service Aspects

A library could choose to narrow the scope of this service by offering a current popular collection of materials in a particular format such as video.

Resource Allocation Issues to Consider

Staff

Staff providing Current Topics and Titles service need to be knowledge-able about popular culture and literature. Staff will need to spend a significant amount of time keeping current with what's *in* and what's *out.* Staff members should have broad personal interests and should frequently read, view, and listen to the types of materials the public is demanding. Skill in marketing and merchandising, including public relations, is an asset.

Collection and Information Resources

Popular demand is the primary criteria for the collection that supports Current Topics and Titles service, and consequently the collection should reflect library user preferences. Nonfiction and fiction titles, paperbacks and hardbound books, popular magazines, and nonprint materials such as video and audio formats should be provided. Libraries may offer CD-ROMs, multimedia kits, puppets, and computer games. Quantities of popular titles in all formats should be sufficient to make the library a dependable source of high-demand items.

Facilities

Display shelving, display end panels, and other furnishings that allow for the effective merchandising of materials should be provided. Broad aisles that encourage browsing should be a standard design feature. A pleasant atmosphere should be created by providing comfortable chairs and excellent lighting. Innovative approaches to creating unique environments, such as coffee bars, should be considered.

Technology

Computers can assist staff in providing a high level of readers' advisory service. For example, library users can be supplied with information about authors, musical performers, or movie producers who share a similar style. Offering this type of special service through a library Web page or pages should be considered. Libraries may offer listening and viewing facilities for browsing and previewing purposes. The online public access catalog should be available by dialing in from home and should offer services such as patron-initiated holds. The library might provide access to commercial online services that provide fiction readers' advisory assistance.

Possible Measures to Consider When Developing Objectives

People Served

Total number of users served (measures the total number of users who used a service during a given time period):

- Number of people who attended programs related to current topics and titles
- Number of people who attended exhibits related to current topics and titles

Number of unique individuals who used the service (measures the total number of unique individuals who used the service during a given time period, regardless of how many times they used the service):

- Number of unique individuals who participated in the library-sponsored new foreign films discussion group

- Number of unique people who participated in at least one of the library-sponsored new books discussion groups

How Well the Service Met the Needs of People Served

- Percent of people who used the current fiction collection who indicated on a survey that the materials were useful to them
- Percent of people who used the video collection who indicated on a survey that the collection met their needs
- Percent of people who used the media collection who indicated on a survey that they almost always were able to find something of interest
- Percent of people who indicated on a survey that they used the library to obtain recreational materials

Total Units of Service Delivered

- Circulation of new books
- Circulation of books on tape
- Number of times the readers' advisory database was accessed
- Number of unique current titles and topics book lists produced
- Number of current topics and titles displays created

Current Topics and Titles Stories

Westlake Porter Public Library

(Westlake, Ohio. Service Population: 30,000)

The Westlake Porter Public Library subscribes to the notion that it takes more than just a good collection of recent materials to offer high-quality Current Topics and Titles service. The library places great emphasis on customer satisfaction in everything it does, and customer satisfaction in this service area requires excellence in readers' advisory service. Each monthly readers' advisory meeting includes a presentation and discussion of a different genre or reading topic. Public service staff members make the presentations on which the discussion is based.

The library also offers Novelist on its Internet stations. Additionally, the library staff have been active in building its own database into a powerful readers' advisory tool that is used independently by the public and by the staff in assisting library customers. The Westlake Porter Public Library distributes 1,000 copies of a publication called *Book Page* each month. The library's name, logo, and information about its services are imprinted on the front and back covers of this commercial tabloid, which covers new and forthcoming titles.

Another example of the library's attention to customer satisfaction is its policy of buying one additional copy of a title for every two reserves that are placed on an item. Additional copies are purchased through local retail outlets if it appears that normal supply channels will delay getting the materials on the shelf. Weeding in the popular materials collection takes place at least five times each year. Surplus copies of popular titles are sold by the Friends of the Library for $3 each while they are still relatively new, but supply exceeds demand.

Churchill County Library
(Fallon, Nev. Service Population: 21,000)

The odds are in your favor if you're looking for something good to read, view, or listen to in Fallon, Nevada. The Churchill County Library prides itself on being very responsive to public demand and has a collection and usage statistics that reflect its success. The library enjoys a circulation per capita of nearly seven in spite of having a staff of less than seven full-time equivalents.

Employment in the Fallon area is dominated by the Navy and by mining companies. Pay scales are relatively low; there are many children and at-home moms in the area; and inexpensive recreational opportunities are fairly limited. The library fills a real need by supplying recreational reading materials, videotapes, books-on-tape, and audio compact discs. Circulation of videos accounts for more than 10 percent of the library's total circulation. The library has also developed significant collections of inspirational and Christian fiction in response to popular demand. The recent addition of public Internet service has added a new dimension to Current Topics and Titles service. Library users can now locate up-to-date information on hot topics such as news, sports, music, and entertainment.

Current Topics and Titles service isn't limited to adults either. The library is an active participant in the Nevada Young Readers program. As part of this program, kids cast votes for their favorite books through their public and school libraries. The library always keeps a good supply of the popular titles identified by the children themselves on hand. The library offers two story times each week for three- to five-year-old children and sees these programs as the means of creating new readers.

Formal Learning Support

Example of Needs Addressed by This Service Response

A library that offers Formal Learning Support helps students who are enrolled in a formal program of education or who are pursuing their education through a program of homeschooling to attain their educational goals.

What the Library Does and Provides

The library will provide informational resources, personal assistance, and educational tools such as computers that further the educational progress of students. Library activities and materials will support the curricular objectives of a teaching institution or institutions. The library will also provide physical facilities conducive to learning.

The library will provide Internet access and may offer access to other instructional technologies such as multimedia computers with educational software, educational videos, and distance education equipment and facilities. Expert assistance with homework, tutoring in specific subject areas, and help with other school projects may be offered. Facilities may include group study rooms and computer laboratories. Formal cooperative agreements and contracts may be in place between the library and educational institutions.

Some Possible Components of Formal Learning Support Service

- Specialized curriculum-based collections
- Homework help center
- Computer laboratory
- Tutoring
- Group study facilities
- World Wide Web site with links to curriculum and other educational sites

Target Audiences and Service Aspects

Target Audiences

Formal Learning Support can be provided for all students in a community or it can be targeted to a specific group or groups of learners. For example, one library may decide to support preschool students, a second may concentrate on students in kindergarten through grade 3, and yet another library may support the learning efforts of community college students. A library could design a program targeted at serving homeschoolers.

Service Aspects

It is possible to focus on an aspect of service such as providing homework assistance or offering tutoring in a particular subject such as reading.

Resource Allocation Issues to Consider

Staff

The staff in a library providing Formal Learning Support service should have a good knowledge of how individuals in their target audience learn and about the topics they are studying. For example, if a library has decided to focus on learning support for very young children enrolled in preschool programs, staff should have a working knowledge of early childhood education principles and methods. Staff need to develop and maintain a good knowledge of the curricular goals of the educational institutions supported.

Collection and Information Resources

The collection and information resources needed to provide Formal Learning Support depend greatly upon the targeted audience. Libraries typically concentrate on providing materials that supplement rather than duplicate the resources available in institutions of formal learning; however, the library may also offer a collection of textbooks (sometimes provided by the schools) for reference purposes. Materials in a variety of nontraditional formats such as instructional videotapes, educational games, educational computer software, models, and multimedia are provided. Graphical World Wide Web access may be provided.

Facilities

Libraries offering Formal Learning Support should provide facilities that are conducive to learning. Space for individual study as well as group study rooms is typically provided. Computer labs or workstations equipped to allow students to complete homework assignments may be offered. Formal classroom space may be offered. The library may be the site from which students participate in coursework offered using distance education technologies. The library may also use this classroom space to offer bibliographic instruction or training related to locating high-quality, relevant information on the Internet.

Technology

The use of technology in teaching has become more closely integrated with content and instruction. Consequently, libraries offering Formal Learning Support should provide appropriate technologies that enable the people in their target audience to learn. World Wide Web access, computer labs, and distance education have already been mentioned above. Library staff members need to be knowledgeable in the use of technological resources and must be able to teach students to use these resources.

Possible Measures to Consider When Developing Objectives

People Served

Total number of users served (measures the total number of users who used a service during a given time period):

- Number of people who attended formal learning support programs

Number of unique individuals who used the service (measures the total number of unique individuals who used the service during a given time period, regardless of how many times they used the service):

- Number of elementary school students registered in the homework help program

How Well the Service Met the Needs of People Served

- Percent of students who used the library for homework assistance who indicated on a survey that the library services and materials met their needs
- Percent of people who used formal learning support information services who indicated on a survey that the information was provided in a timely manner
- Percent of people who attended formal learning support programs who indicated on a survey that the program was satisfactory or excellent

Total Units of Service Delivered

- Number of presentations made in schools that describe and promote the library's formal learning support services
- Number of times the formal learning support Web page was accessed
- Number of unique book lists produced for homeschoolers
- Number of formal learning support displays created
- Number of classes held in the library computer lab

Formal Learning Support Stories

DeForest Public Library
(DeForest, Wisc. Service Population: 6,000)

The DeForest Public Library may not have an imposing building, but what goes on inside the walls of this storefront library may be more important to the future of this middle-class community of 6,000 than anything else that happens in town. Since 1993, the DeForest Public Library, in cooperation with the DeForest Area School District, has been a partner in an extensive program of learning support services to young children and their caregivers.

The partnership began as part of an Even Start program aimed at preparing children for school. The library worked with the school district to design intergenerational storyhour programs in which parents, grandparents, or adult caregivers participate along with their preschoolers. At the end of each session, the participants leave with a small paper bag called a "maker" that contains an interactive family literacy activity based on nursery rhymes or familiar children's stories. The kits, which are designed by library staff, are assembled by high school students studying early childhood development.

The great success and popularity of this program have resulted in an expansion of the partnership between the school district and the public library. For example, "keeper" kits were initially developed in response to heavy demand on library materials that contained ideas for science fair projects. These kits have now been expanded to include activities not just for science but in social studies, reading, math, and history as well. These kits for middle school children, like the kits for preschoolers, contain entertaining learning activities related to the school curriculum that encourage busy parents to become more active in the education of their children.

Houston Public Library

(Houston, Tex. Service Population: 1,702,000)

The Houston Public Library believes that students in kindergarten through twelfth grade (K–12) should ASPIRE to succeed. ASPIRE, which stands for After School Programs Inspire Reading Enrichment, is a neighborhood-based homework help program geared to accommodate the different learning styles and interests of students. While there is a homework help emphasis in most Houston Public Library branch locations, two branches have ASPIRE Centers, with four additional sites opening in the near future. Both peer tutors and adult tutors are available at these centers to help students understand and complete their homework assignments. All children in grades K–12 are eligible for assistance; however, the program places special emphasis on the needs of middle school students.

Special collections, selected to support the curriculum of the Houston Independent School District, are in place at all ASPIRE Centers. Each center has two computer workstations that provide online access to the library's catalog and electronic resources. These computers are also equipped with supplemental educational software that allows students and their tutors to find solutions to their homework-related challenges by entering natural language questions. All workstations provide free graphical Internet access. A paid staff member coordinates ASPIRE activities at each center.

The success of the ASPIRE program is based on an active partnership with the Houston Independent School District. Branch library staff are expected to visit each school in their service area each year. Contacts are made with principals and counselors as well as with classroom teachers. Counselors help the library identify potential peer tutors for the ASPIRE program.

Jasper Public Library
(Jasper, Tenn. Service Population: 26,000)

The library resources at the Marion County campus of Chattanooga State Technical Community College (CSTCC), like those at many satellite locations of community colleges, don't fully meet the needs of the school's population. The Jasper Public Library, working with the CSTCC librarian, helps fill the gap by offering services targeted at the community college's 450 students.

As a result of open policies that offer CSTCC students from three different states full access to resources and an active program of outreach to the college that includes class visits to the library and visits on campus by library staff, the Jasper Public Library is frequently full of students. The library's collections and resources have been strengthened in many areas that mirror the CSTCC curriculum. Educational videotapes and periodical resources are particularly heavily used.

The general public has gained a benefit from the cooperation between the college and the public library as well. In spite of the fact that no formal agreement exists between the public library and CSTCC, the college provides some equipment and CD-ROM reference materials to the library for student use. These materials are available to all.

Wicomico County Free Library
(Salisbury, Md. Service Population: 79,600)

The Wicomico County Free Library serves as a learning resource center for homeschooling families throughout the three-state Delmarva region (Delaware, Maryland, and Virginia). The library provides a wide range of services to support the learning goals of homeschoolers and their parents.

The Wicomico Library purchased a homeschooling curriculum set used by many of the families in their area, and acquires books, videos, and other library materials to support that curriculum for children from preschool age through sixth grade. The library has also developed a program that acquaints the homeschooling community with the world of electronic resources they can use. Intergenerational programs for the public on using the Internet have attracted many homeschooling families. A newsletter, produced locally by a group of homeschoolers, regularly lists information about the library's Internet training programs and the resources available at the library.

The library has identified many World Wide Web sites of interest to students, regardless of whether they are in public, private, or homeschooling settings. Links to these sites, including some specifically related to homeschooling, are available through the library's Kid's Konnection Web page. The Wicomico Information and Learning Library (WILL) provides multimedia computers for use both in the library and at two community centers in the area. Many homeschoolers have commented that they couldn't possibly afford all of the print resources and educational software that the library provides. Families decide which books and instructional media they *do* want to buy for their homeschooling program by first using the materials at the library.

General Information

Example of Needs Addressed by This Service Response

A library that offers General Information helps meet the need for information and answers to questions on a broad array of topics related to work, school, and personal life.

What the Library Does and Provides

The library will offer print, nonprint, and electronic reference resources that cover a broad variety of topics. The library will provide staff skillful in determining users' needs and in locating relevant information that satisfies those needs. Internet access will be provided for staff and public use.

Alternative off-site means of accessing information resources such as dial-in service and computer kiosks in public places may be provided. The library will provide telephone information service and should consider accepting and answering questions via fax and e-mail. The library may locate, organize, and provide access to general information resources on a Web page.

Some Possible Components of General Information Service

- Basic reference resources available through the library Web page
- Twenty-four-hour electronic reference service (ability to e-mail questions)

- Dedicated telephone reference service (not located at reference desk)
- Ready reference answers faxed to home or office
- Desktop videoconferencing (for transmitting schematic drawings, graphics)
- Bibliographic instruction programs

Target Audiences and Service Aspects

Target Audiences

General Information service is typically available to all ages; however, it is possible to target the service to meet the information needs of an age group such as seniors or primary school-aged children.

Service Aspects

Aspects of the service that might be stressed include telephone reference service or other off-site access to basic information resources.

Resource Allocation Issues to Consider

Staff

Staff providing General Information service should be informed about a broad range of topics and should possess a good knowledge of how to retrieve information. In libraries where multiple staff members provide the service, staff with varied formal education backgrounds are desirable. Staff need to become highly skilled in database searching and should be familiar with a variety of computer search engines to access resources on the Internet.

Collection and Information Resources

The entire collection, not just noncirculating books designated as reference, should be considered reference tools. Libraries providing this service should have Internet access available for both staff and the public. Other databases, indexes, and finding tools should be available in many locations throughout the library as well as in the designated reference section. The library catalog and other general information resources should be available twenty-four hours per day through either a dial-in service or through the World Wide Web.

Facilities

Facilities should be provided both for interaction between library staff and library users and for quiet study. Tables and study carrels should be available in numbers that meet demand during the heaviest use period. Individual study rooms and small group study facilities may be provided. Workstations for both standing and seated computer use (short use and extended use) should be provided.

Technology

Computers throughout the library should be able to access a full range of information resources. Single-purpose terminals dedicated to an individual product should be minimized. Technologies such as local and wide area networks should be used to distribute information broadly.

Possible Measures to Consider When Developing Objectives

People Served

Total number of users served (measures the total number of users who used a service during a given time period):

- Number of people who used telephone reference service
- Number of people who attended programs about general information services

Number of unique individuals who used the service (measures the total number of unique individuals who used the service during a given time period, regardless of how many times they used the service):

- Number of unique individuals completing a library-sponsored bibliographic instruction class

How Well the Service Met the Needs of People Served

- Percent of people who used general information reference materials who indicated on a survey that the materials met their needs

- Percent of people who used general information service who indicated on a survey that the information was provided in a timely manner
- Percent of people who attended general information programs who indicated on a survey that the program was satisfactory or excellent

Total Units of Service Delivered

- Number of times the library Web page was accessed
- Number of unique general information pathfinders or book lists produced
- Number of general reference questions answered via fax or e-mail
- Number of general information questions answered

General Information Stories

Skokie Public Library
(Skokie, Ill. Service Population: 59,000)

The people of Skokie, Illinois, know that if they have a question, it's likely that the Skokie Public Library has the answer! The library's information services staff responds to an average of four reference queries per capita each year. General information service has been a priority and a strength of the library for many years. About 24 percent of the library's materials budget is spent on reference materials and electronic resources each year. A number of the information services librarians have an advanced degree in addition to an MLS, and the library is committed to an extensive continuing education program including its initial orientation of new staff members, instruction in the use of each new automated resource before it is made available to the public, and sending staff to area workshops and professional conferences throughout the country.

The information desk is staffed by a minimum of two professional librarians during all hours the library is open. Another staff member tends a telephone reference center that has an automated call distribution system to queue calls and to direct overflow to a secondary location. When the library is not open, calls are directed to a regionally staffed night owl reference service that operates daily until midnight.

The library's extensive local area network (LAN) provides access to a large number of CD-ROM databases from computers located throughout the library. Internet access is also available by reservation and on a walk-up basis when available. The library's online catalog and some databases are available remotely twenty-four hours per day.

The library makes it easy to ask questions as well as to get answers to them. A fax machine is located at the information desk that enables people to request information and receive replies in this way. Information requests can also be submitted and answered electronically through the library's World Wide Web home page.

Montgomery County Department of Public Libraries
(Rockville, Md. Service Population: 819,000)

Offering a high level of General Information service to children seems like an obvious choice to the Montgomery County Library; children are full of questions and the library is full of answers! The library sees reference skill training and a good knowledge of the resources the library has available as the key components of its success in bringing kids and answers together.

Both adult and children's service specialists are cross-trained to serve both children and adults using the Better Communication = Better Reference approach. A knowledge and awareness of how information-seeking behavior differs based on factors such as age and the subject of the question help the staff in their efforts to be responsive to their customers. This responsiveness shows in many ways. For example, library staff are aware that open-ended questions don't work very well with children, and they adjust the reference interview accordingly. Staff also recognize that when an adult and a child approach the reference desk, there may in fact be two questions instead of one. The library tries to make sure that children's questions are taken every bit as seriously as those posed by adults.

The library also recognizes the potential that its entire collection, including children's materials and nonbook formats, has as a source of answers to questions. English is not the first language for many users of the library, and pictures, videos, and other nontext resources often prove valuable in working with this audience as well as with children and with individuals whose reading skills are less developed.

Providing information to adults who work with young children (preschool teachers, child-care workers, etc.) is also seen as an important aspect of the library's information service for children. The Montgomery County Library's strategic plan targets this population for special attention.

Government Information

Example of Needs Addressed by This Service Response

A library that offers Government Information service helps satisfy the need for information about elected officials and governmental agencies that enables people to participate in the democratic process.

What the Library Does and Provides

The library will provide access to a wide selection of information by and about governmental agencies in print and electronic form. The staff will have full Internet access, and Internet access may be provided for public use as well. The library will provide staff knowledgeable in using government documents, searching the Internet, determining users' needs, and locating relevant information that satisfies those needs.

The library may serve as a federal, state, or local document depository. The library may initiate efforts to make local government information available online or through a Web page and may be responsible for collecting, organizing, indexing, and disseminating this information.

Some Possible Components of Government Information Service

- Electronic access to local government information
- Federal, state, and local documents and records depository

- Public hearings and public access television broadcasts of public meetings
- Government contract and procurement center
- Town meetings with government officials
- Patent and Trademark Depository Library

Target Audiences and Service Aspects

Target Audiences

The library could decide to address the specific government information needs of homeowners living within a floodplain area or of retired military in the library's service area.

Service Aspects

Particular aspects of the service that might be emphasized include proceedings of a local city or county government or a focus on making unpublished records information such as tax assessments accessible electronically.

Resource Allocation Issues to Consider

Staff

Staff providing Government Information service need to develop and maintain a good knowledge of government and the political process. An educational background in political science, public administration, or government is an asset. Staff members providing the service need to become highly skilled in database searching and should be familiar with a variety of computer search engines to access resources on the Internet. Good organizational skills and political networking skills are desirable.

Collection and Information Resources

Federal, state, and local documents may all be included in the collection of libraries providing Government Information service. Much government information of interest to the public is also available online. Libraries may be formal depositories for federal, state, and local documents. This designation imposes special requirements regarding retention of records and storage methods. Libraries may also collect information and documents from international sources. The library may create digital collections from print-on-paper formats and may organize and disseminate these documents in a variety of ways including through the Internet.

Facilities

Space needs of libraries providing Government Information service may vary from minimal to extensive, depending on whether the library acts as a full or partial depository of documents and the storage and retention requirements that accompany the designation. Libraries providing Government Information service should provide quiet study spaces.

Technology

Libraries providing Government Information service will make extensive use of technology to access World Wide Web sites maintained by governmental agencies, to access documents stored on CD-ROM, and to provide information through the library's Internet presence.

Possible Measures to Consider When Developing Objectives

People Served

Total number of users served (measures the total number of users who used a service during a given time period):

- Number of people who attended government information programs

Number of unique individuals who used the service (measures the total number of unique individuals who used the service during a given time period, regardless of how many times they used the service):

- Number of unique individuals who completed the library-sponsored patent and trademark classes

How Well the Service Met the Needs of People Served

- Percent of people who used government information materials who indicated on a survey that the materials met their needs
- Percent of people who used government information services who indicated on a survey that the information was provided in a timely manner

- Percent of people who attended government information programs who indicated on a survey that the program was satisfactory or excellent

Total Units of Service Delivered

- Number of times the government information Web page was accessed
- Number of unique government information pamphlets produced
- Number of government information displays created
- Number of government information reference questions answered

Government Information Stories

Pasadena Public Library
(Pasadena, Calif. Service Population: 137,100)

The official name of the Pasadena Public Library is the "Department of Information Services," which acknowledges its broad role in fostering an informed citizenry in the city. The library serves as the Internet node for the city and coordinates the development of an in-depth city World Wide Web site that has as its objective linking local residents to government information. Each department, from the city clerk to human services and from planning to public safety, works with library staff to develop and update relevant government information content.

The city's Web pages include typical municipal information such as city council agendas and job opportunities, but they also include less traditional information such as a citizen's newsletter, e-mail communication with elected officials, and a wealth of neighborhood information. Much of the grassroots information is gathered through the central library and its branches. Each library location has a dedicated area designated as the Neighborhood Information Service (NIS) that collects and submits documents and information from its neighborhood. The library's Web pages have a distinct neighborhood flavor. For example, the information for each branch includes a profile of the community it serves.

Corvallis-Benton County Public Library
(Corvallis, Ore. Service Population: 70,000)

Government Information service at the Corvallis-Benton County Public Library is a two-way street. The library sees itself not only as a provider of government information to the people of its community but as a provider of people information to the government as well. The library actively collects, organizes, and makes available to the public city, county, and school district documents. It also hosts a weekly Council Corner program where citizens can talk to their elected representatives. Every Saturday from 9:00 A.M. to 12:00 P.M., a different councilperson is at the library to talk to constituents. The U.S. congresswoman holds an open session at the library every few months as well. One Saturday each month, the League of Women Voters holds a community issues forum.

Surveys indicate that approximately 84 percent of county residents use the library. Based on this fact, the library serves as the display area for proposals for all kinds of public works and economic development projects. People have had the opportunity to review plans for riverfront redevelopment, for the water mitigation project, and for countless highway and sewer project redesigns. There are typically two displays of this type at the library at any given time, and as many as five have been available for public review on occasion.

The library is also working on getting government employees to use library resources. Both the City Planning Department and the County Parks Department have sent their staff to the library for an orientation and training session in using the library's print and electronic resources.

Information Literacy

Example of Needs Addressed by This Service Response

A library that provides Information Literacy service helps address the need for skills related to finding, evaluating, and using information effectively.

What the Library Does and Provides

The library will provide training and instruction in skills related to locating, evaluating, and using information resources of all types. Teaching the public to find and evaluate information will be stressed over simply providing answers to questions. The library will provide access to information in a variety of formats and will offer public Internet training and access. Library staff will be knowledgeable about how people seek information and learn.

Staff may offer group classes, individual tutoring, or spontaneous one-on-one training in topics such as media literacy or finding resources on the Internet. The library may provide a computer laboratory or classroom.

Some Possible Components of Information Literacy Service

- Classroom space
- Special programs on media literacy

- Computer laboratory
- Listening and viewing multimedia computer stations for critical evaluation of resources
- Basic library skills and bibliographic instruction
- Instructional technology

Target Audiences and Service Aspects

Target Audiences

A library could choose to target its Information Literacy program toward teaching critical thinking skills to children. Another could focus on training adults to use resources found on the Internet.

Service Aspects

Aspects of the service that could be emphasized include teaching effective strategies when using various Internet search engines or instruction in how to perform expert or complex searches on the library's online catalog.

Resource Allocation Issues to Consider

Staff

Staff providing Information Literacy service need to develop and maintain a knowledge of how people seek and process information and a skill in evaluating information resources. Formal education on the topics of information-seeking behavior and how people learn is desirable. Staff should have an excellent range of computer skills and familiarity with different types of software products. Successful teaching experience is also desirable.

Collection and Information Resources

The entire library collection and the entire range of electronic resources available to the library can be used in providing Information Literacy service. Books, periodicals, videotapes, sound recordings, television, radio, and online information resources can all be used to help people understand how to find and critically evaluate information. Information literacy training typically happens either informally, using the materials an individual has already selected, or in a formal classroom or training setting using materials selected by the instructor for illustrative purposes.

Facilities

While Information Literacy service involves more than just computer literacy, training in locating and evaluating online resources is often a major component. Libraries may provide a computer lab to accommodate formal training sessions or they may provide an area in the library that has a large number of computers, some of which can be used for training purposes.

Technology

In addition to the computer lab mentioned, libraries offering Information Literacy service should have access to a full range of instructional technologies for teaching purposes. Specialized equipment such as video equipment capable of frame-by-frame display and computer input video projection units are highly desirable, in addition to more traditional teaching technologies.

Possible Measures to Consider When Developing Objectives

People Served

Total number of users served (measures the total number of users who used a service during a given time period):

- Number of people who attended information literacy classes
- Number of people who accessed computer-based training modules
- Number of people assisted by library technology aides

Number of unique individuals who used the service (measures the total number of unique individuals who used the service during a given time period, regardless of how many times they used the service):

- Number of unique individuals who completed a basic Internet class offered by the library
- Number of unique individuals who attended a class on using computerized reference tools

How Well the Service Met the Needs of People Served

- Percent of people who used information literacy services who indicated on a survey that the information was provided in a timely manner
- Percent of people who attended an information literacy class who indicated on a survey that the class was satisfactory or excellent
- Percent of people attending a class on using technology who indicated on a survey that their confidence in their ability to use computerized reference tools had increased

Total Units of Service Delivered

- Number of times the information literacy Web page was accessed
- Number of unique information literacy publications produced
- Number of information literacy displays created
- Number of basic library skills classes offered

Information Literacy Stories

Farmington Community Library
(Farmington Hills, Mich. Service Population: 85,000)

Michigan is closely associated with the vehicles that traverse our nation's highways, but the library in one Michigan community is more concerned that the residents it serves have what they need to travel the information superhighway. The Farmington Community Library sees the development of digital literacy as one of its service priorities and in response offers extensive computer literacy and Internet training.

Training sessions for people with different levels of computer knowledge and skill are provided six times each week. Two of these sessions (one at each of the library's two locations) are scheduled on Saturday mornings to make sure that people who are unable to attend on weekdays can participate. Objectives for training sessions go beyond the basic how-to in that the classes seek to impart digital literacy competencies such as the critical evaluation of online content. In addition to basic Internet training, sessions are held with groups with special interests such as teachers or businesspeople to acquaint them with Internet resources that may be of special interest to them.

While computer literacy and Internet training are offered for people of all ages, the library targets children and seniors for special attention. The library's Web site includes content and links that are particularly appealing to young people and seniors, since people are more likely to explore the Internet's resources in more depth if they can easily locate content of interest to them. The library's Cyber-Kids and Cyber-Teens pages include games and comics in addition to homework help. Content of special appeal to retirees includes community events, genealogy resources, and a link to the Farmington Historical Museum.

Seattle Public Library
(Seattle, Wash. Service Population: 534,732)

Training people to use the Internet and other electronic resources isn't a sideline for the Seattle Public Library; it's a major activity. The library's Information Literacy service developed from efforts to assist its customers in using the online public access catalog and has grown into a service that includes community learning laboratories in eight libraries located throughout the city.

A large training facility at the main library houses sixteen networked personal computers with full graphical Internet access. Smaller, community library-based installations have six to ten computers. Formal training sessions range from Web basics to specialized sessions in locating Web resources on international business topics and genealogy. The library also offers Web training for employees of other city departments, training for staff members of agencies that work with the Chinese community, and classes in Spanish that feature a wealth of resources in that language.

The library has a designated user education coordinator as well as a full-time lab supervisor. The staff training program is extensive, and approximately sixty staff members, including some clerical staff, have some training responsibilities.

Providence Public Library
(Providence, R.I. Service Population: 160,228)

Lots of children in Rhode Island know IRIS. They met her at one of the ten locations of the Providence Public Library, but IRIS isn't an itinerant storyteller or a substitute children's librarian. Instead, IRIS is the name given to the library's Integrated Reference Information System. IRIS is actually two computer systems, one that contains and distributes reference information and full-text databases, and another that provides public access to productivity software such as word-processing and spreadsheet programs.

An important goal of the library's children's services staff has been to use IRIS as a tool to develop information literacy in children. At the Providence Public Library, information literacy involves more than just basic computer skills. Children learn how information is arranged in reference books, how to listen carefully to a story to gather information, and how to express information in their own words, in addition to learning computer skills.

The library staff identify topics of high interest to children and pull together print and electronic resources children can use to explore the topic. Learning takes on a treasure hunt air as children gather the information they need to answer questions or complete a crossword puzzle.

The library also partners with Providence Public Schools on a number of other family and computer literacy programs that keep IRIS busy all of the time!

Lifelong Learning

Example of Needs Addressed by This Service Response

A library that provides Lifelong Learning service helps address the desire for self-directed personal growth and development opportunities.

What the Library Does and Provides

The library will provide and maintain an extensive collection of circulating materials on a wide variety of topics in which the general public has a sustained interest. Collections will be easily accessible and organized to encourage public browsing by subject area. Staff knowledgeable in subjects and topics of interest to the general public will provide expert assistance in locating materials of all types and in all formats. The library will develop pathfinders or other finding tools to assist library users in learning about specific subjects or topics for which there are frequent requests.

The library may build substantial retrospective collections on some topics and may provide collections in considerable depth in subject areas of local interest. The library may enhance typical subject and keyword access in the online public access catalog through the addition of supplemental user-friendly terms. The library may identify important World Wide Web sites on topics of high interest to the public and may organize them for public access on a Web page.

Some Possible Components of Lifelong Learning Service

- Electronic and printed pathfinders
- How-to programs on topics of general public interest
- Special topical displays of materials and resources
- Artist-in-residence programs
- Demonstrations and exhibits
- History and biography resources

Target Audiences and Service Aspects

Target Audiences

While Lifelong Learning is, by definition, a service that applies to people of all ages, special efforts can be made to encourage specific groups to use library resources to support their informal learning. Examples include programs that introduce very young children to the joy of reading and efforts to provide high-interest, low-vocabulary materials for intermediate-aged children who are hesitant readers.

Service Aspects

A library could concentrate on building exceptional strength in a few specific subject areas. Some examples are travel, antiques, American history, fine arts, biographies, or sports.

Resource Allocation Issues to Consider

Staff

Staff providing Lifelong Learning service should have a broad-based education that prepares them to assist independent learners as they explore a wide range of topics. Formal education in how people learn is highly desirable. Staff providing the service should have good organizational skills that would allow them to develop pathfinders or other guides to using library resources on topics of interest to large numbers of people.

Collection and Information Resources

While the entire collection can be seen as supporting Lifelong Learning service, the nonfiction collection is typically the most critical. Libraries providing the service need in-depth resources in areas of special interest to the public. Electronic resources such as those found on the World Wide Web and other resources that engage multiple senses such as multimedia CD-ROMs can be particularly effective. Self-paced, individualized instruction programs are of special value. The library may be involved in developing Web pages for public use.

Facilities

Libraries providing Lifelong Learning service should provide individual and small-group study spaces. The library may provide meeting spaces for clubs or organizations.

Technology

Online public access computers should be located in and near the collections and should provide enhanced access (additional search terms, keyword searching, etc.). Multimedia computers and other individual educational tools should be provided that can be used for self-paced individualized instruction.

Possible Measures to Consider When Developing Objectives

People Served

Total number of users served (measures the total number of users who used a service during a given time period):

- Number of people who attended lifelong learning programs
- Number of people who attended lifelong learning exhibits

Number of unique individuals who used the service (measures the total number of unique individuals who used the service during a given time period, regardless of how many times they used the service):

- Number of unique children registered in a summer reading program
- Number of unique nursing home residents registered for the books-by-mail program

How Well the Service Met the Needs of People Served

- Percent of people who used library materials who indicated on a survey that the materials were useful to them in meeting their personal lifelong learning goals
- Percent of people who used lifelong learning services who indicated on a survey that the information was provided in a timely manner
- Percent of people who attended lifelong learning programs who indicated on a survey that the programs were satisfactory or excellent

Total Units of Service Delivered

- Number of deposit collections maintained in other community facilities
- Number of times the lifelong learning Web page was accessed
- Number of unique lifelong learning book lists produced
- Number of lifelong learning displays created

Lifelong Learning Stories

Spokane Public Library

(Spokane, Wash. Service Population: 180,000)

Lifelong Learning service at the Spokane Public Library begins at birth. Every newborn in the city and his or her parents receive a Baby Reading Kit. The kit includes a board book and a bib for the child and information about the importance of reading to a child from birth, complete with tips on how to do it for the parents. Information about library locations and getting a library card for the child is also included.

Recognizing the importance of the preschool years in the development of language skills and a lifelong positive attitude toward reading, special efforts are made to reach out to preschoolers, their parents, and caregivers. In addition to storytimes in the library, the library provides monthly storytime visits to preschools and even to home day-care centers in the city. Colorful boxes of books are delivered to the centers to encourage children and their teachers to explore new ideas and stories together. Reading lists for babies, toddlers, and preschoolers are distributed to parents, teachers, and caregivers through the preschools as well. Project Right Start extends the library's reach into home day-care centers. The library offers workshops for home day-care providers, and Right Start kits, containing books selected for preschoolers, are available for check-out by home day-care providers at all branches.

The library offers a wealth of materials and activities to satisfy and foster the curiosity of school-age children. Children's videos, cassettes, magazines, and CD-ROMs supplement high-interest book collections and engage the senses in learning experiences. Many of the library's programs for school-age children feature interesting guests who introduce the children to new topics and the wealth of cultural and educational opportunities that exist in the community. The library's outstanding World Wide Web Kid's Page is colorful, exciting, and full of content for both children and their parents.

Phoenix Public Library

(Phoenix, Ariz. Service Population: 1,210,410)

It's easy to talk about making library resources accessible, but it's much harder to deliver on the promise. When the staff of the Phoenix Public Library talk about providing access to library resources that people need in a way that people can use, the library backs up the words with action. The central library was designed so that all of the adult nonfiction books are located on a single floor with lots of tables and chairs to accommodate users. Further, the library makes extensive use of a wide assortment of assistive technologies and provides training in their use to ensure that the library's resources are available to all residents in the community, including those who have disabilities.

The library operates a Special Needs Center that provides one-on-one training in using the library's resources and the specialized accessibility tools it has available. Through personalized reader advisory service the staff of the Special Needs Center match people with the resources they want and with the means of acquiring the information they're seeking. In addition to large-print computer displays, the library provides video print enlargers, synthetic speech and screen-reading software, voice-activated terminals, computer-generated Braille, Kurzweil Personal Readers, a Computer Assisted Notetaking (CAN) system, and an FM Listening system.

Well-trained library staff members are an integral component in the success of this program. Both central library staff and staff in the branches receive training to make them aware of the devices that are available and how they are used. Library staff members are actively involved with community groups and organizations that work with individuals with disabilities. These organizations refer people to the library for assistance, and the library refers people to them when appropriate. The library also works with other Phoenix city departments to make sure that people with disabilities are able to access the city's other information resources through its home page, Phoenix at Your Fingertips. This is done by helping city departments develop public, Americans with Disabilities Act–compliant workstations and encouraging them to include programs and information for citizens with disabilities.

Local History and Genealogy

Example of Needs Addressed by This Service Response

A library that offers Local History and Genealogy service addresses the desire of community residents to know and better understand personal or community heritage.

What the Library Does and Provides

The library will provide a significant collection of materials and other resources that chronicle the history of the community or region in which the library is located. Family histories and genealogical research tools are provided. The library will provide the equipment required to read, print, and copy all formats in which information is supplied. The library will be actively involved in borrowing and lending historical and genealogical resources with other local, regional, and national libraries and historical societies.

The library may maintain special collections of historical interest including photos and archival materials. The library may digitize these collections and provide computer access to them. Staff knowledgeable in genealogical and historical research methods and in archival and records management will be available to assist library users with their research. Electronic resources including Internet access may be provided.

Some Possible Components of Local History and Genealogy Service

- Instruction in genealogical and historical research methods
- Programs on local history
- Digitization of historic photographs
- Temperature- and humidity-controlled archives vault or room
- Indexing of local newspapers
- Oral histories
- World Wide Web links to history and genealogy sites

Target Audiences and Service Aspects

Target Audiences

While this service is typically associated with older adults, a program of service could be designed to introduce young children to local history or to genealogical research.

Service Aspects

Either the local history or genealogy aspects of this service can be stressed. Historical resources could focus on a municipality or on a region. A special collection such as a famous person's personal papers or a collection of historic photographs might receive special attention.

Resource Allocation Issues to Consider

Staff

Staff providing Local History and Genealogy service need to develop and maintain a good knowledge of history and genealogy. A background or formal training in history and archival management is highly desirable. Special skills in preservation and archival methods are essential if the library performs an archives function.

Collection and Information Resources

Resources supporting Local History and Genealogy service often come from nontraditional sources. Some desirable items are out-of-print, come from small presses, are self-published, or are unpublished documents. Because of the rarity of some items and the fragility of others, many items of interest are available in microform, on CD-ROM, or in other electronic formats. Libraries providing local history and archival functions face special challenges acquiring and maintaining collections of unbound documents such as correspondence, manuscripts, and personal records. Oral histories are also often collected in a variety of formats including sound and video recordings.

Facilities

Libraries providing a high level of Local History and Genealogy service face a number of specialized facilities considerations. Rare, fragile, and archival materials should be housed in a secure and temperature- and humidity-controlled environment. High-density storage units are often used. The library may provide meeting space for genealogical instruction.

Technology

Public Internet access should be provided. Necessary equipment includes computers, printers, and monitors capable of displaying and printing high-resolution graphic images; microform readers and reader/printers; and copying machines.

Possible Measures to Consider When Developing Objectives

People Served

Total number of users served (measures the total number of users who used a service during a given time period):

- Number of people who attended local history programs
- Number of people who attended genealogy programs
- Number of people who attended local history and genealogy exhibits

Number of unique individuals who used the service (measures the total number of unique individuals who used the service during a given time period, regardless of how many times they used the service):

- Number of unique people who register for the genealogy assistance program

How Well the Service Met the Needs of People Served

- Percent of people who used local history materials who indicated on a survey that the materials met their needs
- Percent of people who used genealogy materials who indicated on a survey that the materials met their needs
- Percent of people who used local history information services who indicated on a survey that the services were provided in a timely manner
- Percent of people who attended local history and genealogy programs who indicated on a survey that the program was satisfactory or excellent

Total Units of Service Delivered

- Number of times the genealogy Web page was accessed
- Number of unique local history publications produced
- Number of local history and genealogy displays created
- Number of local history and genealogy reference questions answered
- Number of historic photographs digitized
- Number of local oral history interviews conducted and transcribed

Local History and Genealogy Stories

San Antonio Public Library
(San Antonio, Tex. Service Population: 1,296,000)

An awareness of the ethnically diverse nature of its community permeates virtually every aspect of the San Antonio Public Library's operation, so it's no surprise to discover that Local History and Genealogy service at the library has a distinctly multicultural flair. Library collections chronicle the influence and unique contributions of San Antonio area residents with Mexican, European, and African roots. Primary resource materials in Spanish are available along with *Records of Southern Plantations* and passenger and immigration lists. The many pathfinders and introductory historical research guides the library publishes in both English and Spanish encourage the use of resources by novices as well as by experienced researchers.

While the library has maintained local historical collections for many years, the move into the library's new central library facility in May 1995 signaled a new emphasis on local history and genealogy service. For the first time, a Texana Genealogy Department, with separate staff and facilities, was created. The department now occupies approximately 10,000 square feet, including a 1,900-square-foot climate-controlled vault and a technologically rich public area that seats seventy-six. Seven full-time staff members, one of whom is a certified archivist, provide service, assisted by sixteen volunteers.

The new facilities, coupled with staff dedicated to providing local history and genealogy services, have enabled the library to concentrate on building its resources to reflect the cultural diversity of the area. The oldest genealogical society in San Antonio recently donated its significant collection to the library. In addition, the library has been active in acquiring microfilmed archival collections related to the history of the region.

Richland County Public Library
(Columbia, S.C. Service Population: 285,720)

They say that a picture is worth a thousand words. If so, the Richland County Public Library's historic photo collection speaks volumes. Columbia, South Carolina, prides itself on its history and on its architecture. For more than five years, the library has been building a collection of digitized photographs of historic Columbia. The library's digital photo project began when it received a collection of about 450 historic pictures from the city of Columbia. A search for a method to make these photos accessible while preserving them for posterity led the library to the idea of digitizing the photos, cataloging them, and making them accessible through the library's online catalog. The project has been so well received that the library has expanded the scope of its collection to include the county and the surrounding area. The library expects that it will soon have 2,000 fully cataloged digitized photos of historic significance.

The library works closely with many other organizations in its efforts to coordinate local history service. It is careful not to duplicate the efforts of the State Archives and the University of South Carolina, both of which have extensive historic holdings. The library's focus has been on providing services and resources that supplement what is available from other sources. An additional example of this approach is a collection of videotaped oral history interviews built by the library over the past decade. The library also does a great deal of programming in cooperation with the local historical society's foundation.

Part Three

Tool Kit

GROUPS
Identifying Options

Issues   Library managers must make decisions every day. Sometimes they make those decisions alone; sometimes they give the responsibility for making a decision to a committee or task force. In either case, the first step in any decision-making process is to identify the options to be considered. Regardless of whether the ultimate decision will be made by a single person or a group, it is usually more effective to involve a number of people in the process of identifying options. The greater number of viable options decision makers have to consider, the more likely they are to make effective decisions.

At first glance, it would seem that identifying options would be fairly easy. After all, almost everyone seems to have opinions about almost everything. In reality, when you begin to work with groups to help them identify options, you discover that people's preconceived ideas make it more difficult, not easier, to identify a range of options. Other problems include the tendency to think that there is only one right answer to every question, the difficulty in identifying new options for old problems, the dominance of the group by one or more members, and the effect of peer pressure on group activities that results in a tendency among group members to minimize the appearance of conflict. Finally, it is important to remember the old computer acronym GIGO (garbage in—garbage out). It applies here, too. You have to have the right people involved in the process to identify effective options. The right people, in this instance, include people with some understanding of the problem and some experience or knowledge that provides them with a basis for suggesting solutions. Each of these issues is discussed in greater detail in the following sections.

Searching for the One Right Answer

It is important for the group leader to lay the groundwork carefully for the process to be used to identify options, stressing the need to look at a variety of points of view. Many people are uncomfortable with ambiguity and find the concept of multiple, valid options difficult to understand. Instead they search for the absolute answer to any question. They are inclined to make premature decisions to avoid having to deal with uncomfortable choices. Most groups need periodic reminders that the purpose of this part of the decision-making process is to identify as many options as possible and that even ideas that seem wildly unrealistic at first glance may lead to new insights or choices.

Thinking "Inside the Box"

In general, the more familiar people are with a situation, the more difficult they find it to consider the situation objectively or creatively. This can be a particular problem in libraries because so many staff members have worked in the same system for decades. The group leader will want to encourage people to look with new eyes at the issues under consideration. This might be done in at least three ways.

Move from the specific to the general. Encourage group members to broaden their frames of reference. For instance, instead of thinking about the public library as an institution, broaden the definition to include all libraries, and then broaden it again to include all information providers. Remind the participants of the story of the railroad company executives who defined their business as "railroading." Not much later the competition from trucking and airfreight had pushed them close to bankruptcy. If the executives had understood that they were in the transportation business and not just the railroad business, the executives might well have been able to identify alternative options.

Look at what is happening beyond our own field. We can learn a lot from other organizations, both profit and not-for-profit. For instance, many library managers have benefited from management books written by such authors as Stephen Covey and Peter Drucker even though their books were intended primarily for businesspeople. The United Way has been very involved in helping not-for-profit organizations define the results of the services they provide, and the United Way manual *Measuring Program Outcomes: A Practical Approach* would be a valuable tool for any library manager.[1]

Question everything. James Thurber once said, "It is better to ask some of the questions than know all of the answers." When someone says,

"We've always done it this way," ask "Why?" When someone says, "We can't do that" ask "Why not?" Why can't we provide off-site access to information? Why can't we let users access their e-mail accounts on library equipment? Why can't we use e-book technology to deliver current materials more quickly and cost effectively? Why can't we use wireless technology? Why can't we collaborate with another organization to provide a service?

Dealing with Dominant Behaviors

Every group has one or more dominant members. The source of their dominance varies: Some people control a group by sheer force of personality. Others are dominant because of their positions. Yet others use their expertise (real or perceived) to control a group. Finally, some people dominate groups because they are bullies and attack anyone who disagrees with them or tries to express an alternative point of view.

It is critical for the group leader to make it clear to all group members that each person's opinion is important. This message may have to be repeated several times during the process. Then the group leader must control the behavior of the dominant members in the group. This can be done by waiting until others have spoken before asking the dominant members for their opinions. Another possibility is to divide the group into smaller subgroups, which has the effect of minimizing the impact of the dominant members. These techniques will work in many situations but may not be effective with bullies. It is possible that the group leader will have to talk to the bully privately during a break or after the meeting to ask him or her to respect the opinions of the others in the group. If this direct intervention doesn't work, the leader should consider asking the person who made the appointments to the committee to talk to the bully about his or her disruptive behavior.

Dealing with Peer Pressure

Most people are more comfortable if they feel they are a part of a group and not an outsider. Therefore, people have a tendency to go along with what they think the group believes or values, even if they don't necessarily agree. This can lead to "group think" in which the members place a higher value on agreement than on identifying multiple options. This problem is easiest to deal with at the very beginning of the process by making it clear that the group's task is to identify multiple options. The leader should assure the group that the purpose is not to make the final decision and that success will be defined by the number and creativity of the options identified. This, in turn, creates a group norm that supports and encourages diverse points of view.

Involving the Right People

Several things should be considered when determining whom to involve in the identification of options. First, of course, you want to include people who have something to contribute to the discussion. Their contributions may be based on specialized skills or expertise, on background or experience, or on position or authority. Second, you want to include people who care about the issue being considered. Third, you want to include people who will be affected by whatever option is ultimately selected. Finally, you want people who are reasonably open to change and willing to consider a variety of points of view. If you are careful in your selections (and lucky), most of the participants in whatever process you use to identify options could be included in at least three of these four categories.

Evaluating Methods of Identifying Options

Four methods you might use to help a group identify options are general group discussion, brainstorming, Nominal Group Technique, and the Delphi Method. Each of these methods can be used effectively in certain situations. The important thing is to match the method and the situation. Four measures that can be used to help you decide which method will be most effective for a given situation include the desired

> level of participation from the group
>
> range of the options identified
>
> skill required of the facilitator/leader
>
> time it takes to make the decision

Level of Participation

The first measure to use when deciding which method to use for identifying options is how much participation you need to identify the options for a specific decision. If the options you are to consider relate to a significant change in policy, you will probably want to use a process that encourages the maximum level of participation. On the other hand, if you are developing options for dealing with a situation in a single unit or dealing with a relatively minor change, you may not want or need extensive participation.

Range of Options Identified

The second measure is the range and creativity of the options that are identified. Some problems are intrinsically more difficult to address than others. Consider two committees, one responsible for identifying options for ways to integrate a new technology into the ongoing operations of the library and the second responsible for options for improving the activities for the annual staff day training event. Both are important, but the first will require considerably more flexibility and creativity than the second.

Leadership Skill Required

The third measure is the skill required to develop and lead the process to be used to identify the options. Some of the methods described in this chapter are relatively easy to manage; others require more specialized skills or knowledge.

Time Required

The final measure is the length of time it will take to identify options. The identification of options is just the first step in the decision-making process. There is not much point in expending so much effort on this part of the process that there is no time left to reach agreement on the most effective option to select before the deadline for implementation. Furthermore, some decisions are fairly simple or can only be addressed in a limited number of ways. As a general rule, select the easiest and quickest process that will produce the level of participation and range of options you need.

Methods for Identifying Options

General Group Discussions

Level of participation:
Varies, often low

Range of options identified:
Low to moderate

Leadership skill required:
Low

Time required:
Low

General group discussion is probably the most common method used for identifying options in libraries. Group discussions often occur during meetings that have multiple agenda items. Someone will raise an issue, someone else will suggest a solution, there may or may not be a little discussion, and the suggestion is adopted. The other common setting for group discussion is a special committee meeting called to review a problem and to identify possible solutions.

General group discussions present a number of problems when used as the means to identify options. Because general group discussions often occur extemporaneously, people don't have time to think about the problem and bring suggestions to the meeting. Instead, they are expected to think of options very quickly. The negative effects of peer pressure and the dominance of one or more members of the group are most likely to occur in this situation. Furthermore, the process of identifying options tends to end the first time someone suggests a solution that sounds reasonable to the other members of the group. There is no reward for prolonging the identification process, and there is often considerable pressure to move on to the next item on the agenda.

When to Use

Generally, library managers overuse group discussion. However, group discussion can be an effective way to identify options in several circumstances. The first is when the decision to be made is confidential and the number of people involved in the process of identifying options is small. Two or three people would probably find it difficult and obtrusive to use any of the other methods to identify options. It is also appropriate to use general group discussions to identify options when the group is one that meets regularly and has a shared knowledge base. Branch managers, for instance, often identify options for addressing common problems during their monthly meetings. However, in both instances, the people responsible for leading the process need to be very aware of the problems presented in the preceding paragraph and work with the members of the group to avoid them.

What to Do

1. Identify the issue or question to be addressed.
2. Select the group to address the question. It may be an existing group or committee, or it may be a group convened specifically for this process.
3. Prepare a brief (one-page) description of the issue to be addressed and send it to the members of the group at least one week prior to the meeting in which it will be discussed. Ask the participants to come to the meeting ready to suggest ways to address the issue.
4. At the meeting, briefly review the issue and ask the members to suggest options. Write the options on newsprint as they are presented. Encourage the group to provide as many suggestions as possible. Ask participants to clarify any options that seem ambiguous. Encourage people to combine options that are similar. Do not evaluate the suggestions as they are proposed.
5. When it becomes clear that everyone is finished presenting options, review the list and ask if there are questions or additions. Make needed changes and develop a final list of options.
6. Use the options as the starting point for making a decision about the issue under review.

Brainstorming

Level of participation:
   Moderate to high

Range of options identified:
   Moderate

Skill of facilitator/leader:
   Moderate

Time required:
   Low to moderate

Brainstorming is a method used to identify multiple options by generating a large number of ideas through interaction among team members. The intent is to break free of preconceived ideas by exploring as many alternatives as possible and building on each other's ideas.

As shown in figure 19, in this process a group of people creates a list of ideas by having each member make a suggestion in turn, and the suggestions are recorded with no comment or discussion. Members are encouraged to build on each other's ideas. The actual brainstorming is best done in groups with six to eight members, but large groups can be divided into smaller groups for the initial brainstorming activity and then the suggestions from all of the small groups can be combined.

This is a relatively easy process to manage and, by its very nature, makes it difficult for a few people to dominate the discussion. It is a process that many people enjoy; participants often find the fast-paced generation of ideas by a variety of people stimulating. However, the fast pace of the process can be a problem too. Brainstorming doesn't provide much opportunity for reflection. Participants are encouraged to think of options very quickly, which may mean that more-complex or unusual options are never identified. Participants may also hesitate to make an unusual or creative suggestion for fear that others will laugh at them or think they are strange. There may be a tendency to follow the lead of the first two or three people who offer options rather than suggesting alternates that may be perceived as being in conflict with earlier recommendations.

FIGURE 19
Rules for Brainstorming

RULES FOR BRAINSTORMING

1. Be creative; push the limits.
2. Never criticize anyone's ideas. There are no right answers or wrong answers.
3. The more ideas you contribute the better. Quantity is more important than quality.
4. Free-associate ideas; build on the ideas of others.
5. Don't discuss ideas or stop for explanations.
6. Record all ideas exactly as they are stated.
7. Take turns making suggestions. Contribute one idea each time it is your turn.
8. Pass your turn if you have no further suggestions.

When to Use

Brainstorming is a good method to use to generate a lot of ideas from a group in a fairly short period of time. It works best when it is used to consider a single, focused topic. For example, brainstorming can be an excellent way to identify a list of possible activities to achieve a predetermined goal and objective. However, it is probably not the best way to identify the options for addressing the myriad of issues surrounding access to pornographic sites on the Internet. In the first case, the staff of the library probably have all of the information they need to make suggestions, and any grouping of several dozen activities could be used to accomplish the goal and objectives. In the second case, there aren't dozens of good answers. In fact, there aren't any answers that satisfy everyone involved. Having people with little knowledge of the legal issues or the political environment make suggestions is probably not going to be useful.

What to Do

1. Identify the issue or question to be addressed.

2. Decide whom to include in the process. This may be an existing group or committee or it may be a group convened specifically for this process.

3. Decide if you want to have official recorders for each group or if you want to ask the participants to share the responsibility for recording.

4. Write a short issue statement. This should be specific enough to help participants focus on the issue but open-ended enough to encourage creativity. The statement could include a list of questions that would encourage exploration of the topic.

5. At the beginning of the brainstorming session, review the problem statement with the participants.

6. Prepare a handout with the rules for brainstorming (see figure 19), and distribute it to all participants.

7. If the group has more than eight people, divide it into smaller groups.

8. Establish a specific period of time for the initial brainstorming activity, usually around twenty minutes.

9. If there is more than one group working on the problem, combine their suggestions into a master list on newsprint.

10. Review and discuss the items on the master list, clarifying when necessary and combining when possible.

11. Use the options on the master list as the starting point for making a decision about the issue under review.

Nominal Group Technique

Level of participation:
Moderate to high
Range of options identified:
Moderate to high
Skill of facilitator/leader:
Moderate
Time required:
Moderate

The Nominal Group Technique is used to generate a large number of ideas through contributions of members working individually. Research suggests that more ideas are generated by individuals working alone but in a group environment than by individuals engaged in group discussions.[2] In this process, group members start by writing down their ideas on note cards and posting them for others to read. Members get an opportunity to ask questions to clarify ideas and then they participate in group discussions about all of the ideas presented. Finally, each group member reassesses the ideas presented and selects those that seem most effective. These conclusions are then posted for a final discussion.

The Nominal Group Technique is both more time-consuming and more structured than brainstorming. The investment in time is often repaid because this process generally produces a greater number of more-developed and creative ideas than are produced in a group discussion or brainstorming process. However, people generally feel more comfortable with the fast-paced and open brainstorming process than with the Nominal Group Technique, at least partly because people are more familiar with brainstorming. The Nominal Group Technique structure can be perceived by group members as being artificial and restrictive. Participants may feel that the process drives the content, rather than the other way around, and as a result, they may question the validity of the final list of options.

When to Use

The Nominal Group Technique is a good method to use with a group that has some very strong or opinionated members. Because each participant writes down his or her ideas privately before any discussion begins, the responses are less likely to be driven by the dominant members of the group. Because the facilitator reads the suggestions aloud, the process allows suggestions to be evaluated on their own merits rather than being prejudged based on who made them. The Nominal Group Technique also can be used effectively to identify options for addressing issues that are potentially controversial. For instance, you may be considering how to revise your circulation policies so they support your goal of meeting the public's demand for materials on current topics and titles. This opens up some interesting possibilities, including extending your loan period, allowing patron reserves, etc. Each of these possibilities has proponents and opponents. Using this process, you can develop a comprehensive list of options without a lot of arguments. You can also get a sense of which options are perceived as having the potential for being the most effective.

What to Do

1. Identify the issue or question to be addressed.

2. Decide whom to include in the process. This may be an existing group or committee or it may be a group convened specifically for this process.

3. Write a short problem statement. This should be specific enough to help participants focus on the issue but open-ended enough to encourage creativity. The statement could include a list of questions that would encourage exploration of the topic.

4. At the beginning of the session, describe the process to be used and review the problem statement with the participants.

5. Give the participants five to ten minutes to write down their ideas on note cards without any discussion with others. Ask participants to use a new card for each idea.

6. Collect the cards and read the ideas, one at a time. Write the ideas on newsprint as they are read, so that everyone can see them. There is no discussion during this part of the process.

7. After all of the ideas have been recorded, encourage participants to discuss them. Participants may be asked to clarify their suggestions. They can express agreement or disagreement with any suggestion.

8. Give participants several minutes to select the five options they think are the most effective.

9. Tabulate choices and indicate which options received the most votes. One quick way to tabulate the choices is to use the dot exercise, described in the Groups: Reaching Agreement chapter of the Tool Kit.

10. Discuss the final list of options.

11. Use the options as the starting point for making a decision about the issue under review.

Delphi Method

Level of participation:
High

Range of options identified:
Moderate to high

Skill of facilitator/leader:
High

Time required:
High

The Delphi Method was developed by the RAND Corporation as a way of eliminating the problems of generating ideas in groups: dominant behaviors, peer pressure, etc. In this process the participants never meet face to face, and they normally don't even know who the other members of the group are. The participants are presented with a list of general questions about a specific topic and asked to prepare a written response. The responses are sent to a coordinator who edits and summarizes them into a single report. This report is returned to the participants with a second list of questions intended to clarify differences, and participants are again asked to respond. The responses from the second round are edited and summarized and sent to the participants one final time. In this third round, participants are provided with statistical feedback about how the group responded to particular questions as well as a summary of the group's comments. This makes the participants aware of the range of opinions and the reasons for those opinions. The group is then asked to rank the responses one final time. A final report is developed and sent to all participants.

This is by far the most complex of the methods for identifying options, and most library staff members have never participated in a process that used the Delphi Method. The drawbacks are obvious. The method is quite time-consuming for the participants and extremely time-consuming for the coordinator. Furthermore, this method, more than any of the others, can be seriously compromised if the wrong people are included as participants because their involvement is so much more intensive. However, real benefits can be gained from using the Delphi Method as well. It can be used to gather options from people with significant subject expertise regardless of where they live. It can also be used to facilitate communication among individuals who disagree strongly about the issue being discussed.

When to Use

The Delphi Method is a process that library managers should use sparingly. It is simply too complex and too expensive to be used as a regular tool. However, in some circumstances the effort might well be worth the time and energy invested. For instance, let's say you are the director of a library in a community with a growing Latino population. You want to provide services for this new population group, but you don't know where to start. Some board and staff members feel that you don't have the resources to provide quality services to your "regular" client groups and that it would be foolish to reach out to new groups. In this instance, using the Delphi Method to generate options from board members, staff members, members of the Latino community, and librarians in other communities with established service programs for Latinos might be quite effective. It would minimize the potential for open conflict and maximize the number of options that could be considered. All points of view would be presented, and everyone involved would have a chance to respond. Because the responses are anonymous, participants may be more responsive to other points of view and more open to revising their initial suggestions.

What to Do

1. Identify the issue or question to be addressed.

2. Select a coordinator to manage the Delphi Method, preferably one who has coordinated a similar process before or at least participated in such a process.

3. Select the people to be involved in the process. The majority of Delphi studies have used between fifteen and twenty respondents.[3]

4. Send the participants a description of the process; include the time frame. Participants have to agree to respond to three sets of questions.

5. Prepare a brief description of the issue or problem to be addressed and develop a short list of questions to be answered. Send both to each of the members. The initial questions will probably be general and open-ended.

6. Edit the responses and develop a set of follow-up questions based on the answers to the first questions. These follow-up questions will be more specific than the first open-ended questions. Send the edited responses and the second questions to the participants.

7. Tabulate the responses to each question, edit the comments, and prepare a third report. Send this to the participants for review, and ask them to answer the questions one final time.

8. Tabulate the responses into a final report. Send copies to all participants. Use the information in the report as the starting point for making a decision about the issue under review.

NOTES

1. United Way, *Measuring Program Outcomes* (Alexandria, Va.: United Way of America, 1996).

2. Center for Rural Studies, *Guidelines for Using the Nominal Group Technique*. Available: http://crs.uvm.edu/gopher/nerl/group/a/meet/Exercise7/b.html on 1/2/00.

3. Barbara Ludwig, "Predicting the Future: Have You Considered Using the Delphi Methodology?" *Journal of Extension* (Oct. 1997). Available: http://www.joe.org/joe/1997october/tt2.html on 4/11/00.

GROUPS
Reaching Agreement

Issues   Most public libraries make extensive use of committees and teams to explore options, make recommendations about future services, and review and evaluate existing programs. No matter what their purpose, all committees and teams have one thing in common: to be successful their members must be able to reach agreement on the issues under consideration. As anyone who has ever served on a committee knows, this isn't easy. Problems include lack of a clear committee or team charge, groups that are too large or too small, group leaders with poor facilitation skills, group members with competing agendas, lack of accountability, and the absence of official action on committee recommendations. These issues are discussed in more detail in the following sections.

The Charge

Every committee or team should have a clearly stated charge, and every member of the committee should understand that charge. The charge should include

> an explicit description of what the committee is expected to accomplish
>
> the time frame for the committee's deliberations
>
> the person or group that will receive the committee's report
>
> the process that will be used to review and act upon the committee's work
>
> the time frame for that review and action

Group Size

Committees and teams can range in size from two or three people to as many as twenty or thirty people. The decision concerning the size of the group is a trade-off. Smaller committees are usually easier to work with because fewer people are involved. Communication is quicker, orientation takes less time, discussion and consensus may move more quickly, and smaller committees are less expensive to support. However, smaller groups may be open to potential criticism of narrow thinking or elitism. If the workload you envision for committee members is heavy, a small group may be overwhelmed and burn out before the committee completes its work.

Larger committees usually reflect a wider range of interests and can include people with a variety of expertise. Because the interests of the members may be more diverse, a wider scope of issues might be addressed. On the other hand, meetings will require more time for discussion and reaching consensus. Some committee members may feel lost in the crowd and lose enthusiasm. Large groups are also more difficult to lead. If the group is going to have more than twelve members, it is advisable to make arrangements for a trained facilitator to be the leader.

Leadership

Committees and teams are most effective when they are led by people who understand how groups work and have strong facilitation skills. Most library committees and teams are responsible for problem solving or information gathering. In these types of group activities, leaders are responsible for involving all members of the group in the work of the group and ensuring that everyone has a say in the group's decisions. Generally, group members participate more and take a greater level of responsibility for the group's decisions if the leader focuses his or her energies on *facilitating participation* rather than on providing answers. See figure 20: Group Participation Chart, for more information on group leaders.

Membership

A committee or team is only as strong as its members. Group members normally play one of three roles:

Builders   These people are interested in the work of the committee and focus their energies on the successful completion of the group's charge.

Blockers   These people get in the way of the work of the committee by behaving in ways that block progress. There are dozens of behaviors that can derail an effective meeting. See figure 21: Problem Behaviors in Meetings for more information on blockers.

FIGURE 20
Group Participation Chart

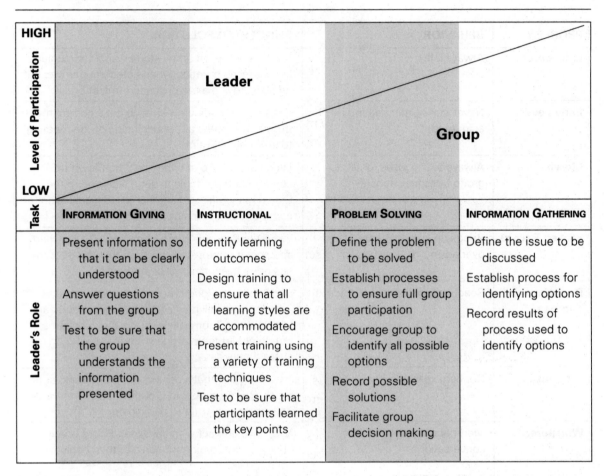

	INFORMATION GIVING	INSTRUCTIONAL	PROBLEM SOLVING	INFORMATION GATHERING
Leader's Role	Present information so that it can be clearly understood Answer questions from the group Test to be sure that the group understands the information presented	Identify learning outcomes Design training to ensure that all learning styles are accommodated Present training using a variety of training techniques Test to be sure that participants learned the key points	Define the problem to be solved Establish processes to ensure full group participation Encourage group to identify all possible options Record possible solutions Facilitate group decision making	Define the issue to be discussed Establish process for identifying options Record results of process used to identify options

Maintainers These people are more interested in maintaining relationships than in the work of the committee. They are the bridge between the builders and the blockers.

Every committee needs builders and maintainers and unfortunately, almost all committees have at least one blocker. It is the leader's responsibility to see to it that the members of the group, no matter what their primary motivation, work together effectively.

Accountability

Committees and teams should be held accountable for their actions, just as individuals are. All too often the old saying, "when everyone is responsible, no one is responsible" comes into play with committees. It is not only possible but desirable to make it clear to a group that they are collectively responsible for specific results.

FIGURE 21
Problem Behaviors in Meetings

PROBLEM	BEHAVIOR	SUGGESTED SOLUTION
Latecomer	Always late	Start meetings on time—don't wait for stragglers. Do not recap meeting when Latecomer arrives but offer to provide a recap during the first break.
Early Leaver	Never stays until meeting is adjourned	Set a time for adjournment and get a commitment from all members at the beginning of the meeting to stay until that time.
Clown	Always telling jokes; deflects group from task at hand	Laugh at the joke and then ask the Clown to comment on the topic under discussion. If the Clown responds with another joke, again ask for a comment on the topic.
Broken Record	Brings up same point over and over again	Write the Broken Record's concern on a flip chart and post it to provide assurance that the concern has been heard and will be addressed.
Doubting Thomas	Reacts negatively to most ideas	Encourage all group members to wait to make decisions until all points of view have been heard. Let Doubting Thomases express their concerns, but do not let them argue with others who do not share that negativity.
Dropout	Nonparticipant	Try asking Dropout's opinion during meeting or at break. Break group into groups of two or three to encourage everyone to participate
Whisperer	Members having private conversations	Make eye contact with speakers. Pause briefly until you have their attention and then begin to speak again.
Loudmouth	Must be center of attention; talks constantly	Acknowledge Loudmouths when they begin to talk and let them have their say. Then, if Loudmouths interrupt others, remind them that they have had their say.
Attacker	Makes very critical comments, often directed at leader	Thank Attacker for the observation; ask other group members what they think. If the person's attacks are directed at another group member, the leader has a responsibility to intervene. It is best to resolve these conflicts privately and not in front of the whole group.
Interpreter	Often says "In other words" or "What she really means"	Check this in public with the original speaker.
Know-It-All	Always has the answer	Remind the group that all members have expertise; that's the reason for meeting. Ask others to respond to Know-It-All's comments.
Teacher's Pet	Tries to monopolize the leader's attention	Be encouraging, but break eye contact. Get group members to talk to one another. Lessen your omnipotence by reflecting "What do you think?" back to the Teacher's Pet.

Action on Recommendations

If you ask any committee or group member what was the most frustrating thing about the group experience, far too many of them will say that they never saw any results from all of their work. Submitting a group report is often likened to Henry Wadsworth Longfellow's words: "I shot an arrow into the air, it fell to earth, I know not where." Library managers who appoint committees or teams to make recommendations have to establish processes for reviewing and acting on those recommendations. All group members should be aware of the review process and be kept informed of the status of the review from beginning to the point at which a final decision has been made.

Evaluating Methods of Reaching Decisions

Three general approaches to reaching agreement in groups are consensus building, voting, and the forced-choice process. Each of these decision-making approaches can be used effectively to lead the group to a decision. The important thing is matching the approach to the situation. Four measures can be used to help you decide which approach will be most effective for the situation: the importance of the quality of the decision made; the time it takes to make the decision; the level of support the members of the group have for the decision; and the learning that takes place while the members make the decision.

Quality of the Decision

The first measure is the importance of the quality of the decision that is produced. For example, a group that decides very quickly to vote to select priorities may not make as informed a decision as a group that spends the time needed to explore all of the options in detail before making a decision. On the other hand, not all situations are equally critical. Decisions such as where the group will eat lunch or when the next meeting will be held don't require extensive discussion.

Time Required

The second measure is the time it takes to reach the decision. To continue with the preceding example, the group that voted quickly obviously made a decision in less time than the group that explored options more fully. There is often a trade-off between the length of time a group spends on a decision and the quality of the final decision. However, that is not always true: At times groups get stuck in a seemingly endless process of data collection and discussion and never do make any decision—good or bad.

Level of Support

The third measure is the desired level of support the group will have for the decision that has been made. Consensus building, by its very nature, creates the highest level of group support for the decisions being made because everyone has to agree with the decisions before they become final. On the other hand, the forced-choice process, which averages choices made by group members to determine priorities, has the potential for resulting in decisions that none of the group supports whole-heartedly.

Development of Expertise

In some cases, it is important that the group members be given an opportunity to develop expertise in the area under consideration. For instance, if a team is going to be involved in making decisions about technology issues for the library for the next year, it is clearly important that the members of the team become knowledgeable about technology options and stay aware of changes in the field. In other cases, there is no need to support the development of such expertise. A committee of children's librarians who are responsible for developing and presenting a puppet show to publicize the summer reading program will probably have the expertise they need to accomplish their charge.

Methods for Reaching Agreement

Consensus Building

Quality of decision:
Normally very good
Time required:
Time intensive
Group support for decision:
High
Development of expertise:
High

Consensus building is a process by which group members seek a mutually acceptable resolution to the issue under discussion. Note that consensus does not mean that everyone agrees that the solution is the best of all possible answers. A group has reached consensus when everyone can and will support the decision.

When to Use

This approach is best suited for making important decisions. Consensus promotes hard thinking that really gets at the issues. It can be slow, and it is occasionally painful; however, when a group finally reaches consensus, it has developed a solution that will have the support needed for implementation. Since consensus requires so much energy, the group should agree that the outcome of the decision is worth the effort. Such outcomes might include long-range planning, the development of a new program or service, or the revision of the library's job descriptions. In each of these situations, people probably care deeply about the outcome, and their support will be required to successfully implement the decision.

What to Do

People reach consensus by talking about issues in a fair and open environment. That means that the group leader will have to ensure that each member of the group has an opportunity to be heard, that no idea is discarded without a thorough review and discussion, and that all members of the group take responsibility for finding a mutually agreeable decision.

The national bestseller *Getting to Yes: Negotiating Agreement Without Giving In* identifies four steps to reaching consensus.[1]

1. *Separate people from the problem.*
   People often feel strongly about issues under discussion, and discussions can shift quickly from issues to personalities. It is important to keep the discussion firmly focused on the problem under review.

2. *Focus on interests, not positions.*
   Positions are the opinions that each group member brings to the discussion before the discussion begins. These positions get in the way of reaching consensus because they tend to be "all or nothing." To reach consensus, group members will have to focus on the problem and their mutual interest in resolving it and not on their preconceived positions.

3. *Generate a variety of options before deciding what to do.*
   There is no one right way to do anything. Consensus building involves identifying and discussing all of the ways the problem might be resolved. This is surprisingly difficult. Most people see problem solving as narrowing the options, not expanding them.

4. *Base decisions on objective criteria.*
   This is a critical step in the consensus-building process. The group members must be able to define the criteria they will use to evaluate the options they have identified. If they can't agree on criteria, the group members are likely to revert to their positions when reviewing the options.

Voting

Quality of decision:
Varies
Time required:
Low to moderate
Group support for decision:
Moderate
Development of expertise:
Low to moderate

When people think about group decision-making processes, the first process that comes to mind is voting. Our whole society is based on the premise that the majority rules. We have all been voting on things since we were children. Voting is democratic, it's generally fair, and it's always quick and easy. However, there are some potential problems with voting. It can short-circuit consideration of all of the options, and if the issue is particularly contentious, it can split the group into winners and losers.

When to Use

If the decision under discussion is not critical and not worth a lot of discussion, it may be easiest to vote with a simple hand count. It is perfectly acceptable to take a hand count to decide where the group will have lunch. Hand counts can be used to make procedural decisions (how long the meetings will last, when the next meeting will be held, etc.).

If the decision is important, the dot exercise voting process is more flexible and allows group members to express their opinions in more detail. It also provides a visual summary of the group members' preferred choices. The dot exercise might be used to identify activities that would help the library achieve the goals and objectives in the long-range plan or identify topics for a staff-day program.

What to Do: Dot Exercise

The basic dot exercise process is quite straightforward. The process allows a large number of people to vote on a variety of options in a short period of time.

1. The leader first lists all the options on newsprint with enough space next to or between the items to allow committee members to place adhesive dots.

2. Each participant is given five self-adhesive colored dots.

3. The group members vote by putting dots on the flip chart sheets next to their choices. Members may vote for five separate items, or they may load their vote, or "bullet vote," by giving an item more than one dot.

4. Count the votes by totaling the number of dots by each item.

5. Share and discuss the outcome of the voting exercise. Does the outcome seem to reflect the earlier discussions? Are clear priorities and consensus emerging? Ask those who voted for items under discus-

sion that received few votes to talk about their reasons for selecting those items under discussion.

A variation on the basic dot exercise helps to balance the effect of "bullet voting," which occurs when members place more than one of their dots by a single option. If the group is large, the bullet votes of one or two people will not have much impact, but if the group is small, those one or two people can essentially set priorities for the entire committee. With a small group you might consider avoiding the impact of bullet voting by asking that committee members use a star to indicate their top priority. Then count votes by totaling the number of dots by each item and the number of stars by each item. Next, they share and discuss the outcome of the voting exercise. What is the difference, if any, between the priorities reflected by the dots and the stars? Does the outcome seem to reflect the earlier discussions? Are clear priorities and consensus emerging?

Forced Choice

Quality of decision:
  Varies

Time required:
  Low

Group support for decision:
  Low to moderate

Development of expertise:
  Low

Most people find it virtually impossible to compare the relative merits of more than three or four items. This process allows people to compare any number of items, each against the other, to determine which are the most important.

When to Use

The forced-choice process is an effective way of helping groups that have become mired in discussion to look at the options under review in a different way. The process does just what its name says: it forces people to make decisions from among a number of competing possibilities. The process also provides the information needed to place the options in priority order, based on the average ranking by each group member. That, however, is also the main weakness in the process. Because the priority of the options is determined by averaging, it is quite possible that the final list will not reflect the opinions of any single individual in the group. However, the process does identify items with little support. These can be excluded from the discussion, and one of the processes discussed in this chapter can be used to allow the group to move forward to reach final agreement on the remaining options.

What to Do

1. List the options under review and number each. It is easier for the group members to vote if each of them has a copy of the options.

2. Prepare a forced-choice workform (see figure 22: Sample Forced-Choice Workform for an example) and make a copy for each group member. The worksheet in figure 22 can be used to prioritize up to ten items. If you are working with more than ten items, you will need to modify the workform to allow for the extra choices.

3. Each of the group members will complete the forced-choice process. (See figure 22 for directions.)

4. After each group member totals the number of times each option was circled, the option with the highest total is the one with the highest priority for that person.

5. The leader will help the group see how the group members' selections compare with one another. This may be done in one of two ways:

Total the points for each choice from all of the group members. The choice with the highest total score is the most important; the next is the second most important, etc.

FIGURE 22
Sample Forced-Choice Workform

Assign a number to each of the activities you are prioritizing. This worksheet will help you evaluate up to 10 items against every other item, each time determining which of your choices is more important. Begin in column A. Compare the first and second items and circle the number of the one you think is more important (1 or 2). Continuing in column A, compare the first item and the third item, again circling the activity you think is more important (1 or 3). Continue through all of the columns.

A	B	C	D	E	F	G	H	I
1 2								
1 3	2 3							
1 4	2 4	3 4						
1 5	2 5	3 5	4 5					
1 6	2 6	3 6	4 6	5 6				
1 7	2 7	3 7	4 7	5 7	6 7			
1 8	2 8	3 8	4 8	5 8	6 8	7 8		
1 9	2 9	3 9	4 9	5 9	6 9	7 9	8 9	
1 10	2 10	3 10	4 10	5 10	6 10	7 10	8 10	9 10

To score your ratings, add the number of times you circled each number, and place the total by the appropriate number below. Note that you must add vertically and horizontally to be sure that you include all circled choices. The item with the highest number is the one you think is most important.

1 = ____   2 = ____   3 = ____   4 = ____   5 = ____   6 = ____   7 = ____   8 = ____   9 = ____   10 = ____

Determine where each of the group members ranked each option by asking how many ranked a given option as the highest priority, how many ranked it as the second highest priority, etc. In this case, the option with the highest average ranking becomes the highest priority.

NOTE

1. Roger Fisher and William Ury, and for the Second Edition, Bruce Patton, *Getting to Yes: Negotiating Agreement without Giving in,* 2d ed. (New York: Penguin Books, 1991), 10–11.

Library Communication

Issues   If practice really did make things perfect, we would all be master communicators. We certainly spend a large part of every day communicating, both as senders and receivers: We chat, write, advise, phone, leave and receive voice mail, remind, e-mail, read, page, meet, listen, lecture—and on and on. In spite of all of this communication, many people still feel uninformed, out-of-the-loop, and misunderstood, particularly in their work environments. There are many reasons for this apparent dichotomy.

Some of the reasons are quite basic. Many people don't fully understand the communication process itself. They are also unclear about the differences between personal and organizational communication and the functions of communication in a work environment. Even people who are familiar with communication theory can have problems putting it into practice. Most people deal with hundreds of messages every day and find it increasingly difficult to process all of the information they receive. Furthermore, there are more ways than ever to transmit information, and people don't always choose the best medium for the messages they are sending. The medium is not the only thing that can get in the way of successful communication. The message itself can be distorted by either the sender or the receiver—or by both. Sometimes the problem is not communication but the lack of communication or having the wrong people involved in the communication loop. These issues are discussed in more detail in the sections that follow.

Defining Communication

Many people think of communication as sending a message. In fact, that is only the first part of the communication process, and even that is not as simple as it might appear on the surface. As shown in figure 23, before

---

FIGURE 23
Effective Communication

EFFECTIVE COMMUNICATIONS OCCURS WHEN

a message

↓

is **understood by** its sender

↓

and **transmitted** through a medium

↓

to one or more **receivers**

↓

who **understand** it

↓

and **are affected** by it

---

a person can send an effective message, he or she has to *understand* the message. That should go without saying, but unfortunately it does not. Think about the number of times you have listened to a speaker who seemed to be confused or unsure of his or her message. If the sender doesn't understand the message, it is virtually impossible for the receiver to understand and act on it.

Once the sender understands the message, he or she has to transmit it through some medium. People can't read our minds (and it is just as well they can't), so we have to tell them what we are thinking. The medium we choose to transmit our message will affect how the message is received. (There is more information on matching the medium and the message later in this chapter.) The communication process does not end when a message is sent. For effective communication to occur, there must be one or more receivers who understand the message and are affected by it. Philosophers have long debated the question "If a tree falls in a forest and no one hears it, does it make a noise?" There is no such debate about communication. If you send a message and no one receives and understands it, you have not communicated.

People sending messages tend to blame the receivers when a message isn't understood or acted upon. However, that's not entirely fair. The responsibility for ensuring that the communication is completed rests with the sender. The person who initiates the communication has a reason for the communication and expects something to occur as a result of the communication. The receiver, who did not initiate the communication, must understand and accept the message to provide the expected response. While this is true in both formal and informal communications, it is more often a problem in the formal communication environment. Informal communications usually occur between two people or in small groups where it is easier to provide feedback and evaluate whether the message has been received. Formal communications, on the other hand, are often third-party communications that go through several layers of the organization. Therefore, there is less opportunity for feedback, and it may take longer to see if the message has been received, understood, and acted upon.

There are two main types of formal communication used in public libraries. One type includes all of the communications about the library to and with the public. The second type includes all internal communications among library staff members. It is this second type of formal communication that is the focus of this chapter.

Internal communications in public libraries have five main functions. They are used to

obtain information to make decisions

clarify job duties and provide feedback to staff

evaluate services and programs

maintain control (both formal and informal) by defining values and sharing the expected norms

meet the social and emotional needs of the staff

When any of these functions are not addressed adequately, library managers and staff find it difficult to provide quality library services.

Managers can do several things to help staff understand the importance of communication within the library. The most obvious is to provide training at all levels. Most staff have attended one or more programs on customer service, and as a part of that training they have received some basic information about communicating, particularly with difficult library users. However, it is also very helpful for all staff to attend at least one training program that focuses on the specific elements of effective communication. A program like this can provide tools to help staff develop messages that are clear and appropriate to the intended receiver, select the best medium for the message, and identify ways to get feedback to ensure that the message was received and understood.

All library managers and supervisors should also receive training in the functions of formal communication that includes discussions of how well each function is being addressed in the library. Follow up this training with meetings among managers to identify ways to improve formal communication in the library. Finally, the library director should include an ongoing review of the status of formal communication in the library as a part of regularly scheduled management meetings. This will help to identify problems early and to resolve them before there are serious consequences.

Sorting through the Cacophony

One of the biggest problems that we all have in receiving, understanding, and acting on incoming communications is that we receive so *many* messages. The sheer volume of information makes it difficult to sort out the messages that are important or urgent from those that are trivial or irrelevant. As already noted, it is up to the sender to help the receiver make these distinctions. The sender can do several things to help the receiver. By far the most important is to select the right medium for the message.

The Message and the Medium

Today there are more ways than ever before to "reach out and touch someone," and most of us haven't given a lot of thought to which way is the most effective in a given circumstance. Consider several things as you match the message and medium:

> Does the intended receiver have easy access to the medium being considered?
>
> Is the message complex, or is it fairly straightforward?
>
> Is the message important, or is it routine?
>
> Is the content ephemeral, or does it need to be maintained as a permanent record for documentation purposes?
>
> Is the message confidential?
>
> How soon does the message need to be received?

Think about these issues in relation to e-mail communications. Many library managers use e-mail as their prime method of communicating with library staff members—regardless of the message. There are several problems with this, not the least of which is that only in rare libraries do all staff members have personal e-mail accounts. Staff do not think of messages sent to a generic agency or unit e-mail address as personal messages. E-mail is also not a good medium to send long messages. As one staff member said, "I hit page down, page down, delete no matter how long the message is. I am not going to read a ten-page memo one screen at a time." E-mail is an ephemeral medium. Most people don't print out e-mail messages, and they don't file them electronically either. Therefore, it is difficult to refer back to an e-mail message if questions arise later. Finally, e-mail isn't a good medium to use for private or confidential messages. It is far too easy to hit the wrong button and send the message to a group instead of a single person or for one person to forward the message to another with a single keystroke.

Figure 24: Match the Message and the Medium lists ten common media used to transmit messages in public libraries in the left column and six criteria to consider when matching the message and the medium across the top of the table. Some of the decisions about matching the medium to the message are based on local conditions or the message itself, and they are labeled "?". For instance, someone wanting to deliver a message to a library director using the phone as the medium has every reason to assume that the director has easy access to a private phone. However, there is no reason to assume that a page or a part-time circulation attendant has that same easy access. As another example, a complex message could be delivered effectively to a small meeting of people who are directly affected by the message, particularly if the meeting is long enough to allow for thorough discussion. The same complex message could not be delivered as effectively to a large group of people consisting of some who are affected by it and others who are not.

It can be helpful for library managers to develop general guidelines concerning the media to be used to transmit certain types of messages. For instance, managers might decide that all messages dealing with human resource issues should be transmitted in written form, either through personal or group memoranda. Sometimes, the guidelines will be more general. The managers in one library developed the following

FIGURE 24

Match the Message and the Medium

MEDIUM	ACCESS	MESSAGE				
	Receiver Has Easy Access	Message Is Complex	Message Is Important	Permanent Record Is Required	Message Is Confidential	Message Is Urgent
Face-to-face conversation	✓	✓	✓		✓	✓
Telephone conversation	?*		✓		✓	✓
Meeting	?	?	✓	?		?
E-mail	?		?			✓
Individual letter or memo	✓	✓	✓	✓	✓	✓
Videotape or audiotape	?	?	?	✓		
Group letter or memo	?	?	?	✓		?
Policy and procedure manual	?	✓	✓	✓		
Web page	?			?		
Notice on a staff bulletin board	✓					

*? = depends on local conditions

preliminary guidelines for the types of messages that should be sent using e-mail:

- general information that can be sent quickly and easily
- nonconfidential messages
- short and concise messages (simple, ephemeral)
- messages that serve as means to send attachments
- scheduling for collaborative projects or meetings
- messages that don't require immediate feedback
- follow-ups to other communications
- reminders

These might not be the guidelines that you would develop in your library, but they can provide a starting place for discussion. The point is that library managers and staff should talk about how communication works in your library environment and what would make it more effective.

Repetition Works

Most experienced public speakers follow this traditional rule: Tell the audience what you are going to say, say it, and then tell the audience what you said. Many speakers also provide the content of their presentation in multiple formats, using both verbal messages (the presentation) and written messages (handouts, overheads, or PowerPoint presentations). These speakers have learned that people need to hear and see information several times before they can fully understand or accept it. This is particularly true if the message contains information that is completely new to the receivers or if the message contains information that the receivers aren't particularly pleased to hear.

It will be worth your time and energy to follow the example set by these speakers. Send important messages several times using several different media. No matter what media you use, remember to rephrase the key points several times and summarize the message in the final paragraph. This improves the odds that the receiver will not only get the message but will understand it and be affected by it. It also provides an opportunity for receivers to verify the information being transmitted. They can check the different versions of the messages they receive to be sure they understand what is being said. One caveat—don't rephrase so much that receivers look for differences, thinking they're getting a new message.

Dealing with Distortion

A message can be distorted by the sender or by the receiver or by both. The sender can distort a message by deliberately filtering the content. For example, a staff member who is unhappy about a new policy might send her supervisor a memorandum describing in detail the complaints she received from two library users about the policy but not mentioning the positive comments she received from ten other users. The sender can also accidentally distort the message in a number of ways. The sender might assume incorrectly that the receiver has certain background information and not provide needed data, or the sender might not understand the content clearly and therefore highlight the wrong data. Finally there is the message's language itself. Because most words have several meanings, some people will interpret a message one way and some another. The easiest way to avoid misinterpretation is to keep professional messages clear, complete, and concise. Use short words and short sentences. Ask several people to review important messages before they are transmitted to the receivers to be sure that the main points are unambiguous.

Receivers can also distort messages. Everyone perceives things a little differently based on his or her experiences, needs, and interests. Emotional reactions may be the most common reason that messages are distorted by receivers. When people are involved in personal crises they are less likely to pay attention to messages that don't deal directly with the crisis at hand. When people are angry or frustrated they are often not responsive to messages from the people or groups that they blame for the anger or frustration. What this means, among other things, is that messages that are likely to evoke strong emotions—especially messages that deal with significant change—have to be even more carefully written and broadly disseminated than other messages.

Lack of Communication

Not all communication problems deal with how a message is framed and delivered. Many staff members say that the biggest problem with communication in their libraries is too *little* communication. Perhaps the most common reason for lack of communication is simple oversight. We are all busy, and most of us feel overwhelmed on occasion. It takes time to communicate, and time is one of our most precious commodities. We also have a tendency to think, "If I know it, everyone must know it." The corollary to that is, "I don't know it, but everyone else must know it because no one else is asking." These two mind sets keep us from transmitting important information to others and from asking for the information that we need to do our jobs.

Sent but Not Received

Sometimes "lack of communication" doesn't mean the message wasn't sent; it may mean that an important message was sent once through a single medium. The sender may feel that the message has been delivered, but, as noted previously, the intended receivers may not have actually received the message. Perhaps the message was sent to branch/department managers who were instructed to pass the message on to their subordinates. If there is no requirement for feedback built into the process, there is no way for the original sender to know if all of the managers in the middle transmitted the message as instructed. It is not at all uncommon for a branch manager to return to the branch from a meeting with information that is to be passed on to all employees. Too often this is what happens:

> The manager sees employee 1 and gives her the complete message. The manager sees employee 2 ten or fifteen minutes later and gives him most of the message. Employees 3 and 4 run into the manager in the break room and get an abbreviated version of the message. Employee 5 doesn't see the manager at all today and is given a very brief summary tomorrow morning. Employee 6, who is out sick all week, never gets the message.

It is clear that employee 6 has been completely cut out of the communication loop, but even employee 1, who received the whole message, has no way of validating what she was told. Everyone but employees 3 and 4 was told something slightly different.

Sent Too Late

Sometimes information is disseminated too late to be useful to a specific audience. Consider this scenario:

January 15	The administrative team considers a policy change, and an individual, committee, or task force is asked to develop a draft of the new policy.
March 1	The draft policy is reviewed by the administration team.
March 15	The draft policy is sent to senior managers for review and comment.
April 15	The administrative team discusses reactions from the senior managers and makes changes in the draft as needed.
May 15	The draft of the policy is sent to branch/department managers for review and comment without explicit instructions that they should share the draft with staff. Consequently some managers share it, and some don't.
July 1	The administrative team discusses reactions from branch/department managers and makes changes in the draft as needed.

August 1   The policy is officially approved by the chief adminis-
            trator and sent to all units.

August 15   The policy is officially scheduled to be implemented.

August 16   Frontline staff, who actually have to implement the pol-
            icy, complain that they were not informed. Managers
            can't understand what the staff are talking about. After
            all, the new policy has been under discussion for more
            than nine months.

Variations on this scenario are played out in libraries across the country over and over again. It is critical to involve the staff who will be affected by a new policy in discussions about that policy early in the planning stages and to be sure that the staff who have to implement policies and procedures are fully trained before the implementation process begins.

Library Intranets

Some library managers are using the library intranet to provide staff with the information they need to do their jobs more effectively. The intranet can be used to provide access to a broad array of information, including policies and procedures, committee/task force information (membership, agendas, minutes, reports), staff directories, training schedules, job post-ings, PR announcements, etc. The most important benefit to providing information through the intranet is that all staff have access to it, and they can access it whenever it is convenient. The second benefit is that information can be loaded on the intranet fairly easily and can be up-dated without a lot of trouble. This is particularly important for library policies and procedures, which are very difficult to keep current at the unit level in paper formats. A third benefit is that, with proper design, most information on the intranet can be searched by key word. This makes finding and using the information much easier.

Evaluating Communication Processes

Four general models that describe the way information is transmitted in libraries include downward communication, downward-and-upward communication, horizontal communication, and diagonal communica-tion. No one of these models is intrinsically superior to the others. At times each is appropriate to use. The important thing to remember is that in libraries with effective communication, all four of these models are used regularly. Four measures can be used to help you decide which model will be most effective for a given situation: distribution of information, ability to verify information, need for acceptance from the receiver, and time required for the transmission.

Distribution of Information

The first measure to use when deciding which model is appropriate is how widely the information needs to be distributed. Does everyone in the organization need to know? Do you need to have some verification that the message has been received? Remember, the more ways you send a message, the more likely it is that the people you are targeting will actually receive, understand, and be affected by the information in the message.

The Ability to Validate Information

The second measure to use when deciding which model is appropriate is the need for the receiver to validate the information being received. Most people have no desire to validate simple messages or messages of little importance. However, people often need to be able to corroborate messages that are complex or messages that contain information they are unfamiliar with or unhappy about.

Need for Acceptance from the Receiver

The third thing to consider when selecting a communication model is the degree to which it is important that the receiver accept the information in the message. Some messages are purely informational, and it doesn't matter a lot to the sender if the receivers accept or reject the information. The announcement that the library board will be holding their regularly scheduled meeting on July 21 is an example of such a message. However, in some instances it is critical to the sender that the receivers not only understand the message but that they accept the information in the message as accurate and valid and act upon the information in a specific way. Suppose a message is disseminated announcing a new policy and procedures for managing patron reserve requests. Staff who receive the message must not only understand the new policy and procedures, they must also put them into practice on a specified date. This is far more likely to occur if staff are familiar with the changes, understand why the changes are being made, and agree that the changes are reasonable and necessary. In general, the more involvement the staff have in the decision-making process, the more accepting they are of the final decision. Therefore, communication models that allow for discussion and interaction are the most effective way to deal with issues that require staff acceptance.

Time Required

The fourth thing to consider when selecting a communication model is time. If there is only one way to do something or if a decision has already been made, then it makes sense to transmit the message in the fastest way possible. Communication processes that allow for staff feedback and for staff involvement in decision making are time-intensive. The more participation you allow, the more time-intensive the process becomes. If the issue under consideration is important and staff involvement is critical, then invest the time needed to resolve it effectively. You will probably find that the initial investment in time pays off in significant time savings during the implementation phase.

Methods for Communicating in Your Library

Downward Communication

Distribution of information:
  Moderate

Ability to verify information:
  Low

Acceptance of receiver:
  Low

Time required:
  Low

Downward communication is also known as "bureaucratic" communication. Messages are sent down the chain of command throughout the library. In many libraries, this is the most frequently used communication model. Downward communication often reflects a centralized managerial style in which decisions are made by senior managers; middle managers and staff are expected to implement those decisions with little or no input. It is rare for centralized decisions that were communicated downward to have a high level of staff acceptance.

The most significant benefit of downward communication is efficiency. It is by far the fastest and easiest of the four communication models. However, that efficiency has a price. There is no way for the sender to be sure that message was distributed throughout the library nor is there a way for the intended receiver to know that he or she didn't receive the message. This is important because there are often breaks in the bureaucratic delivery chain. Some of these breaks are accidental—a manager might be out sick for several days and unable to send the message, but others are deliberate—a manager might disagree with the information in the message and not pass it on. Part-time workers are often unintentionally excluded from the downward communication chain because they aren't at work when messages are being delivered to the rest of the staff. Even messages that are delivered to all intended recipients may be garbled as they move from one level in the organization to the next. Remember the game of "Telephone" in which a message that is passed through a chain of ten people is changed completely by the end of the chain?

When to Use

Downward communications can be used effectively to send simple messages that are intended to distribute general information that requires little or no action on the part of the receiver.

What to Do

1. Make it explicitly clear to managers that they are responsible for ensuring that all downward communications reach all employees.
2. Put all messages to be sent throughout the library in writing.
3. Number each message consecutively, and keep a copy for reference.
4. Clearly label all messages sent downward through the library as "For Your Information."
5. Check periodically to see if messages are being transmitted throughout the library by asking a sampling of people at all levels if they received a given message.
6. Keep each message brief.
7. Start the message with the most important information and then provide supporting data, if needed.
8. Focus on a single topic in each message. If you have several different kinds of information to share, send several separate messages.
9. Post copies of all messages sent downward through the library on the library intranet so that employees can refer to them easily.

Downward-and-Upward Communication

Distribution of information:

Moderate to high

Ability to verify information:

Moderate

Acceptance of receiver:

Moderate

Time required:

Low to moderate

Downward-and-upward communication is also known as "two-way" communication. It follows the chain of command in the library but includes formal processes for ensuring that information flows in both directions. General staff meetings in which downward communications are presented and discussed are one common example of two-way communication.

The most important benefit of two-way communication is that it gives the receivers a chance to verify the data in the message to be sure that they understand it. Downward-and-upward communication provides a mechanism for receivers to formally express their opinions about the information in a message to the people who sent the original message. If the receivers believe that their opinions are taken seriously, they are more likely to accept the content of the message.

There are, however, a number of drawbacks to downward-and-upward communications. Because the process usually follows the structure of the library bureaucracy, the successful transmission of the communication in both directions is dependent on individual managers to provide a conduit for two-way information. Unfortunately, most libraries have at least one manager who blocks the flow of information rather than facilitating it. Even managers who make a good-faith effort to promote two-way communication have differing communication skills and attitudes. As a result, staff in each unit of the library probably get slightly different messages. This model provides no way for staff to validate information among units.

When to Use

Three main categories of messages can be effectively disseminated using two-way communication processes. First, all formal employee-supervisor communications should be both downward and upward. One example is the performance appraisal process in which employees and their supervisors discuss goals and objectives at the beginning of the year and then evaluate progress at the end of the year. Another example is the formal grievance process.

The second category includes all messages that transmit decisions that will affect staff duties and responsibilities. Some of these decisions, such as city or county policies or information about the library budget, will have been made without significant staff input. Other decisions will have been made after extensive discussion using horizontal and diagonal communication processes. Sometimes the participants in committee and task force meetings forget that not everyone has been as involved in the decision-making process as they have. As a result, decisions are made but not formally shared with the entire staff. It is appropriate to share these final decisions using a downward-and-upward communication process. Be sure to include a brief description of the participative process used to reach the decisions in your message.

The final category of messages that can be delivered using downward-and-upward communications are messages containing suggestions from staff and the public for improving services or changing policies. These are messages that originate with staff and are passed up through the chain of command for action. When the recommendations have been acted upon, messages are sent back to the originating staff to inform them of the action taken.

What to Do

1. Personnel communications
   a. Review your performance appraisal process to be sure that it provides a mechanism for two-way communication.

b. Require supervisors to communicate with employees about their performance regularly throughout the year.

c. Ensure that all staff are aware of the grievance process.

2. Disseminating decisions

a. Make it explicitly clear to managers that they are expected to serve as conduits for information—both downward and upward.

b. Provide training to help managers improve their communication skills and learn to facilitate group discussions.

c. Clearly label messages that are intended to be discussed by managers and staff as "For Discussion."

d. Include a date by which feedback and questions about the information in the message are due to be submitted to a single person.

e. Develop a specific format for managers to use to submit feedback, and use it consistently. For example:
   Issue discussed
   Date discussed
   With whom
   General reaction
   Questions
   Suggestions

f. Prepare and distribute a final message that summarizes the feedback and describes what actions, if any, have been taken to respond to the feedback.

g. Monitor the feedback that is received over a period of time. If you notice that some managers rarely provide feedback, speak to them to determine why.

3. Suggestions from the staff and the public

a. Develop a specific form for staff and for public suggestions and make the suggestion forms readily available.

b. Provide a link on the library Web page to a public suggestion form and make sure someone is assigned to retrieve and process the suggestions.

c. Provide an electronic version of the staff suggestion form on the library intranet.

d. Consider posting selected staff and public suggestions on the intranet for staff to review. Include some indication of the disposition of the suggestion.

e. Make sure that staff and the public know when actions are taken as a result of a suggestion.

Horizontal Communication

Distribution of information:
Low to moderate

Ability to verify information:
High

Acceptance of receiver:
High

Time required:
Moderate to high

Horizontal communications in libraries normally take place in regularly scheduled meetings of people with similar positions who work in different units of the library. Common examples include children's librarian meetings, circulation attendant meetings, branch manager meetings, and main library unit manager meetings.

Horizontal groups provide peer support for their members and can significantly improve staff morale. They are the ideal forum for developing new and innovative services or programs and for solving problems in specialty areas that affect more than one library unit. Horizontal groups also provide a mechanism for staff in various library units to verify all kinds of messages that have been distributed downward through the organization.

However, horizontal groups are not always the best way to disseminate information to other staff members in the library. Often the members of the group place far more value on communicating with each other than on communicating with nongroup members. This can cause real problems for library managers who expect horizontal group members to share information with other staff in their units. If a library manager announces a change in circulation policy to the members of the circulation attendant group and asks them to pass the word, that manager cannot assume that everyone who needs to know about the change will be informed. In fact, it is highly probable that some group members will not pass on the message and that some unit managers will be irritated (to say the least) that they were not informed directly.

The primary drawback with horizontal groups is the time they take staff from other activities. Horizontal meetings usually occur monthly. Someone has to plan the meeting, and participants have to travel to a single location for their meeting and then spend one to three hours in the meeting before traveling back to their library unit. Next, someone has to write the minutes from the meeting and pass on any recommendations from the group to the managers who can act on the recommendations. Many library managers resent the scheduling problems that result from staff participation in horizontal meetings.

When to Use

Most participants of horizontal groups benefit from their participation in those groups and use their meetings to discuss ways to improve the services they offer. However, many libraries offer the opportunity to participate in a horizontal group only to selected staff members, generally children's staff and unit managers. Library managers should discuss the benefits that would result from encouraging members of other horizontal groups to meet regularly. Some possibilities to consider are reference staff, staff who serve people with special needs, technical support staff (formal or informal) in each unit, paraprofessional staff, and staff with materials selection responsibilities.

What to Do

1. Provide an opportunity for members of any horizontal group in the library to meet if they wish to and if they can explain the benefits that will result from their meetings.

2. Make sure that all members of a horizontal group are given equal opportunity to meet with the group.

3. Establish a regular schedule for each group to meet.

4. Identify a group leader. This can be an appointed or elected position and can remain the same year after year or change annually.

5. Develop a specific format for horizontal group agendas and minutes, and expect all groups to use it.

6. Ask each group to prepare an agenda (using the standard format) for each meeting and distribute it to all participants and all managers at least one week before the meeting. If you have a library intranet, post all agendas there.

7. Ask each group to have someone responsible for preparing minutes from each meeting (using the standard format) and distributing them to all participants and all managers within one week of the meeting. If you have a library intranet, post all minutes there.

8. Establish a formal process for reviewing the recommendations received from horizontal groups and for acting on those recommendations.

9. Disseminate the final actions taken on recommendations from horizontal groups to all staff members using the downward-and-upward communication model. If for some reason a decision is made not to implement one or more of the recommendations, be sure to explain why.

Diagonal Communication

Distribution of information:
  Moderate to high

Ability to verify information:
  High

Acceptance of receiver:
  High

Time required:
  High

The most common diagonal communication models in libraries are cross-functional work groups that include people with different job classifications who work in different units of the library. The two types of cross-functional groups are task forces and teams. Cross-functional task forces are normally convened for a specific purpose; when the task is completed, the task force is disbanded. Cross-functional teams, on the other hand, generally have continuing responsibilities. For example, a task force might be appointed to coordinate the selection of a new automation system for the library. When the system has been selected, the task force will have completed its work. On the other hand, a cross-functional team might be appointed to monitor library safety issues. The members of the team might change, but the team itself would be ongoing.

Cross-functional teams and task forces are the most open of the communication models. They encourage communication among all staff at all levels. This, in turn, allows staff to verify messages received through any of the other models. Cross-functional teams and task forces also give staff members a very real voice in the decision-making process, which significantly increases staff acceptance of the final decisions.

While cross-functional groups have strengths, they also have some drawbacks. The most obvious drawback is the time it takes to bring disparate people from all over the library system together to discuss a problem and identify possible solutions. In addition, some members of these groups might find it difficult to remember they were appointed to represent a specific constituency and instead promote their personal views. The reverse can be true as well. Sometimes the members of a constituent group don't trust the person selected to represent them. Furthermore, some task forces do not include people with skills and knowledge required to accomplish the task. Others include people with diametrically opposed positions who refuse to consider compromise. Teams and task forces function most effectively if they are led by an experienced facilitator who has credibility with the members of the team and other stakeholders.

When to Use

Most libraries use cross-functional teams and task forces differently. Cross-functional teams are appointed to discuss ongoing issues that affect all staff and to make recommendations when appropriate. Different libraries will have different teams depending on local conditions. Examples of teams include the safety team mentioned previously and staff development teams. Generally the membership of a team changes each year, but the team charge remains the same. Teams give staff members a forum to discuss issues of ongoing interest or concern and provide managers with recommendations for action and with feedback about staff attitudes.

Almost all task forces address some aspect of decision making. Some task forces provide the information needed to reach a decision. Other task forces are responsible for determining how to implement a decision that has been made. Yet other task forces are responsible for actually implementing a decision. The members of each task force must understand both their responsibility and their authority clearly.

Task forces should be used when the decision under consideration or being implemented will have a significant effect on the way most or all staff members do their jobs. Never appoint a task force to consider an issue that you, as a manager, know how you want to handle. More than one library manager has appointed a task force firmly believing the task force would recommend a specific action. When the task force made a different recommendation (and they almost always do), the manager had a serious problem: He could either adopt the task force recommendation even though it was not at all the way he wanted to solve the problem or he could do what he intended to do all along and alienate the members of the task force and the rest of the staff. Neither option is attractive.

What to Do

1. Identify a clear charge for each task force or team that is appointed.

2. Determine which library constituencies should be represented on the task force or team. Make it clear to everyone that the people asked to be members of the task force or team are expected to represent their specific constituencies and not their own personal points of view.

3. Require task force and team members to report regularly to the constituent groups they represent.

4. Establish a time line for each task force that includes a deadline for the receipt of recommendations and a deadline for taking action on those recommendations.

5. Disseminate the charge and membership of every team and task force to all staff. Include information on the time line for all task forces. If any of this information changes, notify all staff that the changes have occurred. If you have a library intranet, this information can be posted there.

6. Develop a specific format for task force and team agendas and minutes, and expect all groups to use it. Consider using the same form used for horizontal groups.

7. Ask each task force and team to prepare an agenda (using the standard format) for each meeting and distribute it to all participants and all managers in the library at least one week before the meeting. If you have a library intranet, post all agendas there.

8. Ask each task force and team to have someone responsible for preparing minutes from each meeting (using the standard format) and distributing them to all participants and all managers within one week of the meeting. If you have a library intranet, post all minutes there.

9. Establish a formal process for reviewing the recommendations received from task forces and teams and for acting on those recommendations.

10. Disseminate the final actions taken on task force and team recommendations to all staff members using the downward-and-upward communication model. If for some reason a decision is made not to implement one or more of the recommendations, be sure to explain why.

Presenting Data

Issues

Public library staff and managers collect a wide variety of information about library services and programs. In theory, five main reasons for collecting all of this data are to

- measure progress toward accomplishing the goals and objectives in the library's strategic plan
- document the value of library services
- make resource allocation decisions
- meet the requirements of a grant project
- meet state library data collection requirements

In practice, much of the information that is collected in libraries is never used at all, and when managers attempt to use the information they collected, they often have problems presenting the information effectively.

The first and most basic problem with presenting data concerns the selection of which data elements to use to support the intended outcomes. This is trickier than it appears. Too little data is unhelpful; too much data is overwhelming; and the wrong data is misleading. The second problem is the difficulty some people have in organizing data. This was a more serious problem when we had to use adding machines and ledgers to analyze data; today we have a variety of computer software programs that help to manipulate and organize data. However, we still have to have a coherent reason for the organizational decisions that we make; otherwise, the data won't make sense. The third problem has to do with the layout and design of the data. It doesn't do any good to select the right data elements and organize the data elements in a logical pattern if you don't present them in a clear and attractive manner. These issues will be discussed in more detail in the following sections.

Selecting the Right Data

Before you can begin to select data for any purpose you have to know who your audience is and what that audience needs to see to make a decision or reach a conclusion. If you are making a presentation intended to encourage seventh grade students to use the library, there isn't much point in telling about the increase in the number of senior citizens who use the library for personal development and ongoing learning. If you are making a presentation to senior citizens about the opportunities for life-long learning at the library, they probably won't be interested in the number of hits on your homework help Web page or the rapidly increasing circulation of game cartridges.

Knowing your audience goes beyond understanding their interests. You also have to have some idea of what they already know and what they don't know. If you present information on document delivery to library managers, you can reasonably assume they will know you are talking about interlibrary loan, reserves, and the delivery of requested items among the various units in the library. If you present information on document delivery to the members of the city council, they may well assume you are talking about services to the homebound.

There are two kinds of data: quantitative and qualitative. Quantitative data is numeric and measures *how much* of something there is and *how often* something happens. Most library data is quantitative (circulation figures, number of reference questions, number of users who log-on to the Internet, number of online searches, etc.). Qualitative data comes from observations or interviews and results in patterns or generalizations about *why* something occurs. The information obtained from a series of focus groups on business services is qualitative data. Both types of data can be effective. Figure 25 lists nine common purposes for collecting data and suggests which type of data would be most effective in each case.

No matter which types of data you decide best meet your needs, be selective about the specific data elements to include. Too much data is worse than too little. However, once you select the data elements you want to use, be sure to include the *entire* data set for each element. Let's say you want to explain to the members of the library board the relation between increased use of electronic resources and decreased print and media circulation. After reviewing all of the possible data elements, you might select *circulation figures* and *number of electronic searches* as the two data elements that would best illustrate what is happening. The data set for circulation includes all of the different categories of circulation you count. You may not want the board to focus on the increase in the circulation of media items, but once you decide to use circulation figures you have to include them all. In the same way, to present an accurate picture of the number of electronic searches, you will have to include all electronic searches that take place using library equipment, both on and off

FIGURE 25
Quantitative and Qualitative Data

PURPOSES	QUANTITATIVE DATA	QUALITATIVE DATA
Measure number of people who use a service or program	✓	
Show reasons for current use		✓
Show trends in the numbers of people who use a service or program	✓	
Show relations between trends in current use	✓	
Show reasons for trends in current use		✓
Measure user satisfaction		✓
Measure units of library service delivered	✓	
Show trends in units of library service delivered	✓	
Measure cost per unit of service delivered	✓	

site, and both CD-ROM and Internet. It is equally important to include the full set of data elements when you use qualitative data. If you decide to report on public reaction to a new service, you have to report all of the reactions, not just the positive ones.

The key to all of this is to be as honest as you can with the statistics you select and present. You will want to be able to explain why you chose the data elements you are using and the source of each. It is also important that you check and double-check your numbers. If one number is inaccurate, it doesn't matter how carefully you selected the data elements you included or how accurate the rest of the numbers are: The single inaccurate number will taint the entire report.

Organizing the Data

Once you have selected the data elements to use, you have to decide how to organize the information so that it is clear and easily understood. Three basic organizational models that you might want to consider are historical order, priority order, and narrative logic. Your choice from among these three options depends on what you are trying to accomplish, what data elements are available, and which of three options seems most logical to you.

What you want to avoid is the fourth option—no particular order. This is just what it sounds like—data elements are arranged without pattern and in no conscious order. This makes it difficult for the person using the data to deliver a coherent presentation and makes it even harder for the audience to understand what is being presented. Think about how hard it would be to follow a presentation about library services that started with juvenile circulation figures, moved to general budget numbers, took a side trip to present data about attendance at the summer reading program, then talked about adult circulation, and finally ended with information about the cost for new electronic resources.

Historical Order

When you use the historical order organizational model, you present information about trends in the areas being considered. These trends provide a context in which to consider data about current services or programs. This is a particularly useful model when you are presenting information about programs or services that are experiencing significant changes. If adult nonfiction circulation has dropped 20 percent in the past five years, that is important information to have when you are considering your materials budget. If media circulation has increased by 15 percent during the same period, that is also important to know. Of course, you can't use historical order if you don't have historical data, which is often the case when you are presenting data about new services or programs.

Priority Order

When you use priority order as the organizational model, you present the most important data first and then provide less important supporting data. This is similar to the journalistic style of the inverted pyramid. It is a useful model if you are presenting a number of different data elements to support a specific proposal. Let's say you are reporting on the use of the library's electronic resources during the eighteen months since you began to allow users to dial in from off-site to use the library's databases and connect to the Internet. The most important data element would be number of log-ons from off-site, and you would start your report with that. You might then choose to include data on the number of searches and the number of items retrieved to give the audience an idea of how the off-site access is actually being used.

Narrative Logic

When you use narrative logic as the organizational model, you arrange the data to tell a story. This model can be very effective when trying to sell a new idea or program. It allows you to create a script that moves the audience from one step to the next until they finally reach the conclusion you want them to reach. Often the story starts with information that the audience already knows (once upon a time . . .). Confirming prior knowledge builds credibility into the sales process. Then you select and present the data that best supports each of the key points in your story.

Designing the Document

The final thing to consider when presenting data is the layout and design of the data. In some ways, this is the most important part of the process. After all, if no one looks at the data you have selected and organized, all of your efforts will have been wasted. The first step in the design process is to create a document that is attractive and visually appealing. The document will have to look inviting enough to encourage busy people to take time to pick it up and start reading it. Next you want to be sure that the information in the document is clear and easy to read. Most of the people in your audience are too busy to spend a lot of time trying to decipher a jumble of confusing words and charts.

Graphic design is visual information management using the tools of layout, typography, and illustration to lead the reader's eye through the page.[1] The layout of the document is the first thing readers will see. They will observe the balance of white space and text and the proportion of text and graphics. A page that has little or no white space is not user friendly; neither is a page filled with a jumble of graphics. You are looking for a balance between text and graphics surrounded by enough white space to provide an effective frame.

Create a basic layout and style sheet and use it consistently throughout the document. Select a single, readable font to use for text and graphics. Match your text and your graphics and try to keep the size of the visuals proportionate. A number of excellent books on graphic design are available that will provide additional suggestions and illustrations to help you create an effective document. Remember, in graphic design, as in so much else, simple is always better. You want the audience to focus on the content, not on the graphics.

Evaluating Methods of Presenting Data

Most library managers present data in three main ways: narrative descriptions, tables, and graphs and charts. Each can be used effectively in certain circumstances. You can also use two or all three of the methods together to improve the chances that your audience will receive and understand the information you are presenting. To help you select the best method or combination of methods for your purpose, think about the following:

How long will it take to develop the presentation, and what level of skill will be required?

How important is it that the information be presented in a visually attractive and interesting way?

How easy will it be to read and understand the final product?

Will the audience be expected to understand the relationship among various data elements?

These questions are addressed in more detail in the following sections.

Time and Skill

The first issue to consider when selecting a method of presentation is the time and skill required to develop the presentation. It can take considerable time and technical skill to create high-quality charts and graphs. Narrative descriptions and tables are normally much easier and quicker to develop. Consider these questions when deciding how much time and energy to invest in developing a presentation:

Is the target audience internal or external? Normally, library managers are willing to invest more time in presentations for external audiences.

Is the data being presented for informational purposes, or do you want it to result in a decision? It makes sense to spend more time on presentations that are intended to help people reach a decision.

How frequently will the final product be used? Some presentations will be used a number of times, while others will be used just once. It is worth investing the time and energy needed to ensure that the template for your monthly report to the city manager is a high-quality product because you will be using it repeatedly.

What is the easiest and simplest method that can be used to achieve what needs to be accomplished?

Visual Appeal

The second issue to consider when selecting a method of presentation is the need to present the information in a visually attractive manner. It is always important that information be readable, but if you are presenting information to staff, you may be less concerned about making it attractive and interesting than you would be if you were presenting the same information to the members of the chamber of commerce. Most library managers routinely "clean things up" for external use. Visual presentations tend to be more appealing and interesting than text presentations. They also usually take considerably longer to develop.

Simplicity and Clarity

The third issue to consider when selecting a method of presentation is the ease with which the data can be read and understood. Some kinds of data are easier to understand than others. A single data point can be presented very nicely using a narrative description. On the other hand, as you will see in figure 26: Narrative Descriptions, it is difficult to use narrative description to present complex historical data about several different categories of information.

Depiction of Relationships

The last question to consider when selecting a method of presentation is whether there are relationships among the data elements that you want to highlight. Most people find it easier to see such relationships when they are presented in graphs and charts rather than in narrative form. The old saying "a picture is worth a thousand words" is as true about data as it is about describing a sunset.

Methods for Presenting Data

Narrative Descriptions

Time and skills:
   Low

Visual appeal:
   Low

Simplicity and clarity:
   Low to moderate

Depiction of relationships:
   Moderate

Narrative descriptions use text to present quantitative and qualitative data and describe the relationship, if any, among data elements. Before library managers had easy access to personal computers and spreadsheet programs, they presented a great deal of library information using narrative descriptions. Even now, some managers rely heavily on narrative descriptions because they are quick and easy to prepare and do not require any special computer skills.

At times narrative descriptions can be effective (see When to Use), but they have some serious drawbacks when used as your primary presentation method. The most obvious problem is that blocks of text aren't very attractive or interesting. It can also be confusing to read about a variety of data elements with no easy way to keep track of them. Although you can use narrative descriptions to describe the relationship among several data elements, the relationship would probably be clearer if you included a table or graph.

FIGURE 26
Narrative Description

CIRCULATION BY TYPE OF MATERIAL

The circulation patterns in the library have changed over the past five years. The most significant change has been in the circulation of nonfiction materials. In 1997, 28 percent of the total circulation in the library came from adult nonfiction items and approximately 12 percent came from children's nonfiction; the combined circulation of children's and adult nonfiction items represented 40 percent of the total circulation. In 2001, the circulation of adult nonfiction materials was 19 percent of the total circulation and an additional 9 percent came from children's nonfiction. The combined circulation of children's and adult nonfiction materials was only 28 percent of the total circulation. That represents a 12 percent decrease over a five-year period.

On the other hand, the circulation of media materials increased from almost 13 percent to almost 20 percent of total circulation between 1997 and 2001. The change in the percentage circulation of fiction materials has been more moderate. In 1997, 25 percent of the total circulation came from adult fiction materials and almost 22 percent of circulation came from children's fiction; total fiction circulation was 47 percent of the overall circulation. In 2001, 27 percent of the circulation came from adult fiction materials and 25 percent came from children's fiction; total fiction circulation was 52 percent, a 5 percent increase.

Figures 26 through 30 present the same data in a variety of ways. Read the description in figure 26, and then look at the table in figure 27 and the graphs and charts in figures 28 through 30. Which of the options do you think presents the information most effectively? Why?

When to Use

Narrative description can be an effective way to present information gathered through focus groups or other qualitative data collection processes because qualitative data is often narrative rather than numeric. Narrative descriptions can also be used effectively to present a few simple statistics and to discuss the relationship among them. You might also find narrative descriptions helpful when you are presenting information that is new or unfamiliar to your audience. The narrative process makes it easy to include background and introductory information.

Whenever you use narrative description to present data, read the final product carefully to see if your points would be clearer if you included one or more tables or charts. In general, narrative descriptions work best when used in conjunction with one of the other methods of presenting data.

What to Do

1. Treat the narrative description as you would any other written presentation. Include an introduction, a body, and a conclusion. If the description is longer than a page, consider using heads and subheads to break up the text.

2. If it takes more than one short paragraph to describe the actual data, consider including a table or graph.

3. Keep it simple. Use short words and sentences.

4. Be very aware of layout and page design. Large blocks of text are boring and can be intimidating.

5. Include the date the narrative description was written.

Tables

> **Time and skill:**
> Low
>
> **Visual appeal:**
> Moderate
>
> **Simplicity and Clarity:**
> Moderate
>
> **Depiction of relationships:**
> Low

Tables present information in a grid format (see figure 27) and provide a relatively easy way to display a considerable amount of information. Library managers often use tables to present data because tables don't require sophisticated computer skills to prepare and can be put together fairly quickly.

Tables are more visually interesting than text, but they can be harder to read and understand than charts or graphs. It is often difficult to identify trends and relationships among the data presented in tables, particularly if the table includes a lot of data. State libraries publish public library statistical reports annually. These reports present data about public library services and

FIGURE 27
Table

CIRCULATION BY TYPE OF MATERIAL

	1997	1998	1999	2000	2001
Media (tapes, CDs, etc.)	38,900	46,650	60,877	63,450	65,980
Adult fiction	78,090	79,950	82,074	85,375	87,430
Adult nonfiction	88,098	84,650	76,220	70,580	63,250
Children's fiction	67,991	71,600	76,909	81,649	83,230
Children's nonfiction	36,500	36,480	34,815	32,112	30,980
Total	**309,579**	**319,330**	**330,895**	**333,166**	**330,870**

resources in tabular form. The tables typically have five or more columns, and they can have hundreds of rows—one for each public library in the state. These endless rows of numbers are very difficult to read, and it is virtually impossible to use them to identify trends or relationships. Most state libraries are now making this statistical data available electronically, which allows the user to manipulate the data to create more focused tables and to develop charts that illustrate trends or relationships.

When to Use

You can use tables to present a variety of information, both numeric and textual. Tables work best when you are dealing with a limited number of data elements and a small set of data. The table in figure 25: Quantitative and Qualitative Data is effective because it presents relatively simple data in an easily read and understood format. If the same information were presented in a narrative description, it would have taken more space and been more difficult to understand. Figure 25 also provides a visual break in a full page of text.

What to Do

1. Select a brief title that clearly identifies the focus of the table.
2. Put borders around tables to make them easier to see and read.
3. Number tables if you are using more than one.
4. Label each row and column clearly using simple words or short phrases.
5. Use different kinds of lines to separate labels from data when possible.
6. Identify the source of data for each table.
7. Round off numbers to the nearest whole number.
8. Use bold or italic type to indicate totals and subtotals.
9. Include the date the table was prepared.

Graphs and Charts

Graphs and charts are visual depictions of numeric data. If you can't count it, you can't graph or chart it.

Every graphic item in a chart represents two pieces of information:

1. the name of a measurable item (called a *category*), which is identified on the chart by a label
2. the quantity associated with the item (called a *data point*), which is plotted on the chart as a value[2]

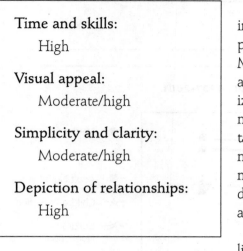

Time and skills:
High

Visual appeal:
Moderate/high

Simplicity and clarity:
Moderate/high

Depiction of relationships:
High

Today, almost all charts and graphs are created using computer software programs, which provide templates for dozens of different types of charts and graphs. Microsoft Word includes fourteen standard chart styles and an additional twenty custom chart styles. Specialized chart and graph software packages provide even more options. Because all of these software programs take time to learn and use, graphs and charts are the most labor- and skill-intensive of the three presentation methods. However, if the message is important and the data is complex, the investment in time required to create graphs and charts is worthwhile.

The three main types of charts and graphs that most libraries use are bar graphs, line graphs, and pie charts. These three styles are illustrated in figures 28 through 30. In general, bar graphs are used to rank the relative size or importance of something over a period of time. Line graphs illustrate trends in several data elements over a period of time. Pie charts show the relationships of parts to the whole; pie charts always present 100 percent of a single category of data.

When to Use

Use graphs and charts when it is important that the audience understand the relationships among various types of information. The most effective graphs and charts focus on a single theme or message and contain only

FIGURE 28
Bar Graphs

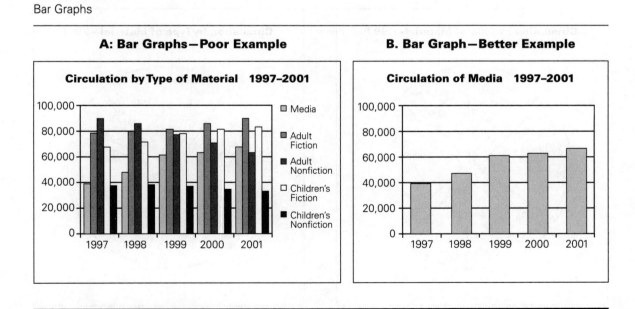

FIGURE 29
Line Graph

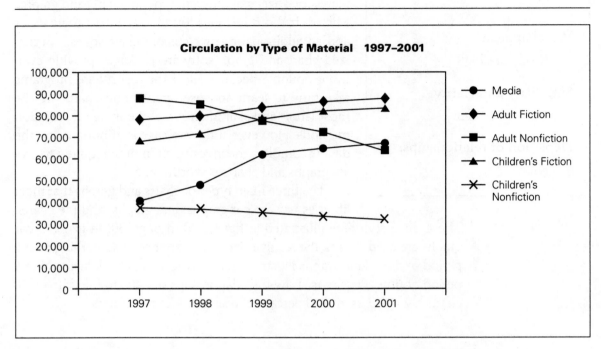

Circulation by Type of Material   1997–2001

Media
Adult Fiction
Adult Nonfiction
Children's Fiction
Children's Nonfiction

FIGURE 30
Pie Charts

A. 1997

B. 2001

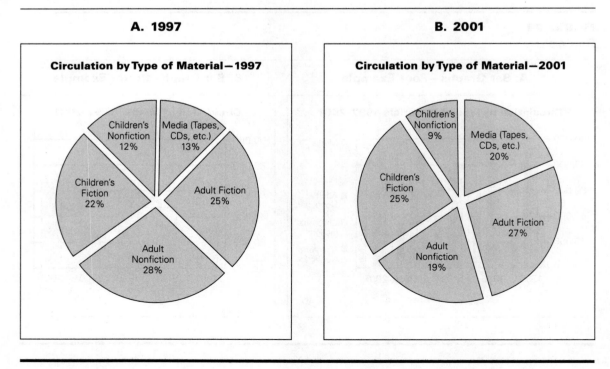

Circulation by Type of Material—1997

Children's Nonfiction 12%
Media (Tapes, CDs, etc.) 13%
Children's Fiction 22%
Adult Fiction 25%
Adult Nonfiction 28%

Circulation by Type of Material—2001

Children's Nonfiction 9%
Media (Tapes, CDs, etc.) 20%
Children's Fiction 25%
Adult Fiction 27%
Adult Nonfiction 19%

the data needed to deliver the message. Be sure to select the right type of graph or chart to present your data. Use graphs to show the relationship between two or more variables. Charts are used to represent data with a single variable.

Bar graphs work best when you want to present data about two variables, normally the changes in a single data element over a period of time. Look at the two graphs in figure 28. Bar graph A is difficult to read and confusing because it tries to present data about multiple data elements over a five-year period. Bar graph B, which presents data on *one* data element over the same five-year period, is much clearer and easier to understand.

Line graphs work well to illustrate the trends in multiple data elements over a period of time. Figure 29 presents exactly the same data as figure 28 A. However, most people would agree that figure 29 is easier to read and understand than figure 28 A. The horizontal lines make it easy to follow the trend in each category of circulation during the five-year period under consideration.

Pie charts are used to present data with a single variable. As noted previously, all pie charts reflect 100 percent of the data in the variable under consideration. Figure 30 A and B illustrate the circulation of materials (the variable) in 1997 and again in 2001. To present the circulation data for 1998, 1999, and 2000, you would need to create three more pie charts. Pie charts are not normally the best format to present multiyear data. However, they are an effective way to illustrate the proportions of the pieces of any given data element.

What to Do

1. Select the right type of chart for the data you are presenting.
2. Keep each chart focused on a single message or theme.
3. Select a brief title that clearly identifies the focus of the chart.
4. Put borders around charts to make them easier to see and read.
5. Number charts if you are using more than one.
6. Identify the source of data for each chart.
7. Keep the background clear, and select simple contrasting patterns to fill bars or slices of a pie chart.
8. Round off numbers to the nearest whole number.
9. The X axis (bottom) and Y axis (left) should meet at 0 for bar and line graphs.
10. Include the date the graph or chart was prepared.

NOTES

1. Patrick J. Lynch, Web Style Guide: Basic Design Principles for Creating Web Sites. Available 5/31/00 at http://info.med.yale.edu/caim/manual/pages/graphic_design100.html.

2. Michael Tolman, "Charts and Graphs: Visualizing Data." Chapter 8 in *Understanding Presentation Graphics* (n.p., n.d.). Available 5/31/00 at http://www.webstudio.com/upg/ch10/ch10.html.

Part Four

Workforms

Instructions: Identify possible members for the planning committee in each of these three broad categories:

Library stakeholders consisting of individuals or groups who can affect or will be affected by an action (library staff members, local funders, etc.)

People with certain skills or areas of expertise (technology, education, etc.)

Community representatives reflecting the diversity of the community (age, race, education, etc.)

Stakeholders	People with Skills/Areas of Expertise	Community Representatives

Completed by _____ Date completed _____

Source of data _____ Library _____

1. How many people live in your community? (If your library serves a significant number of people in neighboring communities, you may wish to keep two sets of population numbers here, one that includes only those within your legal service area and another that includes people in neighboring communities.) _____

    SOURCE: _____

    How is this projected to be different in 5 years? _____

    SOURCE: _____

2. Of the people living in your community, what percent are

	5 years ago	*Now*	*In 5 years*
less than 5 years old	_____	_____	_____
5–13	_____	_____	_____
14–18	_____	_____	_____
19–21	_____	_____	_____
22–65	_____	_____	_____
65 and older	_____	_____	_____

    SOURCE: _____

3. How many single-parent households are there? _____

    5 years ago _____   now _____   projected in 5 years _____

    SOURCE: _____

4. What languages are spoken in the homes of the people in your community? _____

    _____

    SOURCE: _____

5. What ethnic groups are represented in your community? _____

    _____

    SOURCE: _____

    (continued)

6. Who are your community's three largest employers? What do they do?
    How many people do they employ? How is this likely to be different in 5 years?

    1st largest _____   Employs _____

    Make/Do _____

    In 5 years _____

    2nd largest _____   Employs _____

    Make/Do _____

    In 5 years _____

    3rd largest _____   Employs _____

    Make/Do _____

    In 5 years _____

    SOURCE: _____

    What are the major industries in your community (if different from major
    employers listed above)? What do they do? How many people do they employ?
    How is this likely to be different in 5 years?

    Name _____   Employs _____

    Make/Do _____

    In 5 years _____

    Name _____   Employs _____

    Make/Do _____

    In 5 years _____

    Name _____   Employs _____

    Make/Do _____

    In 5 years _____

    SOURCE: _____

7. What percentage of your community is unemployed? _____ %

    SOURCE: _____

(continued)

8. What is the median family income in your community? $ _____

   SOURCE: _____

9. What percent of the families in your community have incomes that are below
   the poverty line? $ _____

   SOURCE: _____

10. Does your community's population change widely during different seasons?
    If yes, describe those shifts.

    Which seasons? _____   +/– how many people? _____

    SOURCE: _____

11. Where do people in your community get their information? Place a check
    mark by each source of information available locally. Then indicate how many
    of each of the information sources are available.

    How many?

    _____ Local newspapers   _____

    _____ Local radio stations   _____

    _____ Local television stations   _____

    _____ Bookstores   _____

    _____ Video stores   _____

    _____ Music stores   _____

    _____ Local community access cable   _____

    _____ Internet service providers (ISPs)   _____

    _____ Other (community organizations, etc.) _____

    SOURCE(S): _____

    Which of the above provide information in languages other than English? _____

    _____

    SOURCE: _____

    (continued)

12. What other libraries are there in your community? Place a check mark
    by each type of library in your community and indicate how many
    of that type of library there are.

    How many?

    _____ Elementary school _____

    _____ Junior high/middle school _____

    _____ High school _____

    _____ Vocational technical _____

    _____ Community college _____

    _____ College or university _____

    _____ Hospital/medical _____

    _____ Law _____

    _____ Special _____

    _____ Other _____

    SOURCE: _____

13. How many public and private schools are in your community? List the number
    of each type of school on the blanks below.

    Preschools _____ public _____ private

    Elementary schools _____ public _____ private

    Middle/junior high schools _____ public _____ private

    High schools _____ public _____ private

    Vocational/technical _____ public _____ private

    Community colleges _____ public _____ private

    Colleges/universities _____ public _____ private

    SOURCE: _____

14. Approximately how many homeschooling families are there in your community? _____

    SOURCE: _____

(continued)

15. What percent of the people in your community age 25 and older have at least a high school diploma or a GED? (Note: this includes all technical school and college grads as well.) _____ %

    SOURCE: _____

    What percent of residents age 25 and older have at least 2 years of college? _____ %

    SOURCE: _____

    What percent of residents age 25 and older have at least 4 years of college? _____ %

    SOURCE: _____

16. How many social service providers are located in your community?

    Nursing homes (extended care) _____

    Day-care centers _____

    Shelters/halfway houses/drug treatment centers _____

    Youth and recreation centers _____

    Other (list) _____

    _____

    _____

    SOURCE: _____

17. List (for small library communities) or estimate the number (for larger communities) and types of the organizations in your community (service groups, clubs, etc.)

    SOURCE: _____

Completed by _____ Date completed _____

Source of data _____ Library _____

Instructions: Picture your community ten years from now. Imagine that the community and its people have been successful beyond belief. It is a place everyone is proud to call home. Now describe the community. What makes it so attractive? Next think about the people. Consider the business community, professional people, parents, people with disabilities, people in the workforce, retirees, children, and teenagers and people in various income groups, various racial and ethnic groups, and various religious groups. Why would they want to live in your community? Using this information, write six to eight sentences articulating elements of your community's vision in the table below. An example has been provided.

Who Will Benefit?	Benefit and Result
All children	will receive the education they need to secure employment that provides a living wage.

(continued)

Who Will Benefit?	Benefit and Result

Completed by _____   Date completed _____

Source of data _____   Library _____

Instructions: Think about your community. Record its strengths and weaknesses below. Then consider the future of your community. Record its opportunities and threats on the next page.

Community Strengths

1.

2.

3.

4.

5.

Community Weaknesses

1.

2.

3.

4.

5.

(continued)

Opportunities for the Community in the Coming Years

1.

2.

3.

4.

5.

Threats Facing the Community in the Coming Years

1.

2.

3.

4.

5.

Completed by _____ Date completed _____

Source of data _____ Library _____

1. Library Users

	5 years ago	Now	In 5 years	*Average of other libraries**
Total number of people registered	_____	_____	_____	_____
Number of residents	_____	_____	_____	_____
Percent of residents	_____%	_____%	_____%	_____%
Number of nonresidents	_____	_____	_____	_____
Percent of nonresidents	_____%	_____%	_____%	_____%

2. Library Hours

How many total (nonoverlapping) hours is the library open per week? _____

How many evening hours (after 6 P.M.) does this include? _____

How many weekend hours does this include? _____

How many evenings (nonoverlapping) is library service available in your community? _____

How many hours is the library open on Sunday? _____

Do these hours appear to meet customer's needs? _____

3. Library Staff

	5 years ago	Now	In 5 years	*Average of other libraries**
Total number of employees	_____	_____	_____	_____
Total number of FTEs	_____	_____	_____	_____
Total FTEs per capita	_____	_____	_____	_____
Number of professional staff	_____	_____	_____	_____
Number of paraprofessional staff	_____	_____	_____	_____
Number of clerical staff	_____	_____	_____	_____
Number of maintenance staff	_____	_____	_____	_____
Number of other employees	_____	_____	_____	_____
Total number of volunteers (in FTEs)	_____	_____	_____	_____
Average weekly volunteer hours	_____	_____	_____	_____

* Available from your state library agency, the National Center for Educational Statistics' annual *Federal-State Cooperative System for Public Library Data*, or PLA's annual *Public Library Data Service: Statistical Report*.

(continued)

Do employees in the following positions reflect the proportion of racial/ethnic groups in the community?

Professional staff	Yes _____	No _____
Paraprofessional staff	Yes _____	No _____
Clerical staff	Yes _____	No _____
Maintenance staff	Yes _____	No _____
Other employees	Yes _____	No _____

What percent of the staff in the following position levels speak the languages of the communities the library serves (other than English)?

Professional staff	_____ %
Paraprofessional staff	_____ %
Clerical staff	_____ %
Maintenance staff	_____ %
Other employees	_____ %

4. Materials/Resources

	5 years ago	Now	In 5 years	Average of other libraries*
Adult books (volumes)	_____	_____	_____	_____
Adult periodicals (titles)	_____	_____	_____	_____
Adult CDs, videos, tapes (volumes)	_____	_____	_____	_____
Other formats (list) _____	_____	_____	_____	_____
_____	_____	_____	_____	_____
Children's books (volumes)	_____	_____	_____	_____
Children's periodicals (titles)	_____	_____	_____	_____
Children's CDs, videos, tapes (volumes)	_____	_____	_____	_____
Other formats (list) _____	_____	_____	_____	_____
_____	_____	_____	_____	_____
YA books (volumes)	_____	_____	_____	_____
YA periodicals (titles)	_____	_____	_____	_____

(continued)

	5 years ago	Now	In 5 years	Average of other libraries*
YA CDs, videos, tapes (volumes)	_____	_____	_____	_____
Other YA formats (list) _____	_____	_____	_____	_____
_____	_____	_____	_____	_____

Electronic resources for public use

CD-ROMs (titles)	_____	_____	_____	_____
for adults	_____	_____	_____	_____
for children	_____	_____	_____	_____
for young adults	_____	_____	_____	_____
Database licenses	_____	_____	_____	_____

Internet access (number of public workstations)

for adults	_____	_____	_____	_____
forchildren	_____	_____	_____	_____
for young adults	_____	_____	_____	_____

5. Other Services You Provide for Public Use (Provide a brief written summary if needed.)

Computers _____

_____

Photocopiers _____

_____

Fax _____

_____

Other (list) _____

_____

* Available from your state library agency, the National Center for Educational Statistics' annual *Federal-State Cooperative System for Public Library Data*, or PLA's annual *Public Library Data Service: Statistical Report*.

(continued)

6. Facility   Age _____   Total Number of sq. ft. _____

	Excellent	Good	Adequate	Poor
Condition	_____	_____	_____	_____
Code compliance	_____	_____	_____	_____
ADA compliance	_____	_____	_____	_____
Electrical wiring	_____	_____	_____	_____
Appearance	_____	_____	_____	_____
Signage	_____	_____	_____	_____
Parking space	_____	_____	_____	_____
Meeting room space	_____	_____	_____	_____
Location of main library	_____	_____	_____	_____
Location of branch libraries (if any)	_____	_____	_____	_____

7. Financial Resources

	5 years ago	Now	In 5 years	Average of other libraries*
Total operating budget	_____	_____	_____	_____
Expenditures per capita	_____	_____	_____	_____
Materials expenditures per capita	_____	_____	_____	_____
Technology expenditures per capita	_____	_____	_____	_____
Staff expenditures per capita	_____	_____	_____	_____
Staff training and development per employee	_____	_____	_____	_____

8. Selected Use Data

	5 years ago	Now	In 5 years	Average of other libraries*
Circulation per capita	_____	_____	_____	_____
Adults	_____	_____	_____	_____
Children	_____	_____	_____	_____
Young adults	_____	_____	_____	_____

(continued)

	5 years ago	Now	In 5 years	Average of other libraries*
Library visits per capita	_____	_____	_____	_____
Adults	_____	_____	_____	_____
Children	_____	_____	_____	_____
Young adults	_____	_____	_____	_____
Reference transactions per capita	_____	_____	_____	_____
Program attendance				
Adults	_____	_____	_____	_____
Total children	_____	_____	_____	_____
Summer Reading Program	_____	_____	_____	_____
Preschool programs in library	_____	_____	_____	_____
Preschool programs in other locations	_____	_____	_____	_____
Young adults	_____	_____	_____	_____
Electronic use				
Number of sessions initiated by off-site users	_____	_____	_____	_____
Number of searches (Internet and CD-ROM)	_____	_____	_____	_____
Number of items retrieved (Internet and CD-ROM)	_____	_____	_____	_____

* Available from your state library agency, the National Center for Educational Statistics' annual *Federal-State Cooperative System for Public Library Data*, or PLA's annual *Public Library Data Service: Statistical Report.*

Completed by _____   Date completed _____

Source of data _____   Library _____

Instructions: If the members of the planning committee have identified needs that they believe the library could address that are not covered in the thirteen service responses, use this form to develop one or more new service responses.

1. What is the community need to be addressed?

2. What could the library do to meet the need?

3. What would be accomplished if the library provided this service?

4. Describe the potential service response.

What will the library do?

Who is the target audience(s)?

(continued)

How will the service be delivered?

What will happen because the library provides this service? (What effect will the service have?)

5. Describe the library resources that will be required to implement the service response.

Staffing

Collections/information resources

Facilities

Technology

(continued)

6. How will you measure the progress you have made toward meeting the needs described in the service response? Write your suggested measures under the appropriate categories below. (For more information on these measures, see Task 6 in chapter 3.)

People served

- Total number of users served

- Number of unique individuals who use the service

How well the service meets the needs of the people served

Total units of service provided by the library

Completed by _____ Date completed _____

Source of data _____ Library _____

Instructions: How would the service responses selected by the planning committee affect current library services and programs? What strengths does the library have in the areas selected as service priorities? What weaknesses does the library have in those areas? Now think about the long-term effect of reallocating resources to accomplish the selected service responses. What opportunities would the library have if resources were reallocated? What threats would the library face if it reallocated those resources?

Library **Strengths** in the Areas Selected as Service Priorities

1.

2.

3.

4.

5.

Library **Weaknesses** in the Areas Selected as Service Priorities

1.

2.

3.

4.

5.

(continued)

Opportunities for the Library if the New Service Priorities Are Selected

1.

2.

3.

4.

5.

Threats to the Library if the New Service Priorities Are Selected

1.

2.

3.

4.

5.

Completed by _____ Date completed _____

Source of data _____ Library _____

Instructions: Every objective for each goal contains the same three elements: a measure, a standard against which to compare that measure, and a date or time frame by which time the standard should be met.

To write an objective, follow these four steps:

1. Decide on the measure you want to use. The information in figure 12 may be helpful to you as you do this.
2. Decide on the standard against which you will compare that measure.
3. Decide when you want to reach the standard.
4. Put the measure, the standard, and the time frame together into a sentence that reads smoothly.

For example:

The measure: *The number of children enrolled in the summer reading program*
The standard: *will increase by 10 percent*
The time frame: *each year*
The completed objectve: *Each year, the number of children enrolled in the summer reading program will increase by 10 percent.*

GOAL: _____

_____

_____

Objective 1

The measure: _____

The standard: _____

The time frame: _____

Completed objective: _____

_____

_____

_____

Objective 2

The measure: _____

The standard: _____

The time frame: _____

Completed objective: _____

_____

_____

_____

Completed by _____   Date completed _____

Source of data _____   Library _____

Instructions: List the activities you have identified that might accomplish one of the objectives in the library's plan. Rank the potential effectiveness of each activity in each of the three categories listed on the table below using the following scale:

1 = High   2 = Moderate   3 = Low

Activity	Relation to Target Audience	Relation to Intended Outcome(s)	Intangibles (See Task 7)
1.			
2.			
3.			
4.			
5.			
6.			
7.			
8.			
9.			
10.			
11.			
12.			

Completed by _____ Date completed _____

Source of data _____ Library _____

Instructions: List the activities you have identified that might accomplish one of the objectives in the library's plan. Rank the effect each activity will have on each of the four resources using the scale below.

1 = Critical resource to accomplish activity

2 = Important resource to accomplish activity

3 = Resource will be affected by the activity but not significantly

4 = Resource will not be affected by the activity

Activity	Staff	Collection	Facility	Technology
1.				
2.				
3.				
4.				
5.				
6.				
7.				
8.				
9.				
10.				
11.				
12.				

Completed by _____   Date completed _____

Source of data _____   Library _____

Service Response/Activity			
(Resource under review)	Have	Need	Gap

Plan for filling the gap or reallocating the surplus

(Resource under review)	Have	Need	Gap

Plan for filling the gap or reallocating the surplus

Completed by _____ Date completed _____

Source of data _____ Library _____

Activity: _____

_____

_____

		Last FY	*Proposed*	*Appropriated*
100	**PERSONNEL SERVICES**			
	101 Salaries	_____	_____	_____
	102 Benefits	_____	_____	_____
	103 Longevity	_____	_____	_____
	TOTAL 100	_____	_____	_____
200	**ADMINISTRATIVE EXPENSES**			
	201 Training	_____	_____	_____
	202 Travel/Mileage	_____	_____	_____
	203 Postage	_____	_____	_____
	204 Printing	_____	_____	_____
	205 Supplies	_____	_____	_____
	206 Other (list)			
	_____	_____	_____	_____
	_____	_____	_____	_____
	TOTAL 200	_____	_____	_____
300	**LIBRARY MATERIALS**			
	301 Print	_____	_____	_____
	302 Media	_____	_____	_____
	303 Electronic	_____	_____	_____
	304 Other (list)			
	_____	_____	_____	_____
	_____	_____	_____	_____
	TOTAL 300	_____	_____	_____

(continued)

		Last FY	Proposed	Appropriated
400	**TELECOMMUNICATIONS**			
	401 Telephone	_____	_____	_____
	402 Fax	_____	_____	_____
	403 Internet access	_____	_____	_____
	404 Other (list)			
	_____	_____	_____	_____
	_____	_____	_____	_____
	TOTAL 400	_____	_____	_____
500	**FACILITIES, FURNISHINGS, AND EQUIPMENT**			
	501 Furniture	_____	_____	_____
	502 Equipment	_____	_____	_____
	503 Relocation/renovation	_____	_____	_____
	504 Other (list)			
	_____	_____	_____	_____
	_____	_____	_____	_____
	TOTAL 500	_____	_____	_____
600	**OTHER**			
	601 _____	_____	_____	_____
	602 _____	_____	_____	_____
	603 _____	_____	_____	_____
	TOTAL 600	_____	_____	_____

Totals

		Last FY	Proposed	Appropriated
100	Personnel	_____	_____	_____
200	Administrative	_____	_____	_____
300	Library Materials	_____	_____	_____
400	Telecommunications	_____	_____	_____
500	Facilities	_____	_____	_____
600	Other	_____	_____	_____
TOTAL FOR ACTIVITY		_____	_____	_____

Completed by _____ Date completed _____

Source of data _____ Library _____

WORKFORM M Forced-Choices Process

Instructions: Assign a number to each of the activities you are prioritizing. This worksheet will help you evaluate up to 15 activities against every other activity, each time determining which of your choices is the more important. Begin in column A below. Compare the first and second activities and circle the number of the one you think is more important (1 or 2). Continuing in column A, compare the first activity and the third activity, again circling the activity you think is more important (1 or 3). Continue similarly through all of the columns.

A	B	C	D	E	F	G	H	I	J	K	L	M	N
1 2	2 3	3 4	4 5	5 6	6 7	7 8	8 9	9 10	10 11	11 12	12 13	13 14	14 15
1 3	2 4	3 5	4 6	5 7	6 8	7 9	8 10	9 11	10 12	11 13	12 14	13 15	
1 4	2 5	3 6	4 7	5 8	6 9	7 10	8 11	9 12	10 13	11 14	12 15		
1 5	2 6	3 7	4 8	5 9	6 10	7 11	8 12	9 13	10 14	11 15			
1 6	2 7	3 8	4 9	5 10	6 11	7 12	8 13	9 14	10 15				
1 7	2 8	3 9	4 10	5 11	6 12	7 13	8 14	9 15					
1 8	2 9	3 10	4 11	5 12	6 13	7 14	8 15						
1 9	2 10	3 11	4 12	5 13	6 14	7 15							
1 10	2 11	3 12	4 13	5 14	6 15								
1 11	2 12	3 13	4 14	5 15									
1 12	2 13	3 14	4 15										
1 13	2 14	3 15											
1 14	2 15												
1 15													

To score your ratings, add the number of times you circled each number and place the total by the appropriate line below. Note that you must add vertically and horizontally to be sure that you include all circled choices. The item with the highest number is the one you think is most important.

1. ____	4. ____	7. ____	10. ____	13. ____
2. ____	5. ____	8. ____	11. ____	14. ____
3. ____	6. ____	9. ____	12. ____	15. ____

Completed by _____ Date completed _____

Source of data _____ Library _____

Index